Lecture Notes in Economics and Mathematical Systems

648

For further volumes:
http://www.springer.com/series/300

Yong Shi • Shouyang Wang • Gang Kou
Jyrki Wallenius

Editors

New State of MCDM in the 21st Century

Selected Papers of the 20th International Conference on Multiple Criteria Decision Making 2009

 Springer

Editors
Professor Yong Shi
Research Center on Fictitious Economy
and Data Science
Graduate University of Chinese Academy
of Sciences
Zhongguancun East Road, No 80
Building 6, Room 203
Beijing, 100190
People's Republic of China
yshi@gucas.ac.cn

and

College of Information Science
and Technology
University of Nebraska at Omaha
Omaha, NE 68182
USA
yshi@unomaha.edu

Professor Gang Kou, PhD
School of Management and Economics
University of Electronic Science
and Technology of China
No 4 Section 2, North Jianse Rd.
Chengdu, 610054
People's Republic of China
kougang@yahoo.com

Professor Dr. Shouyang Wang
Academy of Mathematics
and Systems Science
Chinese Academy of Sciences
Zhonguancun East Road No. 55, Haidian
Beijing, 100190
People's Republic of China
sywang@amss.ac.cn

Professor Dr. Jyrki Wallenius
Aalto University School of Economics
POB 21210
00076 Aalto
Finland
jyrki.wallenius@aalto.fi

ISSN 0075-8442
ISBN 978-3-642-19694-2   e-ISBN 978-3-642-19695-9
DOI 10.1007/978-3-642-19695-9
Springer Heidelberg Dordrecht London New York

Library of Congress Control Number: 2011929784

Cover design: eStudio Calamar S.L.

Printed on acid-free paper

Springer is part of Springer Science+Business Media (www.springer.com)

Preface

This book is the post conference proceedings of MCDM 2009, the Twentieth International Conference on Multiple Criteria Decision Making has been held at Chengdu, China, June 21–26, 2009. The conference has emerged as the global forum dedicated to the sharing of original research results and practical development experiences among researchers and application developers from different multiple criteria decision making related areas. The theme for MCDM 2009 was "New State of MCDM in 21st Century", which is also used as the title of this book. The conference has received more than 350 submissions, out of which 121 were accepted. This included 72 regular papers and 49 short papers. There were more than 250 participants from 31 countries and regions attended the conference.

After a post conference's peer-reviewing process, we selected 17 papers contributed by 35 authors and co-authors from ten countries: Belgium, China, Czech Republic, Denmark, Finland, France, Latvia, Lithuania, Poland and USA to formulate this book. The contents of this book consist of three parts: MCDM Foundation and Theory, MCDM Methodology, and MCDM Applications.

There were four papers in MCDM Foundation and Theory. The first paper "MCDM: In Search of New Paradigms..." is contributed by Milan Zeleny. The second paper "Harmonizing the Omnipresence of MCDM in Technology, Society, and Policy" is written by Yacov Y. Haimes. The third paper "Decision Making on Pareto Front Approximations with Inherent Nondominance", is contributed by Markus Hartikainen, Kaisa Miettinen, and Margaret M. Wiecek, while the forth paper "A New Consistency Index for Comparison Matrices in The ANP" is from Daji Ergu, Gang Kou, Yi Peng and Yong Shi.

MCDM Methodology has four papers. The first paper "Estimating the Robustness of Composite CBA & MCA Assessments by Variation of Criteria Importance Order" is contributed by Anders Vestergaard Jensen, Michael Bruhn Barfod, and Steen Leleur. The second paper "Compromise Based Evolutionary Multiobjective Optimization Algorithm for Multidisciplinary Optimization" is from Benoit Guedas, Xavier Gandibleux, and Philippe Depince. The third paper "A Lower Bound of the Choquet Integral Integrated within Martins' Algorithm" is written by Hugo Fouchal, Xavier Gandibleux, and Fabien Lehuede. The forth paper "Penalty Rules in Multicriteria Genetic Search" is from Grzegorz Koloch and Tomasz Szapiro.

There are nine papers related to various MCDM Applications. The first paper "The Bi-Criteria Approach to Project Cost and Schedule Buffers Sizing" is done by Paweł Błaszczyk, Tomasz Błaszczyk, and Maria B. Kania. The second paper "The Multi-objective Alternative assets Investment Optimization Model on Sovereign Wealth Funds Based on Risk Control" is contributed by Jing Yu, Bin Xu and Yong Shi. The third paper "A New Tool for Feature Extraction and Its Application to Credit Risk Analysis" is written by Paweł Błaszczyk. The forth paper "Algorithm for MCDM in Intelligent Braking Diagnostics System of Railway Transport" is from Anatoly Levchenkov, Mikhail Gorobetz, Leonids Ribickis, and Peteris Balckars. The fifth paper "The Online Advertising Types of Choices Based on DEA Method" is provided by Xianglan Jiang, Yingjin Lu and Wenbo Yang. The sixth paper "Examination of Decision Support Systems for Composite CBA & MCDA Assessments of Transport Infrastructure Projects" is from Michael Bruhn Barfod, Anders Vestergaard Jensen, and Steen Leleur. The seventh paper "An Entropy-weighted Clustering Method for Environmental Pollution Assessment in China" is presented by Gang Kou, Qiaoli Sun, and Yi Peng. The eighth paper "Unconstrained Two-objective Land-use Planning Based-on NSGA-II for Chemical Industry Park" is contributed by Ming Xu and Zongzhi Wu. The last paper "Robustness in Economic Development Studies: The case of Tanzania" is done by Willem Karel M. Brauers and Edmundas Kazimieras Zavadskas.

We wish this book will serve as a useful source for the readers who have interests in the progress of MCDM research and practice.

Chengdu, China   *Yong Shi*
January 1, 2011   *Shouyang Wang*
                                                                              Gang Kou
                                                                        Wallenius Jyrki

Contents

Part I   MCDM Foundation and Theory

1   MCDM: In Search of New Paradigms 3
Milan Zeleny

**2   Harmonizing the Omnipresence of MCDM in Technology,
Society, and Policy** 13
Yacov Y. Haimes

**3   Decision Making on Pareto Front Approximations
with Inherent Nondominance** 35
Markus Hartikainen, Kaisa Miettinen,
and Margaret M. Wiecek

**4   A New Consistency Index for Comparison Matrices
in the ANP** 47
Daji Ergu, Gang Kou, Yi Peng, and Yong Shi

Part II   MCDM Methodology

**5   Estimating the Robustness of Composite CBA and MCA
Assessments by Variation of Criteria Importance Order** 59
Anders Vestergaard Jensen, Michael Bruhn Barfod,
and Steen Leleur

**6   Compromise Based Evolutionary Multiobjective
Optimization Algorithm for Multidisciplinary
Optimization** 69
Benoît Guédas, Xavier Gandibleux, and Philippe Dépincé

**7   A Lower Bound of the Choquet Integral Integrated
Within Martins' Algorithm** 79
Hugo Fouchal, Xavier Gandibleux, and Fabien Lehuédé

8   Penalty Rules in Multicriteria Genetic Search 91
     Grzegorz Koloch and Tomasz Szapiro

Part III   MCDM Applications

9   The Bi-Criterial Approach to Project Cost and Schedule
     Buffers Sizing 105
     Paweł Błaszczyk, Tomasz Błaszczyk, and Maria B. Kania

10   The Multi-Objective Alternative Assets Investment
     Optimization Model on Sovereign Wealth Funds
     Based on Risk Control 115
     Jing Yu, Bin Xu, and Yong Shi

11   A New Tool for Feature Extraction and Its Application
     to Credit Risk Analysis...131
     Paweł Błaszczyk

12   Algorithm for MCDM in Intelligent Braking Diagnostics
     System of Railway Transport 143
     Anatoly Levchenkov, Mikhail Gorobetz, Leonids Ribickis,
     and Peteris Balckars

13   The Online Advertising Types of Choices
     Based on DEA Method 157
     Xianglan Jiang, Yingjin Lu, and Wen-bo Yang

14   Examination of Decision Support Systems for Composite
     CBA and MCDA Assessments of Transport Infrastructure
     Projects 167
     Michael Bruhn Barfod, Anders Vestergaard Jensen,
     and Steen Leleur

15   An Entropy-Weighted Clustering Method
     for Environmental Pollution Assessment in China.......................177
     Gang Kou, Qiaoli Sun, and Yi Peng

16   Unconstrained Two-Objective Land-Use Planning
     Based-on NSGA-II for Chemical Industry Park 189
     Ming Xu and Zongzhi Wu

17   Robustness in Economic Development Studies: The Case
     of Tanzania 199
     Willem Karel M. Brauers and Edmundas Kazimieras
     Zavadskas

Contributors

Peteris Balckars Riga Technical University, 1, Kalku Street, Riga, 1658, Latvia, peteris@dzti.edu.lv

Michael Bruhn Barfod Department of Transport, Technical University of Denmark, Bygningstorvet 115, 2800 Kgs, Lyngby, Denmark, mbb@transport.dtu.dk

Paweł Błaszczyk Institute of Mathematics, University of Silesia, 14 Bankowa Street, 40-007 Katowice, Poland, pblaszcz@math.us.edu.pl

Tomasz Błaszczyk University of Economics in Katowice, ul. 1 Maja 50, 40-287 Katowice, Poland, tomasz.blaszczyk@ue.katowice.pl

Willem Karel M. Brauers Faculty of Applied Economics, University of Antwerp, Birontlaan, 97, 2600 Antwerpen, Belgium, willem.brauers@ua.ac.be

Philippe Depince IRCCyN, Ecole Centrale de Nantes, 1 rue de la Noë, BP 92101, 44321 Nantes Cedex-03, France, Philippe.Depinceg@irccyn.ec-nantes.fr

Daji Ergu School of Management and Economics, University of Electronic Science and Technology of China, Chengdu 610054, China
and
Southwest University for Nationalities, Chengdu 610200, China, ergudaji@163.com

Hugo Fouchal LINA, Universite de Nantes, 2 rue de la Houssini_ere, BP 92208, 44322 Nantes Cedex-03, France, Hugo.Fouchal@univ-nantes.fr
and
IRCCyN, École des Mines de Nantes, 4 rue Alfred Kastler, 44307 Nantes, France

Xavier Gandibleux LINA, Universite de Nantes, 2 rue de la Houssinière, BP 92208, 44322 Nantes Cedex-03, France, Xavier.Gandibleux@univ-nantes.fr

Mikhail Gorobetz Riga Technical University, 1, Kalku Street, Riga, 1658, Latvia, mihails.gorobecs@rtu.lv

Benoit Guedas IRCCyN, Ecole Centrale de Nantes, 1 rue de la Noë, BP 92101, 44321 Nantes Cedex-03, France, Benoit.Guedas@irccyn.ec-nantes.fr

Yacov Y. Haimes L. R. Quarles Professor of Systems and Information Engineering, Center for Risk Management of Engineering Systems, University of Virginia, Charlottesville, VA, USA, Haimes@virginia.edu

Markus Hartikainen Department of Mathematical Information Technology, University of Jyvaskyla, Jyvaskyla, Finland

Anders Vestergaard Jensen Department of Transport, Technical University of Denmark, Bygningstorvet 115, 2800 Kgs, Lyngby, Denmark, avj@transport.dtu.dk

Xianglan Jiang School of Management and Economics, University of Electronic Science and Technology of China, Chengdu 610054, China, xianglan196@yahoo.com.cn

Maria B. Kania Institute of Mathematics, University of Silesia, ul. Bankowa 14, 40-007 Katowice, Poland, mkania@math.us.edu.pl

Grzegorz Koloch Warsaw School of Economics, Al. Niepodleglosci 164, 02-554, Warsaw, Poland, gkoloch@gmail.com

Gang Kou School of Management and Economics, University of Electronic Science and Technology of China, Chengdu 610054, China, kougang@yahoo.com

Fabien Lehuede Ecole des Mines de Nantes, 4 rue Alfred Kastler, 44307 Nantes, France, Fabien.Lehuede@emn.fr

Steen Leleur Department of Transport, Technical University of Denmark, Bygningstorvet 115, 2800 Kgs, Lyngby, Denmark

Anatoly Levchenkov Riga Technical University, 1, Kalku Street, Riga, 1658, Latvia, anatolijs.levcenkovs@rtu.lv

Yingjin Lu School of Management and Economics, University of Electronic Science and Technology of China, Chengdu 610054, China, luyingjin@uestc.edu.cn

Kaisa Miettinen Department of Mathematical Information Technology, University of Jyvaskyla, Jyvaskyla, Finland

Yi Peng School of Management and Economics, University of Electronic Science and Technology of China, Chengdu 610054, China, pengyicd@gmail.com

Leonids Ribickis Riga Technical University, 1, Kalku Street, Riga, 1658, Latvia, leonids.ribickis@rtu.lv

Yong Shi Research Center on Fictitious Economy and Data Sciences, Chinese Academy of Sciences, Beijing 100190, China, yshi@gucas.ac.cn
and
College of Information Science and Technology, University of Nebraska at Omaha, Omaha, NE 68182, USA, yshi@unomaha.edu

Qiaoli Sun School of Management and Economics, University of Electronic Science and Technology of China, Chengdu 610054, China

Tomasz Szapiro Warsaw School of Economics, Al. Niepodleglosci 164, 02-554 Warsaw, Poland, tszapiro@sgh.waw.pl

Margaret M. Wiecek Clemson University, Clemson, SC, USA

Zongzhi Wu China Academy of Safety Science and Technology, Xueyuan Street 29, Haidian District, Beijing 100012, China, wuzongzhi@sina.vip.com

Bin Xu School of Accountancy, Central University of Finance and Economic, Beijing 100081, China

Ming Xu School of Engineering and Technology, China University of Geosciences, Beijing 100083, China, xuming@cugb.edu.cn

Wen-bo Yang School of Management and Economics, University of Electronic Science and Technology of China, Chengdu 610054, China, yangwenbo76@163.com

Jing Yu Research Center on Fictitious Economy and Data Sciences, Chinese Academy of Sciences, Beijing 100190, China
and
Dagong Global Credit Co, Ltd, Beijing 100125, China, yujing3721@163.com

Edmundas Kazimieras Zavadskas Vilnius Gediminas Technical University, Sauletekio av. 11, Vilnius, 10223, Lithuania, edmundas.zavadskas@adm.vtu.lt

Milan Zeleny Fordham University, New York, NY, USA
and
Tomas Bata University, Zlin, Czech Republic, mzeleny@fordham.edu

Part I
MCDM Foundation and Theory

Chapter 1
MCDM: In Search of New Paradigms ...[1]

Milan Zeleny

The field of MCDM has come of age. It is not sufficient to continue improving or refining old concepts and paradigms: we are now facing diminishing marginal returns. It is time for change. In order to assure MCDM future we cannot continue doing the old things better; we have to start doing things differently and, more importantly, doing different things.

We have to return to our MCDM roots and reexamine our basic premises. Forty years is enough time to judge what has worked and what has not. Many of our basic concepts are barely visible under so many layers of algorithmic efficiencies, stochasticities, fuzziness, nonlinearities, dynamics and multimedia and graphics "fireworks", that we are unable to discern the underlying basics, their relevance and efficacy. We are essentially *assuming* that our premises are correct. Yet, paradigms do change and in fact must change, no matter how comfortable. Without paradigm changes our progress would become technical and "cosmetic", with no philosophical depth or application relevance.

The theme of the 2009 MCDM conference in Chengdu was declared as follows: *The New State of MCDM in 21st Century*. Yet, how many contributions even pretend to address this overarching challenge?

A *paradigm* is the generally accepted perspective, frame or matrix of a particular discipline or field of inquiry at a given stage of its evolution. It amounts to a tacit (and often unduly explicit) acceptance of basic premises, definitions, axioms and conventions of the discipline. After a while, such presumed and unquestioned acceptances become straitjackets and barriers to further development. There comes the season of questioning and re-examining the reigning paradigms – in order to bring the new vitality into a stalled area of research.

---

[1]This is a transcript of the keynote speech delivered at the MCDM conference in Chengdu, June 22–26, 2009, addressing its main theme *"The New State of MCDM in 21st Century"*.

M. Zeleny
Fordham University, New York, NY, USA
and
Tomas Bata University, Zlin, Czech Republic
e-mail: mzeleny@fordham.edu

Y. Shi et al. (eds.), *New State of MCDM in the 21st Century*, Lecture Notes
in Economics and Mathematical Systems 648, DOI 10.1007/978-3-642-19695-9_1,
© Springer-Verlag Berlin Heidelberg 2011

1.1   MCDM: Its Roots and Early Beginnings

The First *Multiple Criteria Decision Making (MCDM)* Conference was held at the
Capstone House of the University of South Carolina, *October 26–27, 1972*. About
250 researchers attended, 63 papers were presented. Milan Zeleny, then a PhD student,
was the Chairman of the conference. In 1973, the University of South Carolina
Press published a volume of MCDM proceedings, entitled "Multiple Criteria Decision
Making", edited by James L. Cochrane and Milan Zeleny, then at Columbia
University.

At this conference the name of MCDM was first used, for both the conference
and the volume – the very first of its kind published in the United States. Most
of MCDM founding fathers attended, and most of the MCDM-forming topics and
concepts were established at this famous conference in South Carolina.

Among the first MCDM participants we can find, for example,

C. West Churchman	P.L. Yu
Kenneth R. MacCrimmon	Milan Zeleny
Peter C. Fishburn	Werner Dinkelbach
Ralph L. Keeney	Heinz Isermann
Bernard Roy	Ralph E. Steuer
James S. Dyer	Adi Ben-Israel
Yuji Ijiri	Lotfi A. Zadeh
James P. Ignizio	Ramchandran Jaikumar
Tom Burns	Robyn M. Dawes
Paul E. Green	Ury Passy

as well as many others.

From the titles of presentations we select some *typical concepts and keywords*:
morality in multiple criteria; multiple subjective functions; independence in multiattribute
utility; multidimensional consistency; outranking relations; domination
structures; compromise programming; efficient extreme points; capital budgeting
with multiple goals; optimal control with multiple criteria; tradeoff decisions; multi-group
decision making; multiple criteria in environmental control; multidimensional
scaling; differentially weighted criteria; heuristic algorithms; judgment in medical
efficacy; regression experiments with multiple objectives; etc.

The follow-up conference, *Multiple Criteria Decision Making (MCDM)*, organized
and chaired by Milan Zeleny under the auspices of TIMS, took place on *July
25, 1975* at the Kyoto International Conference Hall. The Proceedings appeared in
1976, under the title "Multiple Criteria Decision Making – Kyoto 1975", edited by
M. Zeleny for Springer-Verlag, vol. 123. This was the second volume of Springer-Verlag,
Lecture Notes in Economics and Mathematical Systems, devoted to
MCDM – after Zeleny's "Linear Multiobjective Programming" in 1974 (vol. 96).

Among the second MCDM-Kyoto 1975 participants we find, for example, such
famous names as:

Jacob Marschak	Anatol Rapoport
Norman C. Dalkey	Kenneth R. Hammond
Robyn M. Dawes	Abraham Charnes
William W. Cooper	Erik Johnsen
Milan Zeleny	Yacov Y. Haimes
Lucien Duckstein	Jared L. Cohon
Elijah Polak	Bernard Roy
Jean-Claude Larréché	Lotfi A. Zadeh

Some *typical concepts and keywords* from the titles of presentations: multi-objective models; multiple objectives in water resources; group decision analysis; multivariate selection; nonlinear goal programming; multi-objective management; guided soul-searching; decision aid; displaced-ideal theory; linguistic approach to multiple criteria, and so on.

We owe it to ourselves and to the future of MCDM to remember its "founding fathers", to honor their memory, and keep expanding their legacy of MCDM knowledge and achievements. Without knowing our roots, the future of MCDM could dissipate or fade away before its time.

1.2 Basic Definitions

It is always necessary to state basic definitions of a field of inquiry. In our case, we have to define what is *decision making* (DM) in general and *multiple criteria decision making* (MCDM) in particular. We conclude that MCDM is a *misnomer* because its adjective "multiple criteria" implies that there is some other form of decision making *without* multiple criteria: there isn't.

All human decision making takes place under *multiple criteria only*. All the rest is measurement and search.

Let us use a simplified example to work out a suitable definition of decision making. In Fig. 1.1 we have a basket of apples, simulating any feasible set of alternatives. Let us determine a single criterion as weight and propose to find (identify, choose, select) the heaviest apple.

How do we solve the problem? First, we *measure*. Then, we *search*. Measurement & search is necessary *and* sufficient for finding the largest apple $\sqrt{}$. So, this

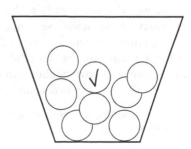

Fig. 1.1 Basket of apples, single criterion

Fig. 1.2 Basket of apples, multiple criteria, with tradeoffs

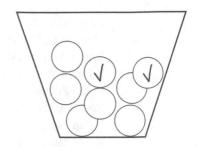

is *not* a problem of decision making or optimization, but a simple task of measurement and search. It is the problem of *computation* (measurement & search), merely a technical challenge. No value or economic judgments, no tradeoffs, no decisions are needed.

Next, we consider *multiple criteria*. In Fig. 1.2 we have the same basket of apples but now we wish to find the heaviest *and* the sweetest apple. Our *criteria* are weight and sweetness.

We use the same necessary procedures of measurement and search and identify the heaviest √ and the sweetest √ apple. In Fig. 1.2 we see that this time measurement & search is *not sufficient*. There are two apples; the criteria are "conflicting". Which apple do we choose? We must go *beyond* the mere *measurement & search* and perform additional functions: we have to *decide*.

Clearly, there can be no decision making without multiple criteria. Decision making is that which must be performed *after* we have measured and searched. Problems with a single objective function, no matter how complex, important or aggregate that function is, are *not* problems of decision making or optimization, but problems of measurement and search only.

So, there is no need for the "MC" in front of DM: all decision making *is* multiple criteria decision making. But we still have to address the question whether all problems with multiple criteria are decision making problems. The answer is: of course not. Let us go to Fig. 1.3 of our basket of apples. It is the same basket and we still search for the heaviest and the sweetest apple. But this time we search "outside the basket" in order to bring new apples in.

Suppose that an apple, both the heaviest and the sweetest, can be added to the basket. In Fig. 1.3, this "heavy and sweet" apple √√ is introduced (as an addition or replacement) into the basket. This particular apple would be preferred by all decision makers aiming to maximize both criteria. All and any processes of measurement & search would safely identify such a prominent apple. Measurement & search can be necessary *and* sufficient even under multiple criteria.

The difference between Figs. 1.2 and 1.3 lies in tradeoffs. There are no tradeoffs in Fig. 1.3, this prominent (or "ideal") alternative now dominates the entire basket and becomes an obvious choice of every rational decision maker. So, the existence of tradeoffs is the key to decision making and we can finally state its definition:

> *Decision making is a function aimed at managing, resolving or dissolving the conflict of tradeoffs.*

Fig. 1.3 Basket of apples, multiple criteria, without tradeoffs

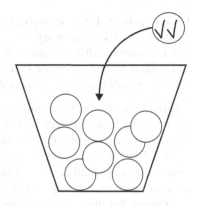

When there are no tradeoffs there can be no decision making – and vice versa. There can be no tradeoffs in situations with a single criterion. The existence of tradeoffs is necessary and sufficient condition for decision making. It is the task and calling of economics, management, decision sciences and (MC)DM: control, reduce or eliminate tradeoffs from decision-making situations. Tradeoffs are not good, they are not preferred or desirable; they are testaments to badly designed, inefficient and wasteful systems. Tradeoffs exist to be eliminated.

1.3 Systems Design of Optimality

In Fig. 1.3 we have encountered a useful "thinking out of the box" through purposefully re-designing the basket of apples (set of feasible alternatives) by introducing targeted desirable options. In fact, this is a key issue of optimization: do we consider feasible set of alternatives to be given and fixed a priori, or do we design or re-design feasible set so that it satisfies certain criteria of optimality?

Optimality and optimization concerns itself precisely with the difference between what is already given or determined and what still remains to be optimized, i.e. designed or determined in an optimal fashion. The two modes: 1. optimizing the given and 2. designing the optimal, are mutually exclusive. In short, one cannot optimize what is already given and fixed.

If somebody puts five lumps of sugar in my coffee I can no longer optimize its sweetness: it is given. If somebody prescribes four operators on a truck, I can no longer optimize its effectiveness: it is given. If I roll four dice, I can no longer roll three dice: *alea iacta est*.

There are at least *four fundamental rules* optimization:

1. What is strictly determined or fixed a priori cannot be subject to subsequent optimization: *it is already given.*
2. What is *not firmly* given can still be selected, chosen or identified and is therefore, by definition, subject to optimization.

3. One cannot optimize a posteriori of fixation. True optimization takes place during the stage of design, i.e. a priori.
4. Consequently, *different optimality concepts* can be derived from differentiating between what is given and what is yet to be determined in problem solving, systems design, optimization or decision making.

Clearly, there is not one optimization concept, but many; we have counted eight different and mutually irreducible such concept (there can be others). In Table 1.1 these eight concepts of optimality are summarized.

In Table 1.1 we list what is given in four rows and the number of criteria (to separate measurement & search from decision making) in two columns. Individual cells then represent the eight optimization concepts.

Observe that the first cell of *Traditional "optimality"* is the only one which does not involve *any* optimization whatsoever, not even a partial one. There is a single given criterion and all alternatives are fixed a priori, either through enumeration or through fixed, well defined constraints. So, there is nothing to be optimized, all is given − like for example in mathematical programming. Observe also that this is a problem of *search only* as the criterion (measurement) is fully (even mathematically) specified. A more precise designation for this cell would be *computation*. One searches given and measured set of alternatives via computational algorithm. The solution is implicit and given by problem formulation, it is made explicit through computation. Nothing else is involved, no optimization takes place.

All other cells of Table 1.1 can be analyzed in a similar way. Of importance is the last cell of the second column, *Cognitive equilibrium*. That is how humans

Table 1.1 Eight Concepts of Optimality

Eight concepts of optimality

Given	Number of Criteria	
	Single	Multiple
Criteria & alternatives	Traditional "optimality"	MCDM
Criteria only	Optimal design (De Novo programming)	Optimal design (De Novo programming)
Alternatives only	Optimal valuation (Limited equilibrium)	Optimal valuation (Limited equilibrium)
"Value complex" only	Cognitive equilibrium (Matching)	Cognitive equilibrium (Matching)

typically make decisions: Very little is given a priori; some alternatives are generated and some criteria chosen to reduce the feasible set. Then additional alternatives are added, some others are dropped, and criteria are re-examined. New sets or combinations of criteria are being tested on changing configurations of alternatives. External points of reference are being sought and evaluated. The complex process of *matching* criteria with alternatives goes through many iterations of narrowing down the choices. Finally, a desirable *equilibrium* between alternatives and criteria is reached and the final prominent or closest to prominent alternative is identified and its feasibility constructed or created.

What is a desirable equilibrium? It is the one when tradeoffs between criteria are either eliminated or significantly reduced by purposeful re-configuration of reconfiguration of alternatives.

Without going into excessive details, one can readily see that the gap between the first and the last cell is formidable indeed. Traditional computation cannot even begin to approximate the complex layers of recurrent optimization involved in the search of cognitive equilibrium. No wonder that traditional "optimization" has had so little resonance in human systems.

1.4   Tradeoffs-Free Management

We have stated that the purpose of decision making is reducing or eliminating tradeoffs. Tradeoffs are a sign of inefficient design and suboptimal solutions. Consumers always abhor tradeoffs because they make their decision making harder, less transparent and loaded with *post-decision regret*.

In MCDM, tradeoffs gave rise to the use of concepts like Pareto efficiency (or optimality), efficiency, non-dominance, non-inferiority, etc. They are all just tradeoffs-based alternatives or solutions. Large, small and vast sets, boundaries, frontiers, etc., of such tradeoffs-based alternatives are being endlessly calculated, graphically displayed, color coded and interactively traversed as a cherished output of analysis – arresting MCDM progress within the second cell of the first row of Table 1.1.

Even more troubling is the notion that such tradeoffs are intimately associated with the criteria or objectives used to evaluate sets of alternatives (baskets of apples). This brings forth often repeated statements about *conflicting objectives*, criteria or goals. So, novices to MCDM speak freely about tradeoffs or conflicts *between objectives* – as if these notions were the properties or attributes of criteria themselves. This often leads to misguided efforts to elicit, reveal, describe or quantify tradeoffs from comparing and analyzing criteria or attributes *alone*. Such results are clearly inapplicable across changing arrays of continually adapted and re-configured sets of feasible alternatives.

It is important to understand at least four principles (there can be more) guiding the concept and properties of tradeoffs in general:

1. Tradeoffs are the *properties of the means* (sets of alternatives), *not* of criteria or objectives.
2. Criteria are merely measures or measure "tapes" for evaluating (measuring) objects of reality (things, alternatives, options, or strategies). There is a fundamental difference between applied *measures* and *measured objects*.
3. *No tradeoffs between measures* (or measure tapes) exist. Measures of cost and quality do not produce tradeoffs – the set of evaluated (measured) choices (alternatives, options) does.
4. It is the *configuration* (shape and structure) of the feasible set (the measured "object") of alternatives, options and strategies that produces or *brings forth all tradeoffs*.

These conclusions are represented in Fig. 1.4 for reader's quick orientation. Two objective functions, f_1 and f_2, are maximized independently over a series of objects of different shapes (baskets of apples, feasible sets). Although both functions are fixed and do not change in the process, their relationship is not characterized by any form of tradeoffs. Depending on the shape of measured objects, tradeoff sets (or boundaries) emerge or disappear accordingly.

The shape, size and properties of tradeoffs (or Pareto, non-dominated and efficient sets) are generated by baskets of alternatives, *not by criteria*. If we combine this understanding with the earlier conclusion that decision making is necessarily about tradeoffs (and their reduction o elimination), then we cannot escape the implication that decision making is primarily about designing a proper (preferably

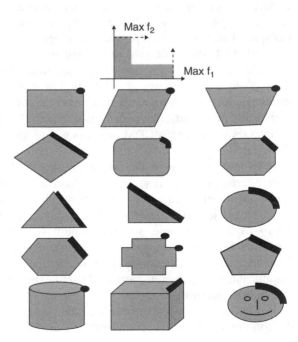

Fig. 1.4 Tradeoffs are properties of measured objects

optimal) set of alternatives. All the rest is valuation or computation. The distinction between design and valuation is emphasized in Table 1.1.

The old idea of *Pareto-efficiency*: that any solution is efficient if it is impossible to move to another solution which would improve at least one criterion and make no criterion worse. The key word here is "impossible". Is redesign of systems impossible? Is efficiency improvement impossible? And if it is, are all our systems perfectly designed for optimality?

Is it possible to define economic efficiency through tradeoffs? That is, at equilibrium, one side, person or criterion can gain only if the other side loses? Is that a desirable state, winning only if other loses? Or is it a direct attack on free-market conditions where both parties to a transaction must realize a gain? At the Pareto-efficient point no free transaction is possible because the gain of one person (or one criterion) implies the loss to the other. How could "efficient allocation" mean that scarce resources are squandered through inefficiency?

Clearly there are many more questions than answers. That is good for all fields of science. Just contemplate the opposite: a dearth of questions but exuberant abundance of answers.

Chapter 2
Harmonizing the Omnipresence of MCDM in Technology, Society, and Policy

Yacov Y. Haimes

Abstract This paper presents historical perspectives on the evolution of the field and discipline of Multiple Criteria Decision Making (MCDM), followed by recognizing MCDM as a philosophy that inspired the development of theory, methodology, and practice of the art and science of MCDM. Except for a brief epilogue, the balance of the paper presents the following Ten Principles for the practice of MCDM: First Principle: MCDM as a harmonizing discipline in science, technology, society, and policy must be holistic; Second Principle: a common denominator bridges risk analysis and MCDM; Third Principle: models and state variables are central to MCDM; Fourth Principle: MCDM must account for risk of low probability with extreme consequences; Fifth Principle: MCDM must account for knowledge uncertainty and variability uncertainty; Sixth Principle: MCDM must account for emergent forced changes; Seventh Principle: multiple models are required to represent the multiple perspectives of a system; Eighth Principle: the imperativeness of selecting representative objectives and the time domain in MCDM; Ninth Principle: the MCDM process must be holistic, adaptive, incremental, and sustainable; and the Tenth Principle: Phantom System Models are required for the effective practice of MCDM, while building on and adhering to all nine principles.

2.1 Historical Perspectives

During the past four or five decades, the consideration of multiple objectives (criteria) in modeling and decision making has grown by leaps and bounds. The 1980s, in particular, saw more emphasis on multiple criteria decision making (MCDM) and a shift from the dominance of single-objective modeling and optimization toward an emphasis on multiple objectives. Indeed, most (if not all) real-world

Y.Y. Haimes
L. R. Quarles Professor of Systems and Information Engineering, Center for Risk Management of Engineering Systems, University of Virginia, Charlottesville, VA, USA
e-mail: Haimes@virginia.edu

Y. Shi et al. (eds.), *New State of MCDM in the 21st Century*, Lecture Notes
in Economics and Mathematical Systems 648, DOI 10.1007/978-3-642-19695-9_2,
© Springer-Verlag Berlin Heidelberg 2011

decision-making problems are characterized by multiple, non-commensurate, and often conflicting objectives. For most such problems, there exists a hierarchy of objectives, sub-objectives, sub-sub-objectives, and so on.

For example, the planning of water and related land resources in a river basin (or a region) is a vital element in the formulation of public policy on this critical resource. Such planning, adhering to the systems-gestalt-holistic philosophy, ought to be responsive to the inherent multiple objectives and goals and should account for the trade-offs among these objectives with respect to myriad objectives, including the following five categories of concern (Haimes 1977, 2009a):

1. Time horizon: short, intermediate, and long term
2. Client: various sectors of the public
3. Nature: aquatic and wildlife habitats
4. Scope: national, regional, and local needs
5. Other considerations: legal, institutional, environmental, social, political, and economic

There are many ways of identifying and classifying objectives and goals for such a planning effort. The U.S. Water Resources Council advocated the enhancement of four major objectives: (1) national economic development, (2) regional economic development, (3) environmental quality, and (4) social well-being.

The Technical Committee study (Peterson 1974) identifies nine goals, which have been divided into two major groups:

1. Maintenance of security: (a) environmental, (b) collective, and (c) individual
2. Enhancement of opportunity: (d) economic, (e) recreational, (f) aesthetic, (g) cultural and community, (h) educational, and (i) individual

In an environmental trade-off analysis, policies should be established to promote conditions where humans and nature can exist in harmony. Resolution of conflicts should be achieved by balancing the advantages of development against the disadvantages to the environment and the aquatic system. The process is one of balancing the total "benefit opportunities," "risks," and "costs" for people and the environment, where the well-being of future generations is as important as that of present ones. Fundamental to multi-objective analysis is the Pareto-optimum concept.

MCDM cannot be practiced effectively, if at all, without models (analytical, conceptual, or simulation). Models, experiments, and simulations are conceived and built to answer specific questions. In general, models assess what is Pareto optimal given what we know, or what we think we know, and where knowledge is needed for an effective decision-making process. Furthermore, mathematical models are the imperative mechanisms with which to perform quantitative MCDM. They are essential for helping analysts and decision makers to better understand and manage a system by relating to its subsystems and its relevant or critical interdependent systems. Modeling is also an art because successful models must build on the artistic traits of experimentation, imagination, creativity, independent thinking, vision, and entrepreneurship. In contrast to scientific knowledge, whose validity can and must be proven, mathematical models cannot always be subjected to such metrics.

In fact, the more complex is the system to be modeled, the lower is the modeler's ability to "verify" or "validate" the resulting models. Some scholars even argue that no complex model can be verified or validated, in part because of the dynamic and probabilistic nature of all natural and constructed systems. Heisenberg's principle is at work here as well; namely, once the system's model is deployed, the essence of the system has been changed.

Therefore, in modeling, it is important to identify this hierarchy of objectives and avoid comparing and trading off objectives that belong to different levels. This fact necessarily leads to the development of hierarchical models and methods that enable the decomposition of an overall system (problem) with its associated objectives into small subsystems, each with its associated sub-objectives. The resulting hierarchical multi-objective decision-making process, which mimics organizational structure, presents a more realistic modeling schema and acknowledges the complexity of the inherent hierarchical multi-objective trade-off analysis (Haimes et al. 1990). In such hierarchical MCDM structures, the subsystems (e.g., department in a major plant or subregions in a regional planning district) generate their own Pareto-optimal strategies and policy options, given the available resources and other constraints. This set of Pareto-optimal options associated with the sub-objectives is forwarded to the next level of the hierarchy of decision making as an input for trade-offs among the overall objectives.

2.1.1 MCDM as a Philosophy That Inspired the Development of Theory, Methodology, and Practice of the Art and Science of Decision Making

The theory, methodology, and practice of the field of MCDM, inspired by the philosophy underpinning MCDM, have experienced a revolutionary process during the past four or five decades. Indeed, MCDM has evolved from a conceptual-theoretical enterprise of interests practiced by a limited number of disciplines and individuals to a universally embraced philosophy. Today, MCDM is being practiced by almost every discipline, including engineering, medicine, economics, law, the environment, and public policy. Furthermore, MCDM has emerged as a philosophy that integrates common sense with empirical, quantitative, normative, and descriptive analysis. It is a philosophy supported by advanced systems concepts (e.g., data management procedures, modeling methodologies, optimization and simulation techniques, and decision-making approaches) that are grounded in both the arts and the sciences for the ultimate purpose of improving the decision-making process. This trend can be traced to the emergent and evolving professional embracing and practicing the gestalt-systems approach, with its appealing representation of the inherent multiple perspectives and comprehensive philosophy by the various disciplines. Consequently, this continuous evolution has necessarily created the need to address the eventual realization of the centrality of multiple objectives that characterize most systems. This is the evolving dominant role of MCDM in harmonizing the disciplines.

Practitioners in the field of MCDM know that an optimum for a single-optimization problem *does not exist in an objective sense per se*. An "optimum" solution exists for a model; however, in a real-life problem it depends on myriad factors, which include the identity of the decision makers, their perspectives, the biases of the modeler, and the credibility of the database. Therefore, a mathematical optimum for a model does not necessarily correspond to an optimum for a real-life problem. This premise also applies to models with multiple objectives in the context of MCDM, as will be discussed subsequently.

In general, multiple decision makers (MDMs) are associated with any single real-world decision-making problem. These MDMs may represent different constituencies, preferences, and perspectives; they may be elected, appointed, or commissioned, and may be public servants, professionals, proprietors, or laypersons; also, they are often associated or connected with a specific level of the various hierarchies of objectives mentioned earlier.

Solutions to a multi-objective optimization problem with multiple decision makers are often reached through negotiation, either through the use of group techniques of MCDM or on an ad hoc basis. The seminal book on the *Art and Science of Negotiation* by Raiffa (1982) is a classic example. Such solutions are often referred to as compromise solutions. However, the pitfalls of a non-win–win compromise solution must be recognized, because one or more decision makers must have lost in the voting or negotiation process. This fact is important because a decision maker in a losing group may be influential enough to sabotage the compromise solution and prevent its implementation. Behind-the-scenes horse trading is a reality that must be accepted as part of human behavior. If a stalemate arises and a compromise solution is not achievable (e.g., if a consensus rule is followed and one or more decision makers objects to a non-Pareto optimal solution that is preferred by all others), the set of objectives may be enlarged or the scope of the problem may be broadened. Finally, it is imperative that decisions be made on a timely basis – a "no-decision" stance could be costly.

What follows are ten Principles that encompass some of the major theoretical, conceptual, and methodological elements that over time have supported MCDM and made it a harmonizing discipline and a field equal to others.

2.2 Ten Guiding Principles for the Practice of MCDM

2.2.1 First Principle: MCDM as a Harmonizing Discipline in Science, Technology, Society, and Policy Must Be Holistic

The multiple perspectives of science, technology, society, and policy, which invariably intersect and often dominate each other, necessarily lead to multi-objective quantitative and qualitative models. This fact positions MCDM as an omnipresence harmonizing philosophy, theory, and methodology of the diverse disciplines. Furthermore, conflicting and competing non-commensurate objectives (criteria)

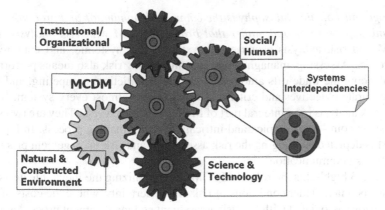

Fig. 2.1 The gestalt-holistic philosophy of MCDM as a harmonizing discipline in science, technology, society, and policy

characterize all disciplines, from engineering, medicine, architecture, agriculture, construction, politics, and education to public policy. MCDM theoreticians and practitioners can benefit from this diversity of users by building on the experiences gained through the domain knowledge of practitioners. The evolving wheels in Fig. 2.1 depict a sample of the multifaceted decision-making process, including the social/human dimension, institutional and organizational behavior, the natural and the constructed environment, and science and technology. All these, among other factors, are interconnected and interdependent systems; thus, the imperativeness of the gestalt-holistic philosophy embraced by MCDM. The analyses of the trade-offs that must be considered in all decision-making processes are depicted by the central wheel – the MCDM driving-force wheel.

2.2.2   Second Principle: A Common Denominator Bridges Risk Analysis and MCDM

The risk assessment and management process should be an integral part of the MCDM modeling effort, and risk management should be an imperative part of the multi-objective decision-making process – not an after-the-fact vacuous exercise. In risk assessment, the analyst often attempts to answer the following questions (Kaplan and Garrick 1981): What can go wrong? What is the likelihood that it would go wrong? What are the consequences? Here we add a fourth question: What is the time frame? Answers to these questions help risk analysts identify, measure, quantify, and evaluate risks and their consequences and impacts. Risk management builds on the risk assessment process by seeking answers to a second set of three questions (Haimes 1991, 2009b): What can be done and what options are available? What are the associated trade-offs in terms of all relevant costs, benefits, and risks? What are the impacts of current management decisions on future options?

The gestalt-holistic philosophy is the common denominator and probably is the most unique integrator and unifier that bridges MCDM with risk analysis. Both MCDM and risk analysis espouse the system-based, systemic, and comprehensive process. Assessing, managing, and communicating risk also means performing and balancing the trade-offs among the multiple conflicting, competing, and non-commensurate objectives and criteria associated with almost every system. By its nature, risk analysis is an integral part of MCDM and vice versa. They are two sides of the same coin – the complex and intricate decision-making process. In Fig. 2.2, MCDM is depicted as bridging the risk assessment and risk management processes through risk communication.

Figure 2.3 highlights the role of MCDM in harmonizing the inevitable decisions that must be made under conditions of risk and uncertainty, where the costs of current decisions associated with the risk assessment and management process are real and certain, but the corresponding beneficial opportunities resulting from reducing and mitigating expected future risks are uncertain.

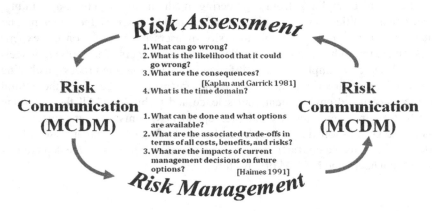

Fig. 2.2 Harmonizing risk assessment, management, and communication through MCDM

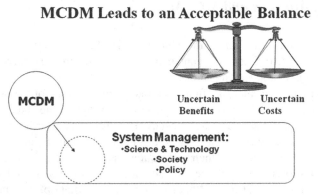

Fig. 2.3 MCDM harmonizes the acceptable balance between remaining residual risks with the costs of risk assessment and management

2.2.3   Third Principle: Models and State Variables Are Central to MCDM

Models are essential for quantitative and qualitative MCDM. Without models, decision makers and the MCDM community at large would be traveling blindly in unknown and often perilous terrains with dire consequences. The systems modeling process relies on the fundamental building blocks of mathematical models: *input, output, state variables, decision (control) variables, exogenous variables, uncertain variables*, and *random variables*. (Note that these building blocks may overlap; for example, *inputs* and *outputs* may be *random*.) Good managers desire to change the states of the systems they coordinate, manage, or control in order to support more effective and efficient attainment of the system's objectives. The choice of the model's state variables selected to represent the essence of the system is, to a large extent, determined and influenced by the model's purpose and the questions it is built to answer, and thus the choice of the decisions that will control the states of the system. Identifying and quantifying (to the extent possible) the building blocks of a mathematical model of any system constitutes a fundamental step in modeling, where the sine qua non is one building block – state variables. This is because at any instant the levels of the state variables are affected by other building blocks (e.g., decision, exogenous, and random variables, as well as inputs), and these levels determine the outputs of the system – primarily the system's objectives and criteria. For example, controlling the production of steel requires an understanding of the states of the steel at any instant – its temperature and other physical and chemical properties. Figure 2.4 depicts the model's building blocks of a farm. Note that at least two state variables are very critical for the optimal growth of the farmer's crops. Knowing the *state* of soil moisture would determine whether the farmer ought to irrigate the crops in non-rainy seasons, and knowing the *state* of soil nutrients would determine the level of fertilizer, if any, that is needed for an optimal growth of the crops. The centrality of state variables in modeling, within and outside the

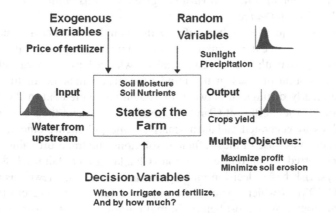

Fig. 2.4 Models and state variables are central to MCDM

MCDM community, has not been sufficiently emphasized. For example, both the vulnerability and resilience of a system are manifestations of the states of the system (Haimes 2006, 2009a, b, c). *Any model should be as simple as possible and as complex as required to answer the expected questions.*

2.2.4 Fourth Principle: MCDM Must Account for Risk of Low Probability with Extreme Consequences

The concerns of the public and most decision makers focus on events with dire and catastrophic consequences, even with low probabilities. Risk is commonly defined as a measure of the probability and severity of adverse effects (Lowrance 1976). With this definition of risk widely adopted by many disciplines, its translation into quantitative terms has been a major source of misunderstanding and misguided use and has often led to erroneous results and conclusions. The most common quantification of risk – the use of the mathematical construct known as the expected-value of risk metric – commensurates low probability of high-consequence events with high probability of low-consequence events – has been playing a decisive role in masking the criticality of these catastrophic events. It is probably the dominant reason for this chaotic situation in the quantification of risk. It is important to recognize the misuse, misinterpretation, and fallacy of the expected value *when it is used as the sole criterion for risk in decision making.* Moreover, the expected value of risk, which until recently has dominated most risk analysis in the field, is not only inadequate, but can lead to fallacious results and interpretations.

The partitioning multi-objective risk method (PMRM) (Asbeck and Haimes 1984; Haimes 2009a), which supplements and complements the expected value measure of risk, isolates a number of damage ranges (by specifying the so-called partitioning probabilities) and generates conditional expectations of damage, given that the damage falls within a particular range. *A conditional expectation is defined as the expected value of a random variable given that this value lies within some prespecified probability range.*

Two challenging questions – how safe is safe enough, and what is an acceptable residual risk? – underline the normative, value-judgment perspectives in risk-based decision making. No mathematical, empirical knowledge base today can adequately model the perception of risks in the mind of decision makers. In the study of MCDM, we clearly distinguish between the quantitative element in the decision-making process, where efficient (Pareto-optimal) policies and their corresponding trade-off values are generated, and the normative value-judgment element, where the decision makers make use of these efficient solutions and trade-off values to determine their preferred (compromise) solution (Chankong and Haimes 1983, 2008). In many ways, risk-based decision making can and should be viewed as a type of stochastic MCDM in which some of the objective functions represent risk functions. This analogy can be most helpful in making use of the extensive knowledge already generated by MCDM (witness the welter of publications and conferences on

Fig. 2.5 MCDM must account for risk of low probability with extreme consequences

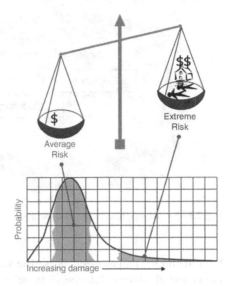

the subject). Probably the most important aspect of considering risk-based decision making within a stochastic MCDM framework is the handling of extreme events. Figure 2.5 depicts the importance of the philosophy, methodology, and practice of MCDM in balancing the average risk with extreme risk.

$$\text{Risk} = function\,(\text{Likelihood}, \text{Consequences})$$

2.2.5 Fifth Principle: MCDM Must Account for Knowledge Uncertainty and Variability Uncertainty

Uncertainty, commonly viewed as *the inability to determine the true state of a system*, can be caused by *incomplete knowledge* and/or *stochastic variability* Paté-Cornell (1996). Two major sources of uncertainty in modeling affect MCDM and other professional fields: (1) *Knowledge Uncertainty*, which manifests itself among other sources in the selection of model topology (structure) and model parameters; and (2) *Variability Uncertainty*, which includes the incorporation into the modeling process of all relevant and important random processes, and other random events and emergent forced changes. Both types of uncertainties markedly affect the quality and effectiveness of the MCDM efforts.

Uncertainty can arise from the inability to predict future events; it dominates most decision-making processes and is the Achilles' heel for all deterministic and most probabilistic models. Clearly, both types of uncertainties markedly affect the quality and effectiveness of the MCDM modeling and analysis efforts and ultimately the decision-making process.

There is a fundamental difference between risk and uncertainty. Risk as a measure of the probability and severity of adverse effects represents an amalgamation of

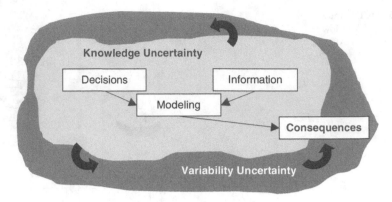

Fig. 2.6 Knowledge uncertainty and variability uncertainty in MCDM

both likelihood and consequences. The very term *risk* refers to a situation in which the potential adverse outcomes can be described in objectively known probability distributions. However, the term *uncertainty* refers only to the likelihood, and commonly refers to a situation in which no reasonable probabilities can be assigned to the potential outcomes.

A significant uncertainty, all too often ignored in the quest for quantitative predictive models, is how well the models used actually represent the real system's significant behavior. This uncertainty can be introduced through the model's topology (structure), its parameters, and the data collection and processing techniques. Model uncertainties will often be introduced through human errors of both commission and omission. In sum, uncertainty caused by variability is a result of inherent fluctuations or differences in the quantity of concern. More precisely, variability occurs when this quantity is not a specific value but rather a population of values. Figure 2.6 depicts the multiple sources of uncertainty.

2.2.6   Sixth Principle: MCDM Must Account for Emergent Forced Changes

Emergent forced changes must be anticipated, tracked, and their precursors be discovered with diligence, so that if and when they cross over (materialize), decision makers would be ready for such an inevitable reality. *The term "emergent forced changes" connotes external or internal sources of risk that may adversely affect the states of the system*, and thus affect the system as a whole. Figure 2.7 presents an example of emergent forced changes based on a 2008 report by the U.S. Department of Transportation, which projects that increased storm intensity due to climate change may lead to increased service disruption and infrastructure damage over the next fifty to one hundred years, and where in the U.S. Gulf coastal area "64% of interstates, 57% of arterials, almost half of the rail miles, 29 airports, and virtually all of the ports are below 7 m (23 feet) in elevation and subject to flooding and possible

Fig. 2.7 An example of
emergent forced changes:
impacts of climate variability

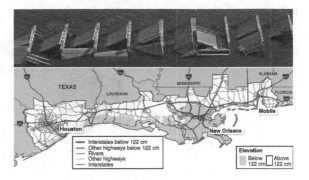

damage due to hurricane surge." Addressing both time and uncertainty when studying emergent forced changes is a sine qua non principle that ought not to be violated
by MCDM practitioners. Emergent forced changes may be manifested through a
continuous spectrum of events, necessarily associated with mostly adverse effects.
These may be caused by natural phenomena or malevolent human actions, including unintended disastrous consequences initiated through local, regional, or global
public policy decisions and actions. Some emergent forced changes are occurring
in today's world. Bayesian analysis constitutes an important element in modeling,
estimating, and tracking over time the precursors to and the emergence of forced
changes. Bayes' Theorem, which provides the basis for Bayesian analysis, translates
probabilistically new knowledge, whether gained by direct observations or through
expert evidence. It incorporates the new probabilistic acquired knowledge within
the prior probabilistic assumptions. Scenario development constitutes a central role
in tracking and estimating precursors to the occurrence of emergent forced changes.
In scenario tracking, both the probabilities and consequences are considered when
evaluating the importance of any specific scenario. The uncertain nature of emergent forced changes requires that appropriate metrics for the quantification of the
risks and uncertainties associated with each objective function (and other parts of
the model) considered in the MCDM process must be adopted and studied. Without such considerations the representativeness and effectiveness and the ultimate
credibility of the entire decision-making process would be questionable.

One important demarcation line between a good or a great decision-making process is the extent to which the known and known-unknown future developments
and emergent forced changes affecting the system enterprise are addressed. These
forces, whose sources may be internal or external to an organization, must be anticipated and tracked, and their precursors discovered with diligence. Then, if and when
they materialize, the decision makers and their tactical and strategic plans will be
ready for such an inevitable reality. In other words, this is a sine qua non principle
that should not be violated by risk analysts and practitioners.

Resilience, which is a manifestation of the states of the system and represents
the ability of the system to withstand a major disruption within acceptable degradation parameters and to recover within an acceptable composite cost and time, is
an important concept in emergent forced changes (Haimes 2009c). This is because

Fig. 2.8 Trade-offs are made between preparedness for emergent forced changes and future system resilience

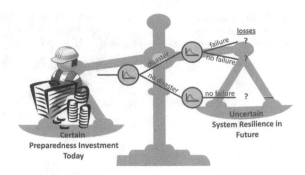

the anticipation of and planning for emergent forced changes through preparedness and other risk management actions necessarily improve the resilience of the system. Figure 2.8 highlights the inherent trade-offs that must be made among certain investments today for preparedness in the quest to address emergent forced changes and the uncertain nature of either the realization of such forced changes or the expected future resilience of the system.

2.2.7 Seventh Principle: Multiple Models Are Required to Represent the Multiple Perspectives of a System

The interconnectedness and interdependencies within and among all large-scale and multi-scale systems defy a single model representation of the multiple systems' perspectives. The included and excluded systems' perspectives implicitly and explicitly affect the ultimate selection of policy options in the MCDM process. Indeed, most organizational and technology-based systems and all military systems are hierarchical in nature; thus their risk management is driven by this hierarchical reality and must be responsive to it. The risks associated with each subsystem within the hierarchical structure are likely to contribute to and ultimately determine the risks of the overall system. Hierarchical considerations and aspects of a system and the multiple objectives associated with that system are dual attributes that should be recognized as such in all serious modeling efforts, and particularly for risk-informed decision making. The ability to model the intricate relationships among the various subsystems and to account for all relevant and important elements of risk and uncertainty renders the modeling process more tractable and the MCDM process more representative and encompassing.

When modeling large-scale and complex systems such as dams and levees, more than one mathematical or conceptual model is likely to emerge; each of these models may focus on a specific aspect of the system, yet all may be regarded as acceptable representations of it.

It is impracticable to represent within a single model all the aspects of a large-scale system, such as physical infrastructure systems, that may be of interest at any given time (to its management, government, or regulators). Hierarchical Holographic Modeling (HHM) (Haimes 1981, 2009a) has emerged from a generalization of Hierarchical Overlapping Coordination (Haimes and Macko 1973; Macko and Haimes 1978). The name is suggested by holography – the technique of lensless photography. The difference between holography and conventional photography, which captures only two-dimensional planar representations of scenes, is analogous to the differences we see between conventional mathematical modeling techniques (yielding what might be termed "planar," limited-perspective models) and the more "multidimensional" HHM schema. In the abstract, a mathematical model may be viewed as a one-sided image of the real system that it portrays. In many respects, HHM is a holistic philosophy/methodology aimed at capturing and representing the essence of the inherent diverse characteristics and attributes of a system it attempts to model – its multiple aspects, perspectives, facets, views, dimensions, and hierarchies. Figure 2.9 presents two perspectives (decompositions) of the Maumee River Basin, within the Great Lakes Basin (Ohio, Michigan, and Indiana): Hydrologic (eight watersheds) and Political-Geographic (five planning subareas) (Haimes, 2009a).

The term *holographic* refers to having a multi-view image of a system when identifying vulnerabilities (as opposed to a single view, or a flat image of the system). The term *hierarchical* refers to the desire to understand what can go wrong at many different levels of the system. HHM recognizes that for the risk assessment to be complete, one must realize that the macroscopic risks that are understood at the upper management level of an organization are very different from the microscopic risks observed at lower levels. In a particular situation, a microscopic risk can become a critical factor in making things go wrong. In order to carry out a complete

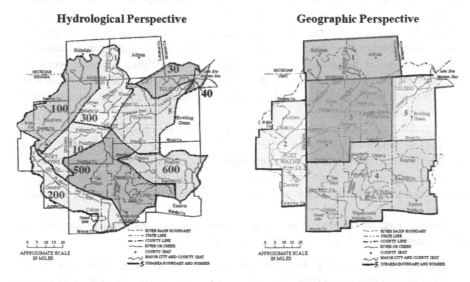

Fig. 2.9 Hydrologic perspective and political-geographic perspective

HHM analysis, the team that performs it must include people who bring knowledge from up and down the hierarchy.

HHM has turned out to be useful in modeling large-scale, complex, and hierarchical systems, such as defense and civilian infrastructure systems. The multiple visions and perspectives of HHM add strength to risk analysis. It has been extensively and successfully deployed to study risks for numerous government agencies. To counter the enormously large scenarios generated for both questions, the Risk Filtering and Ranking Method developed in 1990 for NASA was subsequently extended and modified (Haimes et al. 2002).

2.2.8   Eighth Principle: The Imperativeness of Selecting Representative Objectives and the Time Domain in MCDM

Today, more than ever, it is a mistake to try to optimize a set of objectives that are limited to present needs and aspirations or that are not responsive to emergent or future forced changes. In other words, for an adaptive, incremental, and sustainable MCDM process to be successful, future impacts of present decisions and policies must be incorporated and be an integral part of the trade-offs. Thus, a systemic approach to MCDM should be adopted to (1) continuously assess and evaluate precursors to potential forced changes, (2) balance present objectives with potential or perceived emergent needs and objectives, and (3) add more flexibility to present policy formulation to ensure against adverse emergent or unintended catastrophic or irreversible consequences. For example, evaluating the consequences and future flexibility of two preferred Pareto-optimal policies could dictate a distinct choice between two options presently perceived as seemingly equivalent. The importance of impact analysis is even more critical when considering the time domain that affects all systems – societal, organizational, and technological. Examples are the natural deterioration over time of all physical infrastructures, demographic changes, and advancements in technology. Each stage in this evolving dynamic world is characterized by multiple objectives, and trade-offs among the attainment of present objectives and future flexibility can be incorporated within the overall risk-informed decision-making process.

Should the systems modeler or decision makers always be satisfied with a single-perspective model of the system under study? The answer is no. Invariably single models as discussed in the previous principle cannot adequately capture the multifarious nature of large-scale water resources systems, their bewildering variety of resources and capabilities, their multiple non-commensurable objectives, and their diverse users.

Furthermore, the following too-often overlooked cases constitute major sources of misinterpretation or misuse of Pareto optimality:

1. The number of selected objective functions introduces an implicit bias in the ultimate outcomes generated through the MCDM process. To address this reality, concerted efforts must be devoted to assessing the sensitivity of the resulting

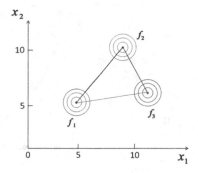

Fig. 2.10 Pareto optimality is dependent on the proper selection of the objective functions

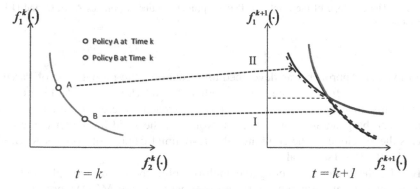

Fig. 2.11 Impact of policies at time $t = k$ on future options at time $k + 1$

policy options to the addition or deletion of one or more objective functions. Figure 2.10 presents three objective functions to be minimized in the decision space and the associated Pareto-optimal solutions (both Proper Pareto-optimal solutions in the interior triangle and Improper Pareto-optimal solutions in the boundaries of the triangle). Note that removing one of the three objective functions would eliminate a significant number of Pareto-optimal solutions, and vice versa.

2. Dynamic systems where the time domain is of paramount importance introduce another challenge to the theory and practice of MCDM. For example, ignoring the changes in the states of a safety-critical dynamic system as time progresses would render static-based decisions misleading, if not disastrous. Recognizing this fact, event trees, decision trees, and process control, among other methods, account for the impacts of current decisions on future options. Figure 2.11 presents impact of policies at time $t = k$ on future options at time $k + 1$, where the dotted line represents a new Pareto-optimal frontier generated at time $k + 1$. Note that if the decision maker were to prefer to operate during period $k + 1$ in Regime I, then Policy B would be inferior to A. Conversely, if the decision maker were to prefer to operate during period $k + 1$ in Regime II, then Policy A would be inferior to B. Clearly, the time domain is critical in the MCDM process.

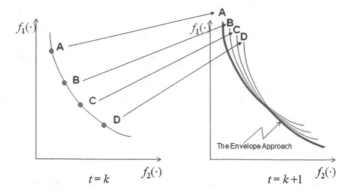

Fig. 2.12 The envelope of the combined Pareto-optimal frontier of policies A, B, C, and D for $k + 1$st period

The Envelope Approach was developed to account for the propagation of Pareto-optimal solutions from one period to another (Li and Haimes 1987). Figure 2.12 extends this concept through the Envelope Approach, where the Pareto-optimal frontier can be generated for n periods. Note that the solid-line outer curve represents the envelope of the combined Pareto-optimal frontier of policies A, B, C, and D for the $k + 1$st period.

Finally, the trade-offs among the multiple objectives must complement and supplement the determination of Pareto optimality in the MCDM process. The process of eliciting the decision makers' preferences must be systemic, repeatable, robust, and based on the evidence generated in the MCDM process. Several methods and approaches have been developed to generate the multiple trade-offs, including the Surrogate Worth Trade-off (SWT) method (Haimes and Hall 1974; Haimes 2009a).

2.2.9 Ninth Principle: The MCDM Process Must Be Holistic, Adaptive, Incremental, and Sustainable

Any characterization of a holistic and multifaceted decision-making process must address, at a minimum, its following attributes: it is dynamic; is fraught with myriad sources of risk and uncertainty, including emergent forced changes; involves a hierarchy of multiple decision makers; often must address multiple conflicting, competing, and non-commensurate objectives, goals, and aspirations; is driven by ever-moving requirements, demands, and targets; and, not least of all, it protects, adheres to, and promotes organizational core values. Thus, the decision-making process must be holistic, adaptive, incremental, and sustainable.

2.2.9.1 Why Holistic?

Can a decision-making process be considered effective and viable if only for randomly selected risks and opportunities, for a fixed time domain, and for only a subset of affected parties? Clearly, the complexity and multi-scale attributes of almost all organizational, societal, and the natural and built environment physical infrastructures require an encompassing and holistic MCDM process. The decision-making process cannot be addressed with a simplistic "one-fits-all" approach, because each system comprises its own unique characteristics and idiosyncrasies. Furthermore, once decisions are made, then the ways and means for *communicating* them to the stakeholders are often as important as the content and impacts of the decisions themselves. In addition, *not all decisions may go well or meet their intended functions.* Holism must be the hallmark of a decision-making process that is impeccable and above reproach.

2.2.9.2 Why Adaptive and Incremental?

Fundamental to the MCDM process is the consideration of present and future opportunities and risks associated with the decisions and trade-offs that are being made. Thus, if we accept the premise that all critical and important decisions are made under uncertain conditions, it follows that as we track the events over time and assess the consequences of the decisions made (positive or negative), some appropriate course correction and adaptation would be imperative. In his book *Good to Great*, Jim Collins (2001 p. 195) writes: "Enduring great companies preserve their *core values and purpose* while their business strategies and operating practices *endlessly adapt to a changing world.* This is the magical combination of 'preserve the core and stimulate progress'" [emphasis mine]. As a corollary, assessing and clarifying the viability of the decisions is dependent on the effectiveness of the MCDM process. In other words, an effective and viable decision-making process does not end when the decisions are made; rather, a systemic post-audit evaluation is required to continuously track the progress being made. *This would reveal future opportunities and unintended adverse consequences that might be encountered.* Furthermore, precursors to emergent forced changes, whose crossovers could adversely affect the system and might counter the original goals and objectives of the decisions being tracked, ought to be assessed and new actions adapted. These activities are commonly made incrementally with appropriate resources allocated for each tracked forced-change scenario commensurate with its projected impacts and consequences.

2.2.9.3 Why Sustainable?

The third edition of The Merriam-Webster New International Dictionary defines sustainability as: "maintained at length without interruption, weakening, or losing in power or quality." An MCDM process must also be sustainable and achieve sustainable results. This means it must maintain the planned and anticipated results from such decisions (in addition to the value derived from being holistic, adaptive, and

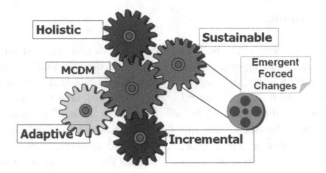

Fig. 2.13 The holistic, adaptive, incremental, and sustainable MCDM process

incremental). Fundamentally, a sustainable decision-making process shares many of the traits of a holistic process, because it also implies that the process must be strategic, encompassing, and well-balanced, involving and communicating with all concerned parties, and responsive to the uncertain world within which the results of the decision will be realized.

An appropriate model ought to be able to answer the following question: *Will the planned-for demands (or stress) on a system be dramatically exceeded by a potential emergent events that could produce a much higher critical demand (or stress) than planned for, thus resulting in extreme or catastrophic consequences?* For an informed confirmation of this scenario, we term this eventuality a "crossover." *Thus, in the context of modeling, crossovers connote situations where during the planning time horizon of a dynamic system, the projected extreme event (e.g., an emergent forced change) can cross from a state of too high an uncertainty to base designs upon to a forecasted state of too high a likelihood of occurring to ignore as an important factor of design.* In addition to focusing on model assumptions, *we must also continue our efforts to develop methods of modeling that can discover and illuminate crossovers, where the output of the model is highly sensitive to the shift in assumptions caused by external forced changes.*

Figure 2.13 depicts the holistic, adaptive, incremental, and sustainable MCDM process that is driven by and responsive to emergent forced changes, where holistic connotes systemic, comprehensive, and encompassing doctrine; adaptive connotes continuously updating the states of the system and the corresponding decisions, and where the time domain is of paramount importance; incremental connotes a step-by-step process that builds on new knowledge; and sustainable connotes a viable and repeatable process.

2.2.10 Tenth Principle: Phantom System Models Are Required for the Effective Practice of MCDM, While Building on and Adhering to All Nine Principles

This Tenth Principle encompasses all nine principles introduced previously. Consider the challenging tasks facing leaders and planners around the world to ensure adequate housing, supply drinking water of safe quality, and myriad other social and economic initiatives, given the emergent forced changes in climate, terrorism, and future population growth. These MCDM-based multi-scale complex systems are not "solvable" in any provable, cost-effective way. Like most complex systems, they require trade-offs across objectives and large-scale integration of scores of research efforts across many dimensions. Indeed, both cases share the urgent need to continue gathering and analyzing actionable information and incorporating it into an evolving policy. Horowitz (2007) provides a definition of multi-scale systems in the context of large-scale systems: "By their nature, large-scale and complex large-scale systems span a number of discrete levels from the highest system level to the lowest component level. As opportunities and risks present themselves, they may have different impacts and require different planned responses at different levels."

No single model can capture all the dimensions necessary to adequately understand, evaluate, and manage the above challenges. For example, it is impossible to represent in a single model all relevant state variables of large- and multi-scale systems. Furthermore, adhering to the nine principles discussed in this paper – and particularly the Ninth Principle, which calls for a holistic, adaptive, incremental, and sustainable MCDM process – requires a new modeling paradigm, referred to as Phantom System Models (PSM) (Haimes 2007, 2009a). (Note that the term PSM will connote the overall modeling philosophy, while PSMs will connote the modeling components.) Indeed, unprecedented and emerging multi-scale systems are inherently elusive and visionary – they are, by and large, phantom entities grounded on a mix of future needs and available resources, technology, forced developments and changes, and myriad other unforeseen events.

The PSM builds on and incorporates input from HHM (see Seventh Principle), and by doing so seeks to develop causal relationships through various modeling and simulation tools; it imbues life and realism into phantom ideas for emergent systems that otherwise would never have been realized. In other words, with different modeling and simulation tools, PSM legitimizes the exploration and experimentation of out-of-the-box and seemingly "far-fetched" ideas and ultimately discovers insightful implications that otherwise would have been completely missed and dismissed. In this sense, it allows for "non-consensus" ideas or an "agree-to-disagree" process for further exploration and study. The output of the HHM is a taxonomy of identified risk scenarios, or multiple perspectives of a system for modeling. Alternatively, the output of the PSM is a justification or rationalization for investment in preparedness or learning activities to protect against critical forced changes or emergent risks – investment that might not otherwise have been approved. *Through logically organized and systemically executed models, the PSM provides a reasoned experimental modeling framework with which to explore and thus understand the intricate relationships that characterize the nature of multi-scale emergent systems.* The PSM philosophy rejects dogmatic problem solving that relies on a single modeling approach structured on one school of thinking. Rather, its modeling schema builds on the multiple perspectives gained through generating multiple scenarios. This leads to the construction of appropriate models to deduce tipping points as well as meaningful information for logical conclusions and future actions.

The multi-model, systems-driven PSM approach can effectively address these emergent challenges at both the national strategic and local tactical levels. Such an approach must be capable of maximally using what is known now and optimally learn, update, and adapt through time as decisions are made and more information becomes available. In the context of the holistic, adaptive, incremental, and sustainable MCDM process, the PSM is a real-to-virtual laboratory for experimentation, a learn-as-you-go facility, and a process for emergent systems that are not yet completely designed and developed.

2.3 Epilogue

The complex social-, technological-, economic-, environmental-, and political-based challenges leaders and planners around the world experience necessarily require a holistic, adaptive, incremental, and sustainable decision-making process, where multiple non-commensurate, competing, and often conflicting objectives must be addressed and reconciled. During the past several decades, MCDM, by its philosophical underpinning and the theory, methodology, and practice that have been developed on the basis of its holistic philosophy, has served as a harmonizing agent in technology, society, and policy. The Ten Principles introduced in this paper are aimed at recognizing this harmonizing trend.

References

Amin, S.M., Horowitz B.M.: Toward agile and resilient large-scale systems: Adaptive robust national/international infrastructures, Global Journal of Flexible Systems Management, 9 Vol. 1, (2008)

Asbeck, E., Haimes Y.Y.: The partitioned multiobjective risk method. Large Scale Syst. 6, L3–38 (1984)

Chankong, V., Haimes Y.Y.: Multiobjective Decision Making: Theory and Methodology, Second Edition. Dover, Mineola (2008)

Collins, J.: Good to Great. HarperCollins Publishers, Inc. NY (2001)

Haimes, Y.Y.: Risk Modeling, Assessment, and Management, Third Edition. Wiley, New York (2009a)

Haimes, Y.Y.: On the definition of resilience in systems. Risk Anal. 29, 498–501 (2009b)

Haimes, Y.Y.: On the complex definition of risk. Risk Anal. 29, 1647–1654 (2009c)

Haimes, Y.Y.: Phantom system models for emergent multiscale systems. J. Infrastruct. Syst. 13, 81–87 (2007)

Haimes, Y.Y.: Total risk management. Risk Anal. 11, 169–171 (1991)

Haimes, Y.Y.: Hierarchical holographic modeling. IEEE Trans. Syst. Man Cybern. 11, 606–617 (1981)

Haimes, Y.Y.: Hierarchical Analyses of Water Resources Systems: Modeling and Optimization of Large-Scale Systems. McGraw-Hill, New York (1977)

Haimes, Y.Y., Hall, W.: Multiobjectives in water resource systems analysis: The surrogate worth trade-off method. Water Resour. Res. 10, 615–624 (1974)

Haimes, Y.Y., Kaplan, S., Lambert, J.H.: Risk filtering, ranking, and management framework using hierarchical holographic modeling. Risk Anal. 22, 383–397 (2002)

Haimes, Y.Y., Macko, D.: Hierarchical structures in water resources systems management. IEEE
    Trans. Syst. Man Cybern. **3**, 396–402 (1973)
Haimes, Y.Y., Tarvainen, K., Shima, T., Thadathil J.: Hierarchical Multiobjective Analysis of
    Large-Scale Systems. Hemisphere Publishing Corporation, New York (1990)
Kaplan, S., Garrick, B.J.: On the quantitative definition of risk. Risk Anal. **1**, 11–27 (1981)
Li, D., Haimes, Y.Y.: The envelope approach for multiobjective optimization problems. IEEE
    Trans. Syst. Man Cybern. **17**, 1026–1038 (1987)
Lowrance, W.W.: Of Acceptable Risk: Science and the Determination of Safety. William Kauf-
    mann, Inc., Los Altos (1976)
Macko, D., Haimes, Y.Y.: Overlapping coordination of hierarchical structures. IEEE Trans. Syst.
    Man Cybern. **8**, 745–751 (1978)
Paté-Cornell, E.: Uncertainties in risk analysis: Six levels of treatment. Reliab. Eng. Syst. Safe. **54**,
    95–111 (1996)
Peterson, D.F.: Water resources planning, social goals, and indicators: Methodological develop-
    ment and empirical tests. Utah Water Research Laboratory, Utah State University, Logan,
    PRWG 131–1 (1974)
Raiffa, H.: The Art and Science of Negotiation. Belknap Press, MA (1982)
(USDOT) United States Department of Transportation, Impacts of climate change and variability
    on transportation systems and infrastructure: Gulf Coast Study, Phase I, 2008

Chapter 3
Decision Making on Pareto Front Approximations with Inherent Nondominance

Markus Hartikainen, Kaisa Miettinen, and Margaret M. Wiecek[†]

Abstract Approximating the Pareto fronts of nonlinear multiobjective optimization problems is considered and a property called inherent nondominance is proposed for such approximations. It is shown that an approximation having the above property can be explored by interactively solving a multiobjective optimization problem related to it. This exploration can be performed with available interactive multiobjective optimization methods. The ideas presented are especially useful in solving computationally expensive multiobjective optimization problems with costly function value evaluations.

3.1 Introduction

In multiobjective optimization (MO), the problem is to find a preferred solution in the presence of several conflicting objectives (see e.g., Hwang and Masud 1979; Miettinen 1999; Sawaragi et al. 1985). In such problems, there is no single well-defined optimal solution but several mathematically equally good solutions, so-called Pareto optimal (PO) solutions, can be identified. To be able to find the most preferred among them as the final solution usually additional preference information is needed from a human decision maker (DM), who knows the problem domain.

According to Hwang and Masud (1979), MO methods can be divided into no-preference methods, a priori methods, a posteriori methods and interactive methods. For details of these different methods see e.g., Miettinen (1999). Interactive methods can be seen as the most prominent – as argued in Miettinen et al. (2008) – because the DM can learn about the problem as e.g., in Eskelinen et al. (2010) and adjust his/her goals accordingly. Because only such PO solutions are generated that are interesting to the DM, interactive methods are generally computationally much less expensive than, for example, a posteriori methods, for which many PO solutions

[†]On sabbatical leave from Clemson University, South Carolina, USA.

M. Hartikainen (✉), K. Miettinen, and M.M. Wiecek
Department of Mathematical Information Technology, University of Jyväskylä, Jyväskylä, Finland

Y. Shi et al. (eds.), *New State of MCDM in the 21st Century*, Lecture Notes
in Economics and Mathematical Systems 648, DOI 10.1007/978-3-642-19695-9_3,
© Springer-Verlag Berlin Heidelberg 2011

must be computed in order for the DM to get enough alternatives for making an informed decision.

If a multiobjective optimization problem (MOP) is computationally very demanding (i.e., function evaluations take a lot of time) even classical interactive methods can have problems, because the DM may get frustrated in waiting while new PO solutions that reflect his/her preferences are computed. This high computational demand occurs often, for example, with so-called black-box MOPs, whose objective functions are not explicitly known as algebraic functions of decision variables but need to be simulated. Approaches based on evolutionary multiobjective optimization methods taylored for finding PO solutions for computationally expensive MOPs have been proposed in Knowles (2006) and Liu et al. (2008). Another way to handle such MOPs is to use design of experiments for constructing surrogate approximations of the objective functions and then solving the surrogate MOP (Yoon et al. 2009; Wilson et al. 2001). However, according to Karakasis and Giannakoglou (2004), the use of surrogate approximations loses its computational benefits as the number of objectives increases. The approaches based on evolutionary algorithms have their issues too; in order to produce a dense Pareto set representation, a large number of solutions must be computed, which is time-consuming or sometimes even impossible. On the other hand, the choice of the final outcome from a large number of PO outcomes is cognitively very demanding as noted in Larichev (1992).

Instead of estimating each objective function with a surrogate, one can estimate the set of PO outcomes (also called the Pareto front (PF)). In Eskelinen et al. (2010), an interactive method called Pareto Navigator is proposed, in which a PF approximation for a convex MOP is constructed based on a relatively small set of PO outcomes. Having constructed the approximation, the preferences of the DM can be reflected in real time by moving on the approximation in a way that resembles the visual interactive Pareto Race method for linear problems (Korhonen and Wallenius 1988). When a preferred point on the approximation has been found, the closest actual PO outcome can be found by means of the achievement scalarizing function (Wierzbicki 1986).

The construction of a PF approximation (that allows consideration of the objective vectors between known PO outcomes) and its exploration with MO methods is a novel approach to computationally demanding MOPs and has some potential benefits. When compared to a posteriori methods, some computational expense can be avoided because a smaller number of PO outcomes is sufficient. The cognitive load of going through a large set of PO outcomes becomes lighter, because the DM is allowed to explore the approximation by iteratively expressing his/her preferences. The DM can also learn about the problem in the process. Finally, since the construction of the PF approximation does not have any special requirements for the initial PO outcomes, they may be generated with any method for finding PO outcomes, and because the DM is not involved in this, the possible computational cost is not a problem. What matters is that when the approximation has been constructed, the DM can be provided with new approximated PO outcomes without delay.

The Pareto Navigator method is, however, only applicable to convex MOPs, because of the type of approximation it uses. The ultimate goal behind our study is to develop a MO method that uses the Pareto Navigator's idea of navigating on the approximation for general continuous nonlinear MOPs. The aim of this paper is to concentrate on the issue of what kind of approximation can be used for the above mentioned exploration. Because interactive MO methods have been proven effective in finding a preferred point on the PF, we want to employ them also for finding a preferred point on the approximation. The process of finding a preferred point on a PF approximation (by using interactive MO methods or other methods) is referred to in this paper as *decision making on the approximation*.

There are numerous methods for approximating the PF of a MOP. A survey (Ruzika and Wiecek 2005) summarizes methods published before 2003. More recent approximation methods for nonlinear MOPs are given e.g., in Bezerkin et al. (2006), Goel et al. (2007), Lotov et al. (2004), and Martin et al. (2005). However, the uses of the PF approximations in decision making have not received the attention that they deserve. Among the few exceptions are Ackermann et al. (2007), Eskelinen et al. (2010), Kaliszewski (1994), Klamroth and Miettinen (2008), Lotov et al. (2004), Miettinen et al. (2003), and Monz et al. (2008). None of these, however, aims at using general interactive MO methods in exploring the PF approximation. The approach of this paper is, thus, different from all the above; we aim at characterizing an approximation for a specific use of exploration with interactive MO methods.

The paper is structured as follows. Some terminology and notation is set in Sect. 3.2. We introduce a new property called inherent nondominance (IND) for a PF approximation and prove its relevant properties in Sect. 3.3. In Sect. 3.4, decision making on the approximation is discussed and an example is given. We also propose an approach to exploring an IND PF approximation by solving a special type MOP. Finally, we draw conclusions in Sect. 3.5.

3.2 Notation and Definitions

In this paper, we study multiobjective optimization problems (MOPs)

$$\min_{\text{s.t. } x \in X} \; (f_1(x), \ldots, f_k(x)), \tag{3.1}$$

where $f_i : X \to \mathbb{R}$ is a function for all $i \in \{1, \ldots, k\}$, $X \subset \mathbb{R}^n$ and $k, n \in \mathbb{N}$. We also define a vector valued function $f : X \to \mathbb{R}^k$, $f(x) = (f_1(x), \ldots, f_k(x))^T$ for all $x \in X$.

The set X is called the feasible decision set of (3.1) and every $x \in X$ is called a (feasible) decision. The set $f(X)$ is the feasible outcome set of (3.1) and every $z \in f(X)$ is called a (feasible) outcome. The set $\mathbb{R}^k$ is called the objective space of (3.1) and every point $z \in \mathbb{R}^k$ is called an objective vector. With the above notation, the MOP (3.1) can be formulated as

$$\min_{\text{s.t. } z \in f(X)} z. \tag{3.2}$$

For any objective vectors $z^1, z^2 \in \mathbb{R}^k$ notation $z^1 \leq z^2$ means that $z_i^1 \leq z_i^2$ for all $i = 1, \ldots, k$ and $z^1 \neq z^2$. If $z^1 \leq z^2$ it is said that z^1 dominates z^2. If $B \subset \mathbb{R}^k$ is a set, then a point $b \in B$ is Pareto optimal (PO) in B, if there does not exist a point $\tilde{b} \in B$ that dominates b. An outcome $z \in f(X)$ is PO for (3.1), if z is PO in $f(X)$. Finally, the Pareto front (PF) of B, $PF(B)$, is the set of PO points in B and the PF of a MOP, PF, is the set of PO outcomes of the MOP. A feasible decision $x \in X$ is a PO solution to (3.1), if $f(x)$ is a PO outcome.

We assume a rational decision maker (DM): he/she always prefers a PO objective vector over a dominated one in any set of possible objective vectors. In other words, for every set $A \subset \mathbb{R}^k$ the preferred objective vectors of the DM belong to $PF(A)$ and, furthermore, the DM is not interested in $A \setminus PF(A)$ if he/she is aware of $PF(A)$.

The starting point of this study is as follows. Assume that we are given a computationally demanding MOP with the above notation. This problem is referred to as the *initial MOP*. If not otherwise defined, the notations PO and PF always refer to this problem. We also assume that we are given a finite set of PO outcomes P. This set is referred to as the *initial set of PO outcomes*. As in Pareto Navigator, the way this set has been generated is not restricted in any way.

3.3 Inherent Nondominance and Inherently Nondominated Approximation of the PF

In this section, we introduce the concept of inherent nondominance and other related concepts. We also present the relevant properties characteristic for an inherently nondominated PF approximation. These properties will be further interpreted in Sect. 3.4.

Definition 1. We say that a set $A \subset \mathbb{R}^k$ is *inherently nondominated (IND)*, if there does not exist two points $a^1, a^2 \in A$ so that $a^1 \leq a^2$.

Definition 2. A set $A \subset \mathbb{R}^k$ is an *inherently nondominated PF approximation (based on P)* if A is IND and $P \subset A$.

According to the following theorem, the actual PF satisfies the IND condition. The actual PF should be suitable as an approximation of itself, because naturally it is the best approximation that one can hope for.

Theorem 1. *The PF is an IND PF approximation based on P.*

Proof. Since P is a set of PO outcomes, then $P \subset PF$. The property that PF is IND is trivial, since if $z^1, z^2 \in f(X)$ so that $z^1 \leq z^2$, then $z^2 \notin PF$.   □

The following theorem gives a sufficient and necessary condition for a set to be IND and could, thus, have been chosen as the definition for an IND set. We, however, chose the definition given above.

Theorem 2. *Let $A \subset \mathbb{R}^k$ be a set. Then the set A is IND if and only if $PF(A) = A$.*

Proof. "$\Rightarrow$": Naturally $PF(A) \subset A$. To show that $A \subset PF(A)$, assume the contrary that there exists a point $a \in A \setminus PF(A)$. This implies a point $b \in A$ so that $b \leq a$. But this is a contradiction, since A is IND.
"$\Leftarrow$": To show that A is IND assume the contrary that there exist distinct points $a, b \in A$ so that $a \leq b$. This would imply that $b \notin PF(A)$ and would thus be a contradiction. $\square$

The following corollary follows directly from Theorem 2. It is, however, considerably important, since according to it an IND approximation *extends P without losing Pareto optimality*.

Corollary 1. *If a set $A \subset \mathbb{R}^k$ is an IND PF approximation based on P, then*

$$P \subset PF(A).$$

Proof. Now $PF(A) = A \supset P$, because of Theorem 2 and Definition 2. $\square$

The above properties of an IND approximation are rather straightforward. Theorem 3 establishes the existence of IND PF approximations.

Theorem 3. *The set of initial PO outcomes P is an IND PF approximation based on P.*

Proof. Because outcomes in P are PO, they do not dominate each other. Also $P \subset P$ trivially. $\square$

The IND approximation P is not, however, interesting, since it does not contain other points than the initial PO outcomes P. We want to construct an IND approximation A that extends P. The outline of our idea to construct such an IND approximation is as follows:

1. Find a family of sets $\mathscr{A} \subset \mathscr{P}(\mathbb{R}^k)$, where $\mathscr{P}(\mathbb{R}^k)$ is the family of all subsets of $\mathbb{R}^k$, that represents geometrical interpolants between known PO outcomes.
2. Find a minimal family $\mathscr{B} \subset \mathscr{A}$ so that the final IND PF approximation $\cup_{A \in (\mathscr{A} \setminus \mathscr{B})} A$ is IND.

Details of this idea are a topic of further research.

The approximation A^2 in the following Example 1 is found by first constructing the convex hulls of all subsets of P (representing the geometrical interpolants) and then the approximation is set as the union of all other convex hulls except the convex hull of the whole set P, which is not included because it is not IND.

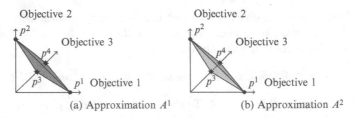

(a) Approximation A^1 (b) Approximation A^2

Fig. 3.1 Two piecewise linear PF approximations constructed with the same initial set of PO outcomes. The approximation A^1 is the convex hull of all points and the approximation A^2 is a union of three triangles

Example 1. Let the set of initial PO outcomes be $P = \{p^1, p^2, p^3, p^4\}$, where $p^1 = (1, 0, 0)$, $p^2 = (0, 1, 0)$, $p^3 = (0, 0, 1)$ and $p^4 = (2/5, 2/5, 2/5)$. We compare two piecewise linear PF approximations $A^1 = \text{conv}(P)$ and $A^2 = \text{conv}(p^1, p^2, p^4) \cup \text{conv}(p^1, p^3, p^4) \cup \text{conv}(p^2, p^3, p^4)$, where $\text{conv}(C)$ is the convex hull of a set C. These are shown in Fig. 3.1. The convex hull of all outcomes in P is used e.g., in Eskelinen et al. (2010) and Monz et al. (2008) for approximating the outcome set $f(X)$ for convex MOPs and has thus been used for getting also a PF approximation. Approximation A^2 is IND, which can be shown analytically. Approximation A^1 is, however, not IND because the point $(1/3, 1/3, 1/3) \in A^1$ dominates the initial PO outcome p^4 that is also in A^1. For this reason, approximation A^1 is not able to capture the non-convex shape implied by the initial set of PO outcomes and, unlike the IND approximation A^2, gives too optimistic estimates.

3.4 Decision Making on the Approximation

In this section, we discuss decision making on the approximation. The underlying reasoning is that once the PF approximation with desired properties has been created, one can navigate on it with significantly lower computational cost than on the PF of the original problem. Once a desired objective vector on the approximation has been found, one can generate the closest corresponding PO solution as in Pareto Navigator.

The problem of finding a preferred point on a PF approximation is similar to finding a preferred outcome of a MOP; like the PF, its approximation A may have many mathematically equally good objective vectors and, thus, there is a need for decision making even on the PF approximation. An important aspect of decision making on an approximation is the question of how well the preferences of the DM on the approximation reflect the preferences on the real PF.

Based on a limited knowledge of the PF in a form of the initial set of PO outcomes P, the accuracy of the approximation cannot naturally be guaranteed outside the initial PO outcomes. What can, however, be done is that a rational DM is given the opportunity to choose any of the initial PO outcomes in P while making rational decisions on the approximation. An undesirable occurrence happens e.g., in non-IND approximation A^1 in Example 1, where a rational DM will not be interested in the initial PO outcome p^4, because this point is not PO on the approximation.

Assuming that the PF approximation discussed above is IND, then we have the following: First of all, all points in the initial set of PO outcomes are now plausible decisions for a rational DM because $P \subset PF(A)$ by Corollary 1. Second, since $PF(A) = A$ by Theorem 2, the diversity of the PO objective vectors on the approximation can be examined directly from A. Since the DM is rational, then the diversity of $PF(A)$, not that of A, is interesting to him/her. If the PF approximation A is non-IND, these are not the same things.

We are left with the question of how to help the DM find a preferred point on a PF approximation. This is another instance where the concept of an IND approximation helps. According to Theorem 4, an IND approximation is the PF of a MOP that also has the set P on its PF.

Theorem 4. *If a set $A \subset \mathbb{R}^k$ is an IND PF approximation based on P, then there exists a MOP with notation (3.1) so that $P \subset PF(f(X))$ and $PF(f(X)) = A$.*

Proof. Assume that $f = I$ (the identity mapping), $X = A$ and $n = k$ in (3.1). Then $PF(f(X)) = PF(X) = PF(A) = A$, where the last equation results from Theorem 2. Also by definition $P \subset PF(f(X)) = A$.   □

The MOP, whose existence is guaranteed by Theorem 4, can be seen as a surrogate MOP for the initial MOP. We define this MOP for a general set, and not just for an IND approximation, and also give it a name.

Definition 3. For any nonempty set $A \subset \mathbb{R}^k$, the MOP

$$\min_{\text{s.t. } z \in A} z \qquad (3.3)$$

is called the *MOP implied by A*. The formulation above is analogous to formulation (3.2) but instead of the set of outcomes $f(X)$, an arbitrary set A in the objective space $\mathbb{R}^k$ is used.

When trying to find a preferred point on an IND PF approximation, we thus propose to solve the MOP implied by A and take the final solution of the former as a preferred point on the approximation A. This approach has a couple of apparent benefits: All methods developed for solving MOPs are now applicable for decision making on the approximation and there is no need to develop new ones for this. Especially we can now use interactive MO methods in solving MOP (3.3). Also, since the PF of the MOP implied by the approximation is explicitly known, the computational expense should be very low while using MO methods in solving this MOP. Furthermore, since all the outcomes of the MOP are actually already on the PF of this MOP, there is no need to be concerned about the convergence to the PF, which also saves computational time. These aspects are clarified below with an example.

Example 2. In Hakanen et al. (2008), a computationally expensive, black-box problem of wastewater treatment planning involving three objective functions is solved with the interactive multiobjective method NIMBUS (Miettinen and Mäkelä 2006; Miettinen 1999). In the optimization process, 11 PO outcomes including the final preferred outcome $(0.72, 332, 524)^T$ were computed. Here we want to produce a PF approximation in the neighborhood of the final outcome and then to formulate a MOP implied by this approximation in a form that could be solved with interactive MO methods. We use the already generated PO outcomes to construct this approximation but we want to emphasize that any appropriate method could have been used to generate the set P. We choose a subset of known PO outcomes (and thus approximate only a part of the PF) for the simplicity of the presentation.

The final outcome and four outcomes closest to it are chosen as the initial set of PO outcomes P. Thus, we have $P = \{p^1, p^2, p^3, p^4, p^5\}$, where $p^1 = (1.7, 326, 506)$, $p^2 = (1.1, 336, 515)$, $p^3 = (0.9, 333, 519)$, $p^4 = (0.7, 332, 524)$, $p^5 = (0.5, 347, 528)$. The set

$$A = \text{conv}(p^1, p^2, p^3) \cup \text{conv}(p^1, p^3, p^4) \cup \text{conv}(p^3, p^4, p^5) \cup \text{conv}(p^2, p^3, p^5)$$

shown in Fig. 3.2 is an IND PF approximation and this can be checked analytically.

The IND PF approximation A can be parametrized with a slack variable $t \in \{0, 1\}^3 \times [0, 1]^2$ and, using this parametrization, the MOP implied by A can be formulated as

$$
\begin{aligned}
\min \ & z(t) \\
\text{s.t.} \ & z(t) = t_1 (t_4 p^1 + t_5 p^2 + (1 - t_4 - t_5) p^3) \\
& \quad + t_2 (t_4 p^1 + t_5 p^3) + (1 - t_4 - t_5) p^4) \\
& \quad + t_3 (t_4 p^2 + t_5 p^3 + (1 - t_4 - t_5) p^5) \\
& \quad + (1 - t_1 - t_2 - t_3)(t_4 p^3 + t_5 p^4 + (1 - t_4 - t_5) p^5) \\
& t = (t_1, \dots, t_5) \in \{0, 1\}^3 \times [0, 1]^2 \\
& 0 \le 1 - t_1 - t_2 - t_3 \text{ and } 0 \le 1 - t_4 - t_5.
\end{aligned}
\tag{3.4}
$$

The MOP (3.4) includes 2 continuous and 3 discrete decision variables, 2 linear inequalities concerning them and also some box constraints. The decision variable t does not have any meaning to the DM, but is merely a product of the parametrization

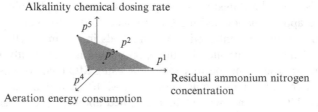

Alkalinity chemical dosing rate

Residual ammonium nitrogen concentration

Aeration energy consumption

Fig. 3.2 The IND PF approximation A

of A. However, the objective function values in the vector $z(t) \in A$ have a meaning to the DM for each feasible t and based on these values he/she can express preferences. Exploration of the PF approximation A means varying the decision variable t based on the preferences of the DM and then showing him/her the resulted objective function values.

Solving MOP (3.4) should be done in the same way as solving the original MOP, if it was not computationally expensive. The MOP can by inputted e.g., to the WWW-NIMBUS implementation of the NIMBUS method.[1] Solving it is computationally inexpensive and the DM can get feedback to his/her preferences quickly unlike with the initial computationally expensive MOP. Thus, the DM could be more inclined to see more new outcomes and this should help him/her obtain a better understanding of the problem.

The ideas presented in this paper are of general nature, but can be seen to be related to some specific MO methods found in the literature. The Pareto Navigator method (Eskelinen et al. 2010) can be interpreted as solving a MOP implied by the convex cone of the Pareto optimal solutions. The surface of this convex cone approximates the PF since for Pareto Navigator the problem is assumed to be convex. The methods of Lotov et al. (2004), on the other hand, can be seen as using a visual technique called the Interactive Decision Map for solving the MOP implied by an approximation (that is constructed by methods mentioned therein) of the feasible outcome set. However, since the approximations used in these methods are not necessarily IND approximations, the benefits mentioned in this section do not apply.

3.5 Conclusion

We have proposed a new approach to solving computationally expensive multiobjective optimization problems. In our approach, we first approximate the Pareto front and then enable the decision maker to explore the approximation with his/her preferences. We have also proposed *inherent nondominance*, a new property for Pareto front approximations which ensures desirable properties for approximations so that exploration can take place.

As further research on this subject, the utilization of the proposed approximation approach requires an algorithm to construct an inherently nondominated Pareto front approximation from a given set of Pareto optimal outcomes. Furthermore, we intend to study which interactive multiobjective optimization methods are best suited for solving the multiobjective optimization problem implied by the approximation. These issues will be considered in our future research, which will also include numerical tests to evaluate the efficiency of our approach to solving computationally expensive multiobjective optimization problems.

---

[1] WWW-NIMBUS System for Multiobjective Optimization, Last accessed: May 26, 2011. http://nimbus.mit.jyu.fi/.

Acknowledgements The research was partly supported by the Academy of Finland, grant number 128495.

References

H. Ackermann, A. Newman, H. Röglin, and B. Vöcking. Decision-making Based on Approximate and Smoothed Pareto Curves. *Theoretical Computer Science*, 378:253–270, 2007.

V.E. Bezerkin, G.K. Kamenev, and A.V. Lotov. Hybrid Adaptive Methods for Approximating a Nonconvex Multidimensional Pareto Frontier. *Computational Mathematics and Mathematical Physics*, 46:1918–1931, 2006.

P. Eskelinen, K. Miettinen, K. Klamroth, and J. Hakanen. Pareto Navigator for Interactive Nonlinear Multiobjective Optimization. *OR Spectrum*, 23:211–227, 2010.

T. Goel, R. Vaidyanathan, R.T. Haftka, W. Shyy, N.V. Queipo, and K. Tucker. Response Surface Approximation of Pareto Optimal Front in Multi-Objective Optimization. *Computer Methods in Applied Mechanics and Engineering*, 196:879–893, 2007.

J. Hakanen, K. Miettinen, and K. Sahlstedt. Wastewater Treatment: New Insight Provided by Interactive Multiobjective Optimization. *Decision Support Systems*, 51:328–337, 2011.

C. Hwang and A.S.M. Masud. *Multiple Objective Decision Making – Methods and Applications: a State-of- the-Art Survey*. Springer, Berlin, 1979.

I. Kaliszewski. *Quantitative Pareto Analysis by Cone Separation Technique*. Kluwer Academic Publishers, Dordrecht, 1994.

M.K. Karakasis and K.C. Giannakoglou. On the Use of Surrogate Evaluation Models in Multi-Objective Evolutionary Algorithms. In P. Neittaanmäki, T. Rossi, S. Korotov, E. Onate, J. Periaux, and D. Knörzer, editors, *ECCOMAS 2004: Proceedings*, Jyväskylä, Finland, 2004. http://www.mit.jyu.fi/eccomas2004/proceedings/pdf/616.pdf, Last accessed: May 26, 2011.

K. Klamroth and K. Miettinen. Integrating Approximation and Interactive Decision Making in Multicriteria Optimization. *Operations Research*, 56:222–234, 2008.

J. Knowles. ParEGO: A Hybrid Algorithm with On-Line Landscape Approximation for Expensive Multiobjective Optimization Problems. *IEEE Transactions on Evolutionary Computation*, 10:50–66, 2006.

P. Korhonen and J. Wallenius. A Pareto Race. *Naval Research Logistics*, 35:615–623, 1988.

O.I. Larichev. Cognitive Validity in Design of Decision-Aiding Techniques. *Journal of Multi-Criteria Decision Analysis*, 3:127–138, 1992.

W. Liu, Q. Zhang, E. Tsang, and B. Virginas. Tchebycheff Approximation in Gaussian Process Model Composition for Multi-Objective Expensive Black Box. In *2008 IEEE Congress on Evolutionary Computation, CEC 2008*, pages 3060–3065, Hong Kong, China, 2008.

A.V. Lotov, V.A. Bushenkov, and G.A. Kamenev. *Interactive Decision Maps*. Kluwer Academic Publishers, Boston, 2004.

J. Martin, C. Bielza, and D.R. Insua. Approximating Nondominated Sets in Continuous Multiobjective Optimization Problems. *Naval Research Logistics*, 52:469–480, 2005.

K. Miettinen. *Nonlinear Multiobjective Optimization*. Kluwer Academic Publishers, Boston, 1999.

K. Miettinen, A.V. Lotov, G.K. Kamenev, and V.E. Bezerkin. Integration of Two Multiobjective Optimization Methods for Nonlinear Problems. *Optimization Methods and Software*, 18:63–80, 2003.

K. Miettinen and M.M. Mäkelä. Synchronous Approach in Interactive Multiobjective Optimization. *European Journal of Operational Research*, 170:909–922, 2006.

K. Miettinen, F. Ruiz, and A. Wierzbicki. Introduction to Multiobjective Optimization: Interactive Approaches. In J. Branke, K. Deb, K. Miettinen, and R. Slowinski, editors, *Multiobjective Optimization: Interactive and Evolutionary Approaches*, pages 27–57. Springer, Berlin, 2008.

M. Monz, K.H. Küfer, T.R. Bortfeld, and C. Thieke. Pareto Navigation — Algorithmic Foundation of Interactive Multi-Criteria IMRT Planning. *Physics in Medicine and Biology*, 53:985–998, 2008.

S. Ruzika and M.M. Wiecek. Approximation Methods in Multiobjective Programming. *Journal of Optimization Theory and Applications*, 126:473–501, 2005.

Y. Sawaragi, H. Nakayama, and T. Tanino. *Theory of Multiobjective Optimization*. Academic Press, Orlando, 1985.

A. Wierzbicki. On the Completeness and Constructiveness of Parametric Characterizations to Vector Optimization Problems. *OR Spectrum*, 8:73–87, 1986.

B. Wilson, D. Cappelleri, T.W. Simpson, and M. Frecker. Efficient Pareto Frontier Exploration using Surrogate Approximations. *Optimization and Engineering*, 2:31–50, 2001.

M. Yoon, H. Nakayama, and Y. Yun. *Sequential Approximate Multiobjective Optimization Using Computational Intelligence*. Springer, Berlin Heidelberg, 2009.

Chapter 4
A New Consistency Index for Comparison Matrices in the ANP

Daji Ergu, Gang Kou, Yi Peng, and Yong Shi

Abstract The inconsistency test is more difficult in the analytical network process (ANP) than in the analytical hierarchy process (AHP) because there are more comparison matrices in the ANP. The consistency ratio (CR) introduced by Saaty for the AHP is used for inconsistency test in the ANP. When the number of comparison matrices increases, the inconsistency test of comparison matrices in the ANP becomes complicated. In an attempt to simplify the inconsistency test, this paper proposes a maximum eigenvalue threshold as the consistency index for ANP, which is mathematically equivalent to the CR method. In addition, a block diagonal matrix is introduced for the comparison matrices in the ANP to conduct inconsistency tests simultaneously for all comparison matrices. An illustrative example is used to show the effectiveness and the simplicity of the proposed maximum eigenvalue threshold method.

Keywords Block diagonal matrix · Inconsistency test · Maximum eigenvalue · Maximum eigenvalue threshold · The analytical network process (ANP)

Y. Peng (✉) and G. Kou
School of Management and Economics, University of Electronic Science and Technology of China, Chengdu 610054, China
e-mail: pengyicd@gmail.com, kougang@yahoo.com

D. Ergu
School of Management and Economics, University of Electronic Science and Technology of China, Chengdu 610054, China
and
Southwest University for Nationalities, Chengdu 610200, China
e-mail: ergudaji@163.com

Y. Shi
College of Information Science & Technology, University of Nebraska at Omaha, Omaha, NE 68182, USA
and
Research Center on Fictitious Economy and Data Sciences, Chinese Academy of Sciences, Beijing 100190, China
e-mail: yshi@gucas.ac.cn

Y. Shi et al. (eds.), *New State of MCDM in the 21st Century*, Lecture Notes in Economics and Mathematical Systems 648, DOI 10.1007/978-3-642-19695-9_4,
© Springer-Verlag Berlin Heidelberg 2011

4.1 Introduction

Decision makers are often facing complicated decision problems which can not be structured hierarchically. Furthermore, the interactions of decision attributes within the same level and the feedbacks between two different levels are important issues that should be considered during the decision making process. Therefore, the AHP method does not work accurately when solving such decision problems (Saaty 1996). The analytical network process (ANP), as an extensive and complementary method of the AHP, was introduced and further developed by Saaty (1996, 1999, 2001, 2003, 2004, 2005, 2006, 2008). Since its introduction, the ANP method is gaining popularity and applied to diverse areas (Lee and Kim 2000; Meade and Presley 2002; Karsak et al. 2003; Niemira and Saaty 2004; Chung et al. 2005; Kahraman et al. 2006; Bayazit and Karpak 2007; Dagdeviren et al. 2008; Despotis and Derpanis, 2008; Peng et al. 2008; Aktar and Ustun 2009; Caballero-Luque et al. 2010; Ergu et al. 2011a,b,c; Peng et al. 2011; Saaty and Zoffer 2011).

Similar to the AHP, the ANP has the consistency issues for its comparison matrices. This issue is more complicated in the ANP than in the AHP since there are more comparison matrices in the ANP. However, to the best of our knowledge, there is no special consistency index designed for the ANP. The goal of this paper is to propose a maximum eigenvalue threshold method, which is based on the original consistency ratio method, as the consistency index for the ANP.

This paper is organized as follows. The next section briefly analyzes the consistency ratio method and the issues of inconsistency test in the ANP. In Sect. 4.3, a threshold of maximum eigenvalue method is introduced as the consistency index for ANP. Then a block diagonal matrix to test the consistency of all comparison matrices simultaneously and the judgment process of the proposed method are presented. A numeric example is illustrated using the proposed method in Sect. 4.4. Section 4.5 concludes the paper and discusses future research directions.

4.2 Analysis of the Consistency Ratio Method and the Issues of Inconsistency Test in the ANP

4.2.1 Analysis of the Consistency Ratio Method

During the process of making decisions, there will be inconsistency issue occurring when comparing different attributes or criteria as the decision problems are complicated in nature. For instance, suppose attribute A is 2 times important as attribute B, and attribute B is 3 times important as attribute C, however, attribute A is only 4 times important as attribute C instead of 6 times. Likewise, the values of A is bigger than B, B is bigger than C, however C is bigger than A, namely, $A > B, B > C$, but $C > A$. Both of these issues are called inconsistency (Saaty 1991). Therefore, the inconsistency test is necessary for comparison matrix before the vector priority

Table 4.1 The average random index

N	1	2	3	4	5	6	7	8	9	10
RI	0	0	0.52	0.89	1.11	1.25	1.35	1.4	1.45	1.49

of the comparison matrix can be calculated. If the inconsistency test for the comparison matrix is failed, the inconsistent elements in the comparison matrix has to be revised, otherwise, the result of decision analysis process is meaningless.

The most widely used consistency index is the consistency ratio (CR) (Saaty 1991), that is,

$$C.R. = \frac{C.I.}{R.I.} < 0.1 \tag{4.1}$$

where $C.I. = \frac{\lambda_{max} - n}{n-1}$ is the consistency index, $R.I.$ is the average random index based on Matrix Size shown in Table 4.1, λ_{max} is the maximum eigenvalue of matrix A, and n is the order of matrix A.

According to rule of thumb, the comparison matrix is consistent only if the value of CR is less than 0.1. The inconsistency test includes the following four steps:

Step 1: Calculate the λ_{max} of one comparison matrix.

Step 2: Calculate the value of CI using the formula $C.I. = \frac{\lambda_{max} - n}{n-1}$.

Step 3: Calculate the CR using the formula $CR = \frac{CI}{RI}$ and Table 4.1.

Step 4: Compare the value of CR with the consistency threshold 0.1 to judge whether the comparison is consistent.

There is a major shortcoming when using CR as the consistency index for comparison matrices, as above steps has to be calculated repeatedly for each comparison matrix to test the consistency.

4.2.2   The Issues of Inconsistency Test in the ANP

The ANP is an extensive and complementary method of the AHP. Therefore, the consistency of each comparison matrix need to be tested using the CR method. If the comparison matrices pass the inconsistency test, then the priorities derived from the comparison matrices are added as parts of the columns of the supermatrix of a network (Saaty 2008), which is shown in Fig. 4.1. Otherwise, this comparison matrix has to be revised by experts.

Therefore, the inconsistency tests will be much more complicated in the ANP than in the AHP since, in the ANP, there are more comparison matrices derived from the following supermatrix of a network.

Assume $W_{ij} \neq 0$ for all $1 \leq i, j \leq N$. Hence, both inner-clusters and outer-clusters have interactions. In the supermatrix, there are two kinds of comparison matrices in the ANP, the inner-clusters comparison matrices and the outer-clusters comparison matrices. From the C_1 cluster to the C_N cluster, the number of the comparison matrices in the inner-cluster is n_1 with order n_1, n_2 with order $n_2, \ldots,$ and

Fig. 4.1 The supermatrix of a network

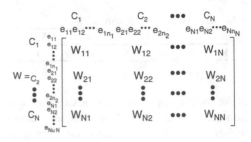

n_N with order n_N respectively. The number of the comparison matrices in the outer-cluster includes: $(N-1)n_1$ with orders $n_2, n_3, \ldots, n_N$; $(N-1)n_2$ with orders $n_1, n_3, \ldots, n_N$; $(N-1)n_3$ with orders $n_1, n_2, n_4, \ldots, n_N$; $\ldots$; $(N-1)n_N$ with orders $n_1, n_2, n_3, \ldots, n_{N-1}$.

Inner-cluster comparison matrices in the ANP	
Quantity	**Matrices order**
n_1	$n_1 \times n_1$
n_2	$n_2 \times n_2$
$\vdots$	$\vdots$
n_N	$n_N \times n_N$

The total number of Inner-cluster comparison matrices is $n_1 + n_2 + \cdots + n_N$

Outer-cluster comparison matrices in the ANP	
Quantity	**Matrices order**
$(N-1)n_1$	$n_2 \times n_2, \quad n_3 \times n_3, \ldots, \quad n_N \times n_N,$
$(N-1)n_2$	$n_1 \times n_1, \quad n_3 \times n_3, \ldots, \quad n_N \times n_N,$
$\vdots$	$\vdots$
$(N-1)n_N$	$n_1 \times n_1, \quad n_3 \times n_3, \ldots, \quad n_{N-1} \times n_{N-1}$

The total number of Outer-cluster comparison matrices is $(N-1)(n_1 + n_2 + \cdots + n_N)$.

Therefore, the total number of all the comparison matrices in the ANP is $N(n_1 + n_2 + \cdots + n_N)$. Hence, the CR method has to calculate the CRs $N(n_1 + n_2 + \cdots + n_N)$ times for all comparison matrices.

To sum up:

1. The consistency ratio is calculated repeatedly for each comparison matrix in the CR method.
2. The CRs of the comparison matrices in the ANP needs to be calculated $4N(n_1 + n_2 + \cdots + n_N)$ times since the total number of the comparison matrices is

$N(n_1 + n_2 + \cdots + n_N)$ from C_1 cluster to C_N cluster which contain n_1 elements to n_N elements respectively.

Therefore, the traditional CR method is very complicated in practice, especially for the ANP.

4.3   The New Consistency Index for the ANP

4.3.1   The Maximum Eigenvalue Threshold as the Consistency Index for the ANP

In the formula $CR = \frac{\lambda_{max} - n}{(n-1)R.I.}$, CR is only dominated by the λ_{max} for the comparison matrices in the same order, which are commonly occurred in the ANP. Therefore, we can derive the following corollary.

Corollary 1. *The inequality $CR < 0.1$ is mathematically equivalent to the inequality $\lambda_{max} < \lambda^n_{max\ threshold}$ or $\Delta\lambda_{max} < 0$, where λ_{max} denotes the maximum eigenvalue of the comparison matrix with order n, $\lambda^n_{max\ threshold}$ represents the corresponding maximum eigenvalue threshold with order n, which is listed in Table 4.2, $\Delta\lambda_{max}$ denotes the bias between the maximum eigenvalue and its corresponding threshold. The proofs can be done as the following:*

Proof. If

$$CR = \frac{CI}{RI} = \frac{\lambda_{max} - n}{(n-1)RI} < 0.1 \tag{4.2}$$

That is

$$CR = \frac{CI}{RI} < 0.1 \Leftrightarrow CI < 0.1RI \tag{4.3}$$

$$\Leftrightarrow \frac{\lambda_{max} - n}{n - 1} < 0.1RI \tag{4.4}$$

$$\Leftrightarrow \lambda_{max} - n < 0.1RI(n - 1) \tag{4.5}$$

$$\Leftrightarrow \lambda_{max} < 0.1RI(n - 1) + n \tag{4.6}$$

where the symbol "$\Leftrightarrow$" denotes equivalence. Let the right value be the maximum eigenvalue threshold $\lambda^n_{max\ threshold}$ (in short $\lambda^n_{max\ thrd}$), namely,

Table 4.2 The threshold $\lambda^n_{max\ thrd}$ of the maximum eigenvalue and the corresponding RI

N	1	2	3	4	5	6	7	8	9	10
RI	0	0	0.52	0.89	1.11	1.25	1.35	1.4	1.45	1.49
$\lambda^n_{max\ thrd}$	1	2	3.104	4.267	5.444	6.781	7.81	8.98	10.16	11.341

$$\lambda^n_{\max\ thrd} = 0.1RI(n-1) + n \tag{4.7}$$

Therefore

$$CR < 0.1 \Leftrightarrow \lambda_{\max} < \lambda^n_{\max\ thrd} \tag{4.8}$$

$$\Leftrightarrow \nabla\lambda_{\max} = \lambda_{\max} - \lambda^n_{\max\ thrd} < 0 \tag{4.9}$$

Introduce the corresponding value of RI in Table 4.1 in formula (4.7). The corresponding values of $\lambda^n_{\max\ thrd}$ of the comparison matrices with order n can be easily obtained, as in Table 4.2.

Therefore, the maximum eigenvalue threshold $\lambda^n_{\max\ thrd}$ can be used as a new consistency index for the ANP to test whether a comparison matrix is consistent. The specific principal of inconsistency test can be defined as follows:

Inconsistency test principal: If $\lambda^i_{\max} < \lambda^n_{\max\ thrd}$, that is, $\Delta\lambda^i_{\max} < 0$, the ith comparison matrix passes the inconsistency test. If $\lambda^i_{\max} \geq \lambda^n_{\max\ threshold}$, that is, $\Delta\lambda^i_{\max} \geq 0$, the ith comparison matrix fails the inconsistency test. The ith comparison matrix should be revised.

4.3.2 The Analysis and Comparison

Although it is proved that the CR method developed by Saaty is mathematically equivalent to the $\lambda^n_{\max\ threshold}$ method, that is, $CR = \frac{CI}{RI} < 0.1$ is equivalent to $\lambda^n_{\max} < \lambda^n_{\max\ thrd}$ or $\Delta\lambda^n_{\max} < 0$. However, the maximum threshold $\lambda^n_{\max\ threshold}$ method is easier to implement than the CR method according to the following analysis and comparison.

The principals of inconsistency test of the CR method and the $\lambda^n_{\max\ thrd}$ method are showed in inequalities (4.10) and (4.11) respectively:

$$CR = \frac{CI}{RI} = \frac{\lambda_{\max} - n}{(n-1)RI} < 0.1 \tag{4.10}$$

$$\lambda_{\max} < \lambda^n_{\max\ thrd} \quad \text{Or} \quad \Delta\lambda^n_{\max} < 0 \tag{4.11}$$

The detailed processes of the CR method and the $\lambda^n_{\max\ thrd}$ method are shown as the Figs. 4.2 and 4.3.

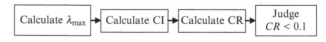

Fig. 4.2 The calculation processes of the CR method

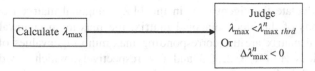

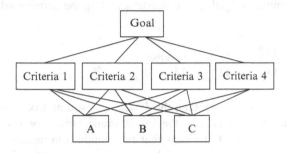

Fig. 4.3 The calculation processes of the $\lambda_{max\ thrd}^n$ method

Fig. 4.4 The typical hierarchy structure in the AHP

In $\lambda_{max\ thrd}^n$ method, it is no need to calculate the two middle steps, which saves $2N(n_1 + n_2 + \cdots + n_N)$ times in calculation comparing to the CR method.

4.3.3   The Block Diagonal Matrix and Judgment Process

To further simplify the processes of the inconsistency test in the ANP, a block diagonal matrix, based on the comparison matrices in the same level or different levels, is introduced. As the AHP is a special case in the ANP, without losing generality, the block diagonal matrix is constructed for a typical AHP model in Fig. 4.4.

In this hierarchy structure, there are five comparison matrices in all: One with order four for the criteria with respect to the goal in the first level, denoted by A, and four with order three for the three alternatives with respect to the four criteria in the second level, denoted by $C1, C2, C3$ and $C4$. The inconsistency test for the comparison matrix A can be tested. The other four comparison matrices with the same order can be tested simultaneously. The processes of the inconsistency test include the following three steps:

Step 1: Construct the following block diagonal matrix (B in short) using these five comparison matrices as the entries in the main diagonal:

$$B = \begin{pmatrix} A & & & & \\ & C1 & & & \\ & & C2 & & \\ & & & C3 & \\ & & & & C4 \end{pmatrix} \tag{4.12}$$

Step 2: Calculate the eigenvalues in the block diagonal matrix B. According to the notations of the block diagonal matrix, the maximum eigenvalues in the block diagonal matrix are the corresponding maximum eigenvalues of the comparison matrices A, $C1$, $C2$, $C3$ and $C4$ respectively, which are denoted by $\lambda_{max}^i (i = 0, 1, 2, 3, 4)$.

Step 3: Calculate the maximum eigenvalue bias $\Delta\lambda_{max}^i (i = 0, 1, 2, 3, 4)$ using the following formula, and judge its consistency using the corresponding condition mentioned above.

$$\Delta\lambda_{max}^0 = \lambda_{max}^0 - \lambda_{max\ thrd}^4 \tag{4.13}$$

$$\Delta\lambda_{max}^i = \left(\lambda_{max}^1 \quad \lambda_{max}^2 \quad \lambda_{max}^3 \quad \lambda_{max}^4\right) - \lambda_{max\ thrd}^3 \tag{4.14}$$

If $\Delta\lambda_{max}^i < 0$ $(i = 1, 2, 3, 4)$, then the ith comparison matrix passes the inconsistency test, otherwise, it fails to the inconsistency test. For instance, assume $\Delta\lambda_{max}^2 < 0$ and $\Delta\lambda_{max}^4 > 0$, it means that the comparison matrix $C2$ passes the inconsistency test and is consistent while the comparison matrix $C4$ failed to the inconsistency test, and it is suggested to recheck its elements.

4.4 Illustrative Example

For simplicity, an example selecting the best computer system firstly introduced by Triantaphyllou and Mann (1995), which has the typical hierarchy structure mentioned above, is used to test the proposed method. Suppose there are three alternative configurations, system A, system B, and system C. There are also four criteria, hardware expandability, hardware maintainability, financing available, and user friendly characteristics of the operating system and related available software, denoted by C1, C2, C3, and C4 respectively.

Then follow above three steps using the comparison matrices provided by Tirantaphyllou and Mann, that is:

Step 1: Construct the block diagonal matrix B showed below using the matrices A, C1, C2, C3 and C4.

Step 2: Calculate the eigenvalue of block diagonal matrix B, and obtain the maximum eigenvalues of the corresponding block diagonal sub-matrix A, C1, C2, C3 and C4. That is:

$$\lambda_{max}^0 = 4.2365, \lambda_{max}^1 = 3.1356, \lambda_{max}^2 = 3.2470, \lambda_{max}^3 = 3.1356, \lambda_{max}^4 = 3.0858$$

Step 3: Test the consistency using the maximum eigenvalue threshold method. That is:

$$\Delta\lambda_{max}^0 = \lambda_{max}^0 - \lambda_{max\ thrd}^4 = 4.2365 - 4.267 = -0.0305 < 0$$

The result shows that the comparison matrix A is consistent.

$$\Delta\lambda^i_{max} = \left(\lambda^1_{max}, \lambda^2_{max}, \lambda^3_{max}, \lambda^4_{max}\right) - \lambda^3_{max\ thrd}$$
$$= (3.1356, 3.2470, 3.1356, 3.0858) - 3.104$$
$$= (0.0316, 0.143, 0.0316, -0.0182)$$

Obviously, only $\Delta\lambda^4_{max} < 0$, which mean only the comparison matrix $C4$ is consistent, and others are inconsistent.

4.5 Conclusions

In this paper, a new consistency index for the ANP is proposed, because the consistency ratio (CR) method is quite complicated for the ANP. The proposed maximum eigenvalue threshold is mathematically equivalent to the CR method, but easier and simpler than the CR method in practice as the consistency index for the ANP. A block diagonal matrix is also introduced to simplify the process and conduct the inconsistency tests of several comparison matrices all together. An illustrative example is used to demonstrate the processes of the inconsistency test using the proposed method.

Although the inconsistent comparison matrices can be identified using the proposed index, the identification and adjustment of the inconsistent elements in the comparison matrices still remain to be studied, which is another research direction in the future.

Acknowledgements This research has been supported by grants from the National Natural Science Foundation of China (#70901011, #70901015, and # 70921061).

References

Aktar D.E. and Ustun O (2009). Analytic network process and multi-period goal programming integration in purchasing decisions. *Computers and Industrial Engineering*, 56(2), pp.677–690.

Bayazit O. and Karpak B. (2007) An analytical network process-based framework for successful total quality management (TQM): An assessment of Turkish manufacturing industry readiness. *International Journal of Production Economics*, 105(1), pp.79–96.

Caballero-Luque, A., Aragonés-Beltrán, P., García-Melón, M., and Dema-Pérezc, (2010). Analysis Of The Alignment Of Company Goals To Web Content Using ANP, Int. J. Inform. Technol. Decision Making, 9(3), 419–436.

Chung S.H., Lee A.H.I. and Pearn W.L. (2005). Analytic network process (ANP) approach for product mix planning in semiconductor fabricator. *International Journal of Production Economics*, 96(1), pp.15–36.

Dagdeviren M., Yuksel I. and Kurt M. (2008). A fuzzy analytic network process (ANP) model to identify faulty behavior risk (FBR) in work system. *Safety Science*, 46(5), pp.771–783.

Ergu G., Kou, G., Peng, Y., and Shi, Y. (2011a). A Simple Method to Improve the Consistency Ratio of the Pair-wise Comparison Matrix in ANP, DOI:10.1016/j.ejor.2011.03.014, *European Journal of Operational Research*, 213(1), 246–259.

Ergu G., Kou, G., Shi, Y. and Shi, Y. (2011b). Analytic Network Process in Risk Assessment and Decision Analysis, DOI: 10.1016/j.cor.2011.03.005, Computers & Operations Research

Ergu G., Kou, G., Peng, Y., Shi, Y. and Shi, Y. (2011c). The Analytic Hierarchy Process: Task Scheduling and Resource Allocation in Cloud Computing Environment, DOI: 10.1007/s11227-011-0625-1, The Journal of Supercomputing

Despotis, D.K., and Derpanis, D., (2008) A Min–Max Goal Programming Approach To Priority Derivation In Ahp With Interval Judgements, Int. J. Inform. Technol. Decision Making, 7(1), 175–182.

Karsak E.E., Sozer S., and Alptekin S. Emre (2003). Product planning in quality function deployment using a combined analytic network process and goal programming approach. *Computers and Industrial Engineering*, 44(1), pp.171–190.

Kahraman C., Ertay T., and Buyukozkan G (2006). A fuzzy optimization model for QFD planning process using analytic network approach. *European Journal of Operational Research*, 171(2), pp.390–411.

Lee J.W. and Kim S.H. (2000). Using analytic network process and goal programming for interdependent information system project selection. *Computers and Operations Research*, 27(4), pp.367–382.

Meade, L.A., and Presley, A. (2002). R&D project selection using ANP...the analytic network process. IEEE, volume 21, Issue 2, pp: 22–28.

Niemira M.P., and Saaty T.L. (2004). An Analytic Network Process model for financial-crisis forecasting. *International Journal of Forecasting*, 20(4), pp.573–587.

Peng, Y., Kou, G., Shi, Y. and Chen, Z. (2008). A Descriptive Framework for the Field of Data Mining and Knowledge Discovery, *International Journal of Information Technology & Decision Making*, 7(4), 639–682.

Peng, Y., Kou, G., Wang, G., Wu, W. and Shi, Y. (2011). Ensemble of software defect predictors: an AHP-based evaluation method, DOI: 10.1142/S0219622011004282, *International Journal of Information Technology & Decision Making*, 10(1), 187–206.

Saaty, T.L. (1991) Some mathematical concepts of the analytic hierarchy process. Behaviormetrika. No. 29. 1–9.

Saaty, T.L. (1996). Decision Making with Dependence and Feedback: The Analytic Network Process. Pittsburgh, Pennsylvania: RWS Publications. ISBN 0–9620317–9–8.

Saaty, T.L. (1999). Fundamentals of the analytic network process. ISAHP 1999, Kobe, Japan, August 12–14.

Saaty, T.L. (2001). Decision Making with the Analytic Network Process (ANP) and Its "Super Decisions" Software: The National Missile Defense (NMD) Example," *ISAHP 2001 Proceedings*, Bern, Switzerland, August, 2–4.

Saaty, T.L. (2003). Theory of the Analytic Hierarchy and Analytic network process- Examples Part 2.2, *The International Journal of Systems Research and Information Technologies*, 2.

Saaty, T.L. (2004). Fundamentals of the Analytic Network Process: Dependence and Feedback in Decision-Making with a Single Network, *Journal of Systems Science and Systems Engineering*, published at Tsinghua University, Beijing, Vol. 13, No. 2, pp. 129–157.

Saaty, T.L. (2005). Theory and Applications of the Analytic Network Process: Decision Making with Benefits, Opportunities, Costs and Risks. Pittsburgh, Pennsylvania: RWS Publications. ISBN 1–888603–06–2.

Saaty, T.L. (2006). Rank from Comparisons and from Ratings in the Analytic Hierarchy/Network Processes, *European Journal of Operational Research*, 168, pp. 557–570.

Saaty, T.L. (2008). The Analytic Network Process, *Iranian Journal of Operations Research*, Vol.1, No.1, pp.1–27.

Saaty, T. L., Zoffer, H.J., (2011) Negotiating the Israeli-Palestinian Controversy from a new perspective, in press, Int. J. Inform. Technol. Decision Making, 10(1), Jan 2011.

Triantaphyllou, E. and Mann, S.H. (1995). Using the analytic hierarchy process for decision making in engineering applications: Some challenges. Inter'l Journal of Industrial Engineering: Applications and Practice, Vol. 2, No. 1, pp. 35–44, 1995.

Part II
MCDM Methodology

Chapter 5
Estimating the Robustness of Composite CBA and MCA Assessments by Variation of Criteria Importance Order

Anders Vestergaard Jensen, Michael Bruhn Barfod, and Steen Leleur

Abstract This paper discusses the concept of using rank variation concerning the stakeholder prioritising of importance criteria for exploring the sensitivity of criteria weights in multi-criteria analysis (MCA). Thereby the robustness of the MCA-based decision support can be tested. The analysis described is based on the fact that when using MCA as a decision-support tool, questions often arise about the weighting (or prioritising) of the included criteria. This part of the MCA is seen as the most subjective part and could give reasons for discussion among the decision makers or stakeholders. Furthermore, the relative weights can make a large difference in the resulting assessment of alternatives (Hobbs and Meier 2000). Therefore it is highly relevant to introduce a procedure for estimating the importance of criteria weights. This paper proposes a methodology for estimating the robustness of weights used in additive utility models.

Keywords COSIMA · Decision-support tool · Multi-criteria analysis · Rank order distribution · Stakeholder preference

5.1 Introduction

When assessing larger transport infrastructure projects often several non-monetised impacts could be relevant to include in the appraisal (UNIVERSITAET STUTTGART 2009). For many decision makers and stakeholders the task of setting the criteria weights for several criteria can be very difficult. To overcome this, the proposed method uses importance weights based on rankings of the criteria, by the use of Rank Order Distribution (ROD) weights (Roberts and Goodwin 2002). This reduces the problem to assigning a rank order value for each criterion. A method for

A.V. Jensen (✉), M.B. Barfod, and S. Leleur
Department of Transport, Technical University of Denmark, Bygningstorvet 115,
2800 Kgs. Lyngby, Denmark
e-mail: avj@transport.dtu.dk

Y. Shi et al. (eds.), *New State of MCDM in the 21st Century*, Lecture Notes
in Economics and Mathematical Systems 648, DOI 10.1007/978-3-642-19695-9_5,
© Springer-Verlag Berlin Heidelberg 2011

combining the MCA with the cost-benefit analysis (CBA) is applied as described by Salling et al. (2007). This methodology, COSIMA, uses a indicator which expresses the trade-off between the CBA and MCA part resulting in a total rate expressing the attractiveness of each alternative. However, it should be mentioned that the proposed procedure for estimating the importance of criteria weights is not limited to the ROD and COSIMA methods described above.

The proposed framework is applied to the case of choosing a light railway line to be implemented in the Swedish town Malmö. The decision concerns which of the three identified lines should be built and put into operation first. Preliminary studies have found eight non-monetised criteria, which are not all included in the conducted CBA. The alternatives are compared to each other with respect to each criterion by using the REMBRANDT methodology. With 8 criteria there are 40,340 (8!) possible combinations of ranking the criteria. The proposed method calculates all combinations and produces a set of rank variation graphs for each alternative and for different values of the trade-off indicator. This information is relatively easy to grasp for the decision-makers. The result is compared with the results from a conducted decision conference about the decision problem. During the decision conference the different stakeholder preferences were unveiled by the participants who had to assign weights.

The proposed method also introduces a more constrained approach. In this approach the stakeholders/decision makers have the possibility to set up some constraint to the decision problem. This could for example be that criterion XX cannot assume a rank lower than three or criterion XX always have to be ranked higher than criterion YY. This would mean that the outcome of the method is a subset of the total solution space.

The paper finishes up with a discussion and considerations about how to present the results. The question whether to present a single decision criterion, such as the benefit-cost rate or the net present value, or instead to present graphs showing the robustness of the decision analysis is discussed. Furthermore a perspective, for estimating the robustness of weights using other MCA methodologies (and weighting methods) than the proposed framework, is discussed.

5.2   Case Study: Public Transport System

For testing the proposed methodology, a case study has been examined. It concerns the introduction of a new public transport system in the Swedish town Malmö, located in the southern part of Sweden. The case study was conducted under the project "An overall evaluation of public transport investments" (Hiselius et al. 2009). The new transport system consists of several light railway lines, which are planned to be introduced in different stages and in the first stage three different lines have been chosen to be further examined. The three lines run in different parts of the city and therefore differ in which impacts they result in. As a preliminary analysis the municipality of Malmö had a cost benefit analysis (CBA) conducted (Hiselius

Table 5.1 Results from the cost benefit analysis (costs and benefits in M SEK)

Line	Costs	Benefits	BCR
A	652	1,475	2.26
B	603	1,978	3.28
C	296	579	1.96

et al. 2009). The CBA was carried out following the national Swedish standard for transport project appraisal (Table 5.1).

The result from the CBA indicated that all three lines are economically feasible with line B as the most feasible with at benefit-cost-rate (BCR) on 3.28. In addition the municipality also conducted a wider analysis of the three lines covering impacts which not are included in the CBA, all these impacts could not be assessed in a monetary way. This wider analysis of the three alternatives was performed by a working group formed by the municipality and consisted of ten different stakeholders. However, the municipality had difficulties in making an overall assessment of the three lines taking all the impacts into consideration. Consequently, there was a need for a more comprehensive assessment. This assessment was done using a decision support system called COSIMA, which is a composite model for assessment of transport projects. Using decision models which make use of both CBA and MCA in combinations have been recommended to give complementary insights (Macharis et al. 2008).

5.2.1 Composite Assessment

In order to conduct a composite assessment of the three alternatives the COSIMA (COmpoSIte Model for Assessment) framework was used (Salling et al. 2007). As with other composite models COSIMA is an extension of a traditional CBA to a more comprehensive analysis, which seeks to meet the demands from the decision makers. The COSIMA analysis is characterized by the way it includes, in addition to the CBA, missing impacts which have relevance for the examined project. These impacts are often not possible to express by monetary values and thereby they are excluded from the CBA, but by including them in the assessment a better foundation for a decision can be achieved.

As mentioned the COSIMA consists of two parts, a CBA and a MCA and the total result of the COSIMA can be expressed by the Total Rate of Return (TTR). By using this approach the MCA part has to be additive to the CBA part. The additive MCA part is expressed by a MCA percentage. This percentage expresses the MCA part of the total analysis in relation to the CBA part. In a situation where the MCA part is regarded as just as valuable as the CBA part, the MCA percentage would be 50% (see Fig. 5.1). The decision makers have to make this value judgment in order to calculate the TRR.

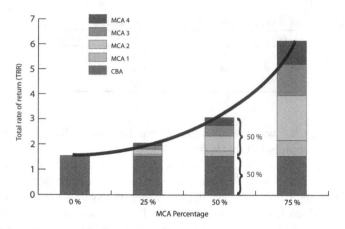

Fig. 5.1 The total rate of return (TRR) as a function of the MCA percentage

The COSIMA framework uses pair wise comparisons for rating of the alternatives, either the Analytical Hierarchy Process (AHP) or the REMBRANDT technique is used. For setting the criteria weights Rank Order Distribution technique is used (Roberts and Goodwin 2002). The ROD technique provides importance weights based on the rankings of the criteria, thereby the weight approximation problem is reduced to rank the criteria after importance. The ranking of the criteria reveals the decision maker's perception of how important the criterion is relative to other criteria under consideration (Monat 2009).

5.2.2 Decision Conference

In order to capture the stakeholders' preferences a decision conference was conducted with the purpose of finding the most attractive alternative seen from the involved stakeholders' point of view (Phillips 2006). The decision conference was tailored in order to capture all the different perspectives of the decision problem and to give input to the COSIMA model. One of the advantages with involving the stakeholders (and the decision makers) are that many stakeholders tend to reject decision criteria that appear to provide the "right" answer through a single number coming out an economic mode. They want the flexibility of implementing their own value judgments in the decision (DeCorla-Souza et al. 1997). Furthermore, a decision made during a decision conference has a higher probability of acceptance than a decision made based on complex decision process (Goodwin and Wright 2004).

The decision conference was conducted with ten participants, which all were stakeholders of the project. All the stakeholders were also part of the working group formed by the municipality in order to find the most appropriate light railway line to build first. Prior to the decision conference the CBA was conducted. The set-up of the decision conference was: presentation of the alternatives, presentation of the CBA, defining the criteria, description of the criteria, ranking of the criteria after importance, evaluating the alternatives (pair wise comparisons), setting the MCA percentage and finally a presentation of the results from the decision conference. All the participants had opportunity to make an individual ranking of the criteria and setting an individual MCA percentage.

After some discussion the group agreed on a ranking of the criteria, the pair wise comparisons and a MCA percentage of 60%. The resulting total rate of return is illustrated in Fig. 5.2. The TRR for the three alternatives show that alternative B has the highest TRR – based on the preferences the group could agree upon.

To test the result sensitivity for changes in the MCA %, all TRRs was calculated for MCA % in the range from 0% (only contribution from the CBA) to 80%. The sensitivity test is illustrated in Fig. 5.3. The figure shows that with any MCA percentage up to approximately 75% it makes no difference to the overall result. This result does not differ from the result from the CBA, which also had alternative B

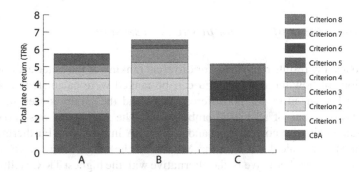

Fig. 5.2 The group's consensus with a MCA percentage on 60%

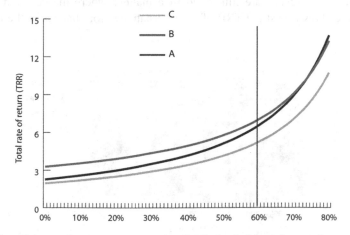

Fig. 5.3 Sensitivity test for changes in the MCA %. The bar indicates the group's consensus on a MCA percentage

as the most attractive alternative. However, this composite analysis gives valuable information to the decision makers anyway. A possible decision about building line B first would be based on a better foundation than just the CBA. The municipality is better prepared for eventual criticism of the decision because they can publish a comprehensive analysis taking a wide range of impacts into account.

The sensitivity analysis showed that many of the disagreements or uncertainties found during the decision conference had no impact on the overall result, line B is the most attractive alternative. However, during the decision conference the participants had difficulties in agreeing on a consensus about the ranking of the criteria after importance. So the individual criteria weights, which also were recorded, were compared to the criteria weights agreed upon in consensus. All the participants had ranked the same criteria as most important and there seemed to be most agreement about the higher ranked criteria and more disagreement with the lower ranked criteria. This disagreement gave reason for also testing the TRRs robustness for variation in the ranking (importance order) of the criteria.

5.2.3 Robustness of the Composite Assessment

In order to test the results robustness for different ranking of the criteria all possible combinations of how the eight criteria can be ranked were calculated. The eight criteria can be ranked in 40,320 different ways and the group consensus on the ranking was only one of all these combinations. The simulation was carried out with the same pair wise comparisons and same CBA information. Furthermore, all combinations were calculated with the MCA% in the range from 0% to 80%. A simulation result for alternative B, the alternative with the highest TRR, is illustrated in Fig. 5.4.

The simulation results are illustrated in a manner where the decision makers easily can see how robust the TRR of the alternative is for changes in the ranking,

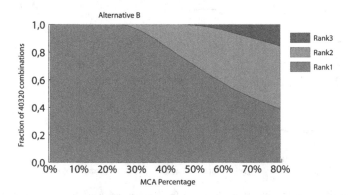

Fig. 5.4 Simulation results for alternative B

and thereby weighting, of the criteria. For alternative B it can be seen that in the range of a MCA % on 0% to approximately 25%, it does not matter how the criteria are ranked after importance – alternative B will be ranked as number 1 among the alternatives in all cases. In the case of a MCA % set to 60, which was chosen by the group, alternative B is ranked as the most attractive alternative in approximately 58% of all possible rankings. The group did choose a ranking which put alternative B as the highest ranked alternative, but other rankings of the criterion would put either alternative A or C as the most attractive alternative. Similar illustrations could also have been made for the other alternatives.

However, the decision conference revealed a tendency in the ranking of the criteria, and this information could be used in the simulation. All the participants ranked the same criterion as the most important, so a simulation with this criterion fixed as ranked number 1 could be made. Furthermore, there was also a tendency in which criterion was ranked as second most important. These tendencies can be simulated and the results can either confirm that the decision makers (in this case the participants of the decision conference) have a robust result that points out a certain alternative as being the most attractive or that the result is sensitive to changes in the ranking of the criteria. Figure 5.5 illustrates the results from three different simulations at a MCA percentage at 60%. The first bar shows the simulation results with all combinations, where in 58% of all the combinations alternative B would be ranked as number 1. The next bar is the result from a simulation with criterion 1 fixed as ranked number 1. It can be seen that there is a lower fraction of all combinations giving alternative B the highest rank than in the simulation with all combinations. The reason for this result is that alternative B has the lowest score among the alternatives for criterion 1 and ranking this criterion as number 1 is then a disadvantage for alternative B. The next bar shows the results for the simulation with criterion 1 and 2

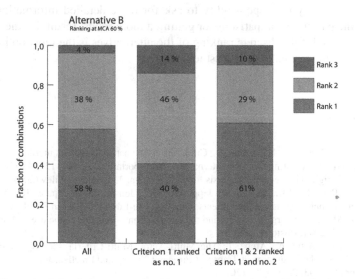

Fig. 5.5 Constrained simulation approach with one or two criterion rankings fixed

fixed as ranked as number 1 and 2. This simulation shows the highest fraction of all possible combinations giving alternative B the highest rank (61%). A reason for this can again be found in how the alternative B is scoring on the criterion. Alternative B has the highest score on criterion 2, together with alternative A, this gives alternative B a advantage when the criterion is fixed as the next most important criterion.

This approach provides an opportunity to deal with disagreement among the participant about the ranking of the criteria. If the group have difficulties in ranking one or more criteria, a simulation can be made based on keeping all the agreed upon rankings fixed.

5.3   Conclusion and Perspectives

This paper has introduced a method of using rank variation concerning the stakeholders' perception of criteria importance for exploring the sensitivity of criteria weights in MCA. The method preserves the CBA information and applies ROD weights based on the stakeholders' ranging the criteria after importance. The method has shown that it is possible to conduct a sensitivity analysis by using rank variation and the analysis gives useful information to the decision makers.

The combination of a technical solution (COSIMA model) that captured the different perspectives with a social process (decision conference) that engaged the stakeholders was a successful process where the stakeholders were confident with the final results (see also Phillips and Bana e Costa 2005 for similar conclusions).

A further research task is to consideration if the robustness test should be revealed for the decision makers or not? This might give reason for not trusting the model results among the decision makers. However, if kept away from the decision makers, it will be the analyst's responsibility to ask for more detailed information of for example the pair wise comparisons for getting a more robust result. Furthermore, it can be discussed if the discrete ranking of the alternatives is the most optimal way of presenting the results of the robustness test.

References

DeCorla-Souza, P., Everett, J., Gardner, B., Culp, M.: Total cost analysis: An alternative to benefit-cost analysis in evaluating transport alternatives. Transportation 24, 107–123 (1997)

Goodwin, P., Wright, G.: Decision Analysis for Management Judgement. Wiley (2004)

Hiselius, L., Barfod, M.B., Leleur, S., Jeppesen, S.L., Jensen, A.V., Hjalte, K.: An overall evaluation of public transport investments. University of Lund (2009) – In Swedish.

Hobbs, F.B., Meier, P.: Energy decisions and the environment – A guide to the use of Multicriteria Methodes. Kluwer, Boston (2000)

Macharis, C., De Witte, A., Ampe, J.: The Multi-Actor, Multi-Criteria Analysis Methodology (MAMCA) for the Evalutaion of Transport Projects: Theory and Practice. Journal of Advanced Transportation. 43, 2, 183–202 (2008)

Monat, J. P.: The Benefits of global scaling in multi-criteria decision analysis. Judgement and Decision Making 4, 6, 492–508 (2009)

Phillips, L.D., Bana e Costa, C. A.: Transparent prioritization, budgeting and resource allocation with multi-criteria decision analysis and decision conferencing. Working paper LSEOR 05.75 (2005)

Phillips, L. D.: Decision Conferencing. A working paper LSEOR 06.85 (2006)

Roberts, R., Goodwin, P.: Weight approximations in multi-attribute decision models. J. Multi-Crit. Decis. Anal. 11:291–303 (2002)

Salling, K. B., Leleur, S., Jensen, A.V.: Modelling decision support and uncertainty for large transport infrastructure projects: The CLG-DSS model of the Øresund Fixed Link. Decision Support Systems 43:1539–1547 (2007)

UNIVERSITAET STUTTGART: HEATCO - Developing Harmonised European Approaches for Transport Costing and Project Assessment. EU Sixth framework Programme 2002–2006. http://heatco.ier.uni-stuttgart.de/. Accessed 24 February 2009

Chapter 6
Compromise Based Evolutionary Multiobjective Optimization Algorithm for Multidisciplinary Optimization

Benoît Guédas, Xavier Gandibleux, and Philippe Dépincé

Abstract Multidisciplinary Design Optimization deals with engineering problems composed of several sub-problems – called disciplines – that can have antagonist goals and thus require to find compromise solutions. Moreover, the sub-problems are often multiobjective optimization problems. In this case, the compromise solutions between the disciplines are often considered as compromises between all objectives of the problem, which may be not relevant in this context. We propose two alternative definitions of the compromise between disciplines. Their implementations within the well-known NSGA-II algorithm are studied and results are discussed.

Keywords Compromise solutions · Evolutionary algorithm · Multidisciplinary optimization · Multiobjective optimization · Preferences.

6.1 Introduction

The design and optimization of complex engineering systems, such as aircrafts, cars or boats, require the collaboration of many engineering teams from different disciplines. These problems are referred to as Multidisciplinary Design Optimization (MDO). This work deals with a class of MDO problems, where each discipline is a Multiobjective Optimization Problem (MOP – see Ehrgott (2005) for notations and definitions). For instance, the design of a wing of an airplane involves two strongly coupled disciplines: aerodynamics and structure. Both may have several objectives to achieve. For example, the minimization of the drag and the maximization of the

B. Guédas (✉) and P. Dépincé
IRCCyN, École Centrale de Nantes, 1, rue de la Noë, BP 92101, 44321 Nantes Cedex 03, France
e-mail: Benoit.Guedas@irccyn.ec-nantes.fr, Philippe.Depince@irccyn.ec-nantes.fr

X. Gandibleux
LINA, Université de Nantes, 2, rue de la Houssinière, BP 92208, 44322 Nantes Cedex 03, France
e-mail: Xavier.Gandibleux@univ-nantes.fr

Y. Shi et al. (eds.), *New State of MCDM in the 21st Century*, Lecture Notes
in Economics and Mathematical Systems 648, DOI 10.1007/978-3-642-19695-9_6,
© Springer-Verlag Berlin Heidelberg 2011

lift for aerodynamics and the minimization of the weight and of the deflection for the structure. The goal of such a MDO problem is to propose compromise solutions to the decision maker between the disciplines. In other contexts, compromises solutions have to be found between several possible scenarios (see for example Better et al. (2008) for an application to risk management). A compromise solution can be understood as a preferred solution for the decision problem.

6.2 Context and Goal

Classical MDO methods (Tosserams et al. 2009) do not consider problems where the disciplines have multiple objectives each. Recently, Evolutionary Multiple Objective (EMO) optimization methods such as EM-MOGA (Gunawan et al. 2003), COSMOS (Rabeau et al. 2007) and others (see Guedas (2010) for a description of these methods), were designed to solve optimization problems where each discipline has multiple objectives. But these approaches consider the problem as a unique MOP composed with all the objectives of the disciplines optimized simultaneously. Hence, the solutions found by those methods are the efficient solutions of the following problem:

$$\min_{x \in X}(f_{1,1}(x), \ldots, f_{1,p_1}(x), \ldots, f_{q,1}(x), \ldots, f_{q,p_q}(x)) \qquad (6.1)$$

where q is the number of disciplines and p_i the number of objectives of the ith discipline. The function $f_{i,j}$ represents the jth objective of the ith discipline. We will assume that all the disciplines are defined on the same decision space.

We will note C_0 the first compromise which consists in solving the MOP described (6.1). Unfortunately, C_0 does not give relevant solutions in MDO problems, as illustrated by the following didactic example composed by two disciplines. Each discipline has two objectives to minimize: $f_{1,1}$ and $f_{1,2}$ for the first discipline and $f_{2,1}$ and $f_{2,2}$ for the second one. Let $f_1(x) = (f_{1,1}(x), f_{1,2}(x))$ and $f_2(x) = (f_{2,1}(x), f_{2,2}(x))$ be respectively the objective functions of the first and the second discipline, and $X = \{x_a, x_b, x_c\}$ the feasible set of solutions in the decision space. The performances of these solutions are reported in Table 6.1.

Considering independently the disciplines, we have two efficient solutions by discipline (see Fig. 6.1): x_a and x_c in the first discipline, and x_a and x_b in the second one. As x_a is an efficient solution in both disciplines, x_a is expected to be

Table 6.1 The performances of the feasible solutions by f_1 (resp. f_2) defined for discipline 1 (resp. discipline 2)

x	Discipline 1		Discipline 2	
	$f_{1,1}(x)$	$f_{1,2}(x)$	$f_{2,1}(x)$	$f_{2,2}(x)$
x_a	1	3	2	1
x_b	3	2	1	3
x_c	2	1	3	2

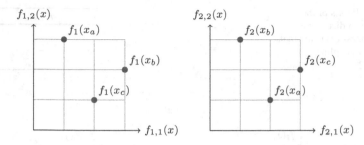

Fig. 6.1 The objective spaces of the two disciplines of the didactic minimization problem: discipline 1 is on the *left* and discipline 2 on the *right*

the only efficient compromise solution of this problem and reported as the unique output of the algorithm. But if we consider the four objectives problem (6.1), all the feasible solutions are efficient because their 4-dimensions performance vectors are mutually non-dominated: the C_0 compromise solution set is thus X. Indeed, solving the MOP can be interpreted as finding solutions between objectives without taking into account the grouping of the objectives within the disciplines. For instance, x_a would be preferred over x_b in the first discipline and over x_c in the second one but this information is missing in the C_0 compromise. We propose two compromises which are more relevant in this context: C_1 and C_2.

6.3 Computing a Compromise

6.3.1 C_1: Ordering the Solutions in Disciplines

The first idea we propose – also presented in Guédas et al. (2009) – is to transform each disciplinary MOP into a single objective using a measure of solutions quality inside each discipline.

Ranking procedures are frequently used in multiobjective genetic algorithms for evaluating the fitness of the solutions. Goldberg (1989) first introduced the rank to bias the selection operator based on the evaluations of the objective function. This idea has then been used by Srinivas and Deb (1994) in the NSGA algorithm in order to sort the individuals for a multiobjective problem. Other ranking procedures have been proposed for multiobjective genetic algorithms, such as the one proposed by Fonseca and Fleming (1993). Definition 1 presents the rank as it is defined in ordered sets theory. This definition is the same as the one used by Srinivas and Deb.

Definition 1. Let $O = (E, \leq)$ be an ordered set. For $e \in E$, the rank $r(e)$ of e is defined as follows:

- $r(e) = 1$, if e is a minimum.
- $r(e) = n$, if the elements of rank $< n$ have been assigned and e is a minimum in the ordered set $P \setminus \{x \in P : r(x) < n\}$.

Table 6.2 Ranks of the points in each discipline: $r_1(x)$ (resp. $r_2(x)$) is the rank of x in the discipline 1 (resp. discipline 2)

x	$r_1(x)$	$r_2(x)$
x_a	1	1
x_b	2	1
x_c	1	2

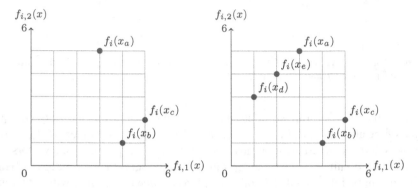

Fig. 6.2 Using the rank to define an order relation between elements of a discipline i, the order relation depends on the other elements: the rank of $f_i(x_a)$ is less than the rank of $f_i(x_c)$ in the *left chart* whereas this relation is reversed in the *right chart*

The compromise C_1 consists in using the rank as the only objective of each discipline. The corresponding multidisciplinary optimization problem can be formulated as the following MOP:

$$\min_{x \in X}(r_1(x), \dots, r_q(x)) \tag{6.2}$$

where $r_i(x)$ represents the rank of x in the ith discipline. The efficient solutions of (6.2) are the C_1-compromise solutions.

For instance, in the didactic example introduced in the previous section (Table 6.1, Fig. 6.1), each point is ranked in each discipline separately. The results are presented in Table 6.2. Considering these ranks as performances of the solutions in each discipline, we can define a compromise solution as a non-dominated ranks vector. There is only one non-dominated rank vector $(1, 1)$, so the only C_1-compromise solution to this problem is x_a.

Unfortunately, a compromise based on ranks has an important drawback if implemented within an EMO algorithm because of its stochastic behavior: the order relation between two performance vectors depends on the spread of the performance vectors of the other individuals in the population. Thus, as the population evolves, the performance vectors move. Figure 6.2 shows that on the first chart, $f_i(x_a)$ is ranked 1 and $f_i(x_c)$ is ranked 2, whereas $f_i(x_a)$ is ranked 3 and $f_i(x_c)$ is ranked 2 on the second chart. Between the first and the second chart, only two points, $f_i(x_d)$ and $f_i(x_e)$ have been added, but it results in a reverse of the order of $f_i(x_a)$ and $f_i(x_c)$: $f_i(x_c)$ was greater than $f_i(x_a)$ on the first chart whereas it is less than $f_i(x_a)$ on the second one.

6.3.2 C_2: Taking into Account Incomparability in the Disciplines

Another approach is to take into account the incomparabilities in the dominance relation: an element $f(x)$ dominates $f(x')$ if $f(x)$ dominates $f(x')$ in at least one discipline, and $f(x')$ never dominates $f(x)$:

$$f(x) \preceq f(x') \iff \begin{cases} \exists i \in \{1, \ldots, n\} & f_i(x) \leq_i f_i(x') \\ \nexists j \in \{1, \ldots, n\} & f_j(x') \lneq_j f_j(x) \end{cases} \tag{6.3}$$

where $\leq_i$ is the componentwise order in the discipline i, and $\lneq_j$ is the Pareto-dominance relation in the discipline j. Let us call C_2 the compromise such that the compromise solutions are such that their performance vectors in each disciplines are non-dominated according to the transitive closure of the $\preceq$ relation.

In the didactic example presented Fig. 6.1, let $f(x) = (f_1(x), f_2(x))$. The point $f(x_a)$ dominates $f(x_c)$ and $f(x_c)$ dominates $f(x_b)$ in one discipline each, and there are no other domination relations. So we have $f(x_a) \preceq f(x_c) \preceq f(x_b)$. Thus, x_a is the only solution to this problem. On this example, the solutions of C_2 are equivalent to C_1. Moreover, this compromise is expected to be less sensitive when implemented within an EMO algorithm, because it does not introduce new order relations in the disciplines depending on the spread of the population.

6.4   EMO-MDO Algorithm

The proposed algorithm, called EMO-MDO (Algorithm 1), is a generalization of the NSGA-II algorithm (Deb 2001). Its particularity lies in the ranking procedure which can be computed on any preordered set[1], and not only the performance vectors of the individuals. It allows to modelize different kind of compromises such as C_0, C_1 and C_2. In particular, EMO-MDO used with C_0 is identical to NSGA-II. It also shares its genetic operators: real coded genes, SBX crossover (crossover routine), polynomial mutation (mutation routine), crowded binary constrained tournament selection (selection routine) and non-constrain-dominated sorting procedure with crowding (generation routine) (Deb 2001).

The initial population of size N is created from solutions randomly picked from the feasible set. The *preorder* between the individuals is then computed by the compromise function according to the population *pop* and the compromise $c \in \{C_0, C_1, C_2\}$. This *preorder* is used to compute the *ranks* of the individuals in the *population*. A *parents* population is selected from *pop* according to their *ranks*. Crossovers and mutations are performed to create an *offspring* population. The *offspring* is then added to the current population *pop* to create a $2 \times N$

---

[1] Ordered sets which are not necessarily antisymmetric.

Algorithm 1 EMO-MDO

Require: compromise c
Ensure: solution population
  population ← `initialization()`
  preorder ← `compromise`(c,population)
  ranks ← `compute_ranks`(preorder)
  for $i = 1$ to max_iteration **do**
    parents ← `selection`(population,ranks)
    offspring ← `mutation`(`crossover`(parents))
    population ← population ∪ offspring
    preorder ← `compromise`(c,population)
    ranks ← `compute_ranks`(preorder)
    population ← `generation`(population,ranks)
  end for
  return population

---

population on which the compromise relation is computed. The `generation` function selects the new individuals which will belong to the next generation.

6.5 Numerical Experiments

A series of experiments were performed on the EMO-MDO in order to study its behavior on C_0, C_1 and C_2 compromises.

6.5.1 Test Problem

This test problem comes from Engau and Wiecek (2007). It is composed of two bi-objective disciplines defined on the feasible set X. Here, all the feasible solutions are efficient for C_0 compromise.

$$D_1 \begin{cases} \min_{(x_1,x_2)\in X} f_{1,1}(x_1,x_2) = (x_1 - 2)^2 + (x_2 - 1)^2 \\ \min_{(x_1,x_2)\in X} f_{1,2}(x_1,x_2) = x_1^2 + (x_2 - 3)^2 \end{cases} \tag{6.4}$$

$$D_2 \begin{cases} \min_{(x_1,x_2)\in X} f_{2,1}(x_1,x_2) = (x_1 - 1)^2 + (x_2 + 1)^2 \\ \min_{(x_1,x_2)\in X} f_{2,2}(x_1,x_2) = (x_1 + 1)^2 + (x_2 - 1)^2 \end{cases} \tag{6.5}$$

with $X = \{(x_1, x_2) \in \mathbb{R}^2 : x_1^2 - x_2 \leq 0, x_1 + x_2 - 2 \leq 0, -x_1 \leq 0\}$

6.5.2 Test Protocol

Two reference sets of solutions are computed by filtering the solutions satisfying the compromises from a sampling of the feasible set of decision variables. The first sampling corresponds to a uniform discretization of the feasible set, whereas the second sampling is a simple random sampling. For each test, 300 solutions are evaluated.

The three compromises have been compared with the filtering methods and the EMO-MDO algorithm. The latter has been performed in two conditions: with or without the phenotypic diversity procedure enabled (crowding) in the `selection` and the `generation` functions.

The EMO-MDO algorithm as been run with the following combinations of population sizes and iterations numbers: 10×50, 20×15, 20×20, 50×50 and 50×500. Three simulations of each combination have been done to verify the stability of the algorithm.

From these experiments, we want to compare the solutions found by the genetic algorithms to the reference solutions, and to compare C_1 and C_2 compromises to C_0. As far as we know, there is no quality measure of the solutions of such problems as they exist in the field of evolutionary multiobjective genetic algorithms.

6.5.3 Results and Discussion

The crossover and mutation probabilities are respectively 0.8 and 0.2. The η and σ parameters for the SBX crossover and mutation are respectively 2 and 4. Other set of parameters have been tested and they produce comparable results:

- We observe that the compromise solutions found with C_1 with the uniform sampling (Fig. 6.3a) are uniformly distributed in an area approximately equal to the half of the image of the feasible set.
- A random sampling of the feasible set (Fig. 6.3b) does not give the same results: the compromise solutions still belong to the same area but are not spread uniformly. This shows that the solutions of the compromise C_1 are dependent to the spread of the population as stated in Sect. 6.3.
- The C_2 solutions are more largely spread with the simple random sampling than the uniform discretization (Fig. 6.3a,b). Nevertheless, the solutions are in the same area, and this spread decrease as the sampling size increase.
- The EMO-MDO algorithm did not converge to the expected area when used with C_1 (Fig. 6.3c,d). This is more salient when phenotypic diversity is disabled (Fig. 6.3d).
- The EMO-MDO algorithm converged to the expected area when used with C_2 (Fig. 6.3c,d).
- The phenotypic diversity of NSGA-II is not adapted to this kind of problem: many solutions have the same performances within a discipline (Fig. 6.3c). Nevertheless, phenotypic diversity still improves the solutions: they are less diversified when disabled (Fig. 6.3d).

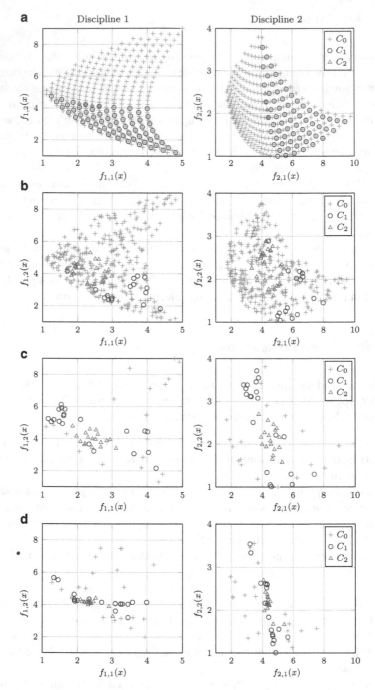

Fig. 6.3 Results of the test problem using compromise C_0, C_1 and C_2 with filtering on uniform sampling (**a**), and simple random sampling (**b**) of 300 points. Results with EMO-MDO with phenotypic distance enabled (**c**), and disabled (**d**). Population size is 20, and 15 iterations were performed

We also observed that the compromise C_2 is less sensitive to the algorithm parameters than the compromise C_1.

6.6 Conclusions and On-Going Work

MDO problems are often composed of disciplines which have several objectives each. The compromise solutions are then often defined as the efficient solutions of the MOP (C_0). This can be interpreted as a compromise between the objectives instead of a compromise between the disciplines.

We propose a first compromise (C_1) based on the preferences of the disciplines using the ranks of the solutions. Unfortunately, this does not suit to an EMO algorithm because ranks will not change uniformly as the population evolves. To overcome this problem, we propose another compromise (C_2) allowing a non total order of the preferences of the disciplines. C_0 C_1 and C_2 have been implemented into an EMO algorithm. C_2 gives satisfying results and is less sensitive to the algorithm parameters than C_1.

The proposed compromises have been defined on a simplified class of MDO problems without local variables and coupling functions between disciplines. Our future research will extend the compromises to more complex problems.

Acknowledgements The authors would like to thank the regional council of the Pays de la Loire (France), MILES project, for their support of this research.

References

Better M., Glover F., Kochenberger G., Wang H.: Simulation optimization: application in risk management. *International Journal of Information Technology & Decision Making* **7**(4):571–587 (2008).

Deb K.: *Multi-objective optimization using evolutionary algorithms.* Wiley (2001). 518 p.

Ehrgott M.: *Multicriteria optimization.* Springer, Berlin Heidelberg, 2nd edition (2005). 323 p.

Engau A., Wiecek M.M.: 2D decision-making for multicriteria design optimization. *Structural and Multidisciplinary Optimization* **34**(4):301–315 (2007).

Fonseca C., Fleming P.: Genetic algorithms for multiobjective optimization: formulation discussion and generalization. In : *Proceedings of the 5th International Conference on Genetic Algorithms*, pp. 416–423, San Francisco, CA, USA (1993).

Goldberg D.E.: *Genetic algorithms in search, optimization and machine learning.* Addison-Wesley, Reading, Massachusetts (1989). 432 p.

Guédas B.: *Proposition de compromis pour le calcul de solutions préférées à l'aide d'un algorithme évolutionnaire multiobjectif en optimisation multidisciplinaire.* Ph.D. Thesis, École Centrale de Nantes, France (2010).

Guédas B., Dépincé P., Gandibleux X.: Vers une notion de compromis en optimisation multidisciplinaire multiobjectif. In: *Book of abstracts of the ROADEF 2009 Conf.*, Nancy, France (2009).

Tosserams S., Etman L.F.P., Rooda J.E.: A classification of methods for distributed system optimization based on formulation structure. *Structural and Multidisciplinary Optimization* **39**(5):503–517 (2009).

Gunawan S., Farhang-Mehr A., Azarm S.: Multi-level multi-objective genetic algorithm using entropy to preserve diversity. In: Fonseca C.M., Fleming P., Zitzler E., Deb K., Thiele L. (eds) *Evolutionary Multicriterion Optimization*, LNCS 2632, pp. 148–161 (2003). Springer, Berlin Heidelberg.

Rabeau S., Dépincé P., and Bennis F.: Collaborative optimization of complex systems: a multidisciplinary approach. *International Journal on Interactive Design and Manufacturing* **1**(4):209–218 (2007).

Srinivas N., Deb K.: Multiobjective optimization using nondominated sorting in genetic algorithm. *Evolutionary Computation* **2**(3):221–248 (1994).

Chapter 7
A Lower Bound of the Choquet Integral Integrated Within Martins' Algorithm

Hugo Fouchal, Xavier Gandibleux, and Fabien Lehuédé

Abstract The problem investigated in this work concerns the integration of a decision-maker preference model within an exact algorithm in multiobjective combinatorial optimization. Rather than computing the complete set of efficient solutions and choosing a solution afterwards, our aim is to efficiently compute one solution satisfying the decision maker preferences elicited a priori. The preference model is based on the Choquet integral. The reference optimization problem is the multiobjective shortest path problem, where Martins' algorithm is used. A lower bound of the Choquet integral is proposed that aims to prune useless partial paths at the labeling stage of the algorithm. Various procedures exploiting the proposed bound are presented and evaluated on a collection of benchmarks. Numerical experiments show significant improvements compared to the exhaustive enumeration of solutions.

Keywords Choquet integral · Multiobjective optimization · Shortest paths

7.1 Introduction

Real-world optimization problems often require the use of more than one objective for evaluating the impact of alternatives. For example, the evaluation of the cost and the quality of the solutions may not in general be aggregated on a single metric

H. Fouchal (✉)
LINA, Université de Nantes, 2 rue de la Houssinière, BP 92208, 44322 Nantes Cedex-03, France
and
IRCCyN, École des Mines de Nantes, 4 rue Alfred Kastler, 44307 Nantes, France
e-mail: Hugo.Fouchal@univ-nantes.fr

X. Gandibleux
LINA, Université de Nantes, 2 rue de la Houssinière, BP 92208, 44322 Nantes Cedex-03, France
e-mail: Xavier.Gandibleux@univ-nantes.fr

F. Lehuédé
IRCCyN, École des Mines de Nantes, 4 rue Alfred Kastler, 44307 Nantes, France
e-mail: Fabien.Lehuede@emn.fr

Y. Shi et al. (eds.), *New State of MCDM in the 21st Century*, Lecture Notes
in Economics and Mathematical Systems 648, DOI 10.1007/978-3-642-19695-9_7,
© Springer-Verlag Berlin Heidelberg 2011

representative of the original problem. In front of such a situation, the design of a decision-making process based on multiobjective optimization (see Ehrgott and Gandibleux (2000) for notations and definitions) is relevant. Moving from a single to multiple objective optimization implies that the decision-maker (DM) no longer has a unique optimal solution, but a set of efficient solutions as output of the decision making process. Computing rapidly the complete set of efficient solutions remains a challenge in multiobjective optimization (see Przybylski et al. (2008)). Unfortunately, this set may be large and solutions are incomparable to each other without any preferential information provided by the DM. Also, the exhaustive computation of this set may not be relevant when a DM can provide his preferences about the expected solutions. A resolution method handling DM preferences is usually tagged *a priori, interactive or a posteriori* (Evans 1984) according to the articulation of preferences with the computing phase(s). This concerns the domain of MultiObjective Preference-based Optimization (MOPO).

MOPO is at the frontier between MultiCriteria Decision Aid (MCDA) and MultiObjective Programming (MOP). MCDA aims at building a preference model in order to help the DM to find a preferred solution within an explicit set of solutions. MOP is mainly focused on mathematical models, methods and algorithms for computing rapidly a (maximum or minimum) complete set of efficient solutions. The scientific community is active on MOPO, and the literature has become abundant. For example, in the multiobjective metaheuristic field, Branke et al. (2008) proposes solutions to integrate preferences inside evolutionary algorithms. In robust optimization (Kouvelis and Yu 1997), the preference models favour well-balanced solutions inside multiobjective problems. Perny and Spanjaard (2005) proposes to use a non-classical preference model, and (Galand and Spanjaard 2007) an OWA aggregation function. Lehuédé et al. (2006) uses the Choquet integral in a constraint programming context.

Despite an important number of applications, little research has investigated the field of MOPO for MultiObjective Combinatorial Optimization (MOCO – see Ehrgott and Gandibleux (2000) for an extensive presentation of this field). This is the scope of our work. The proposed approach is an a priori method where the preferential information from the DM is first elicited. The preferences are then exploited inside the algorithm for computing a preferred solution, without generating the complete set of efficient solutions. The preference model is based on the Choquet integral (Grabisch 1995) and the MOCO problem is the shortest path problem with multiple objectives (MOSP). A pioneer work in this context has been proposed by Galand et al. (2007; 2010) where the Choquet integral is used to find balanced solutions for the MOSP problem.

This paper is devoted to a lower bound of the Choquet integral which generalizes the work in Galand and Perny (2007). This bound aims to prune useless partial paths at the labeling stage of the Martins' algorithm. Various procedures exploiting the proposed bound are presented and benchmarked on a collection of numerical instances. Experiments are reported and a comparative analysis is discussed.

The paper is organized as follows. Section 7.2 provides definitions for the MOSP problem, for preference model and introduces related work. The definition of a lower bound and its integration in the Martins' algorithm is presented in Sect. 7.3. Section 7.4 reports numerical results provided by using the lower bound inside Martins' algorithm. Finally, Sect. 7.5 presents our conclusions and suggests several directions for future research.

7.2 Problem Formulation

Let $G = (N, A)$ be a directed and connected *graph*, where $N = \{1, \ldots, n\}$ is the set of *vertices* with cardinality $|N| = n$ and $A = \{(i_1, j_1), \ldots, (i_m, j_m)\}$ is the set of *arcs* with cardinality $|A| = m$. The directed arc linking vertices i and j is denoted by (i, j), and the vector $(c_1(i, j), \ldots, c_p(i, j))$ represents p non-negative "cost" values associated with the arc (i, j). In the set N, we identify a *source vertex* s and a *sink vertex* t.

A *path* r from s to t in G is a sequence of arcs and vertices from s to t, where the tail vertex of a given arc coincides with the head vertex of the next arc in the path. The *decision space* is denoted by $R_{s,t}$, the set of all paths from s to t in G, or by $R_{s,\bullet}$ the set of all paths from s to all others vertices $N \setminus \{s\}$ in G. We consider a set $P = \{1, \ldots, p\}$ of p objectives[1] to be minimized. Let $z_k(r) = \sum_{(i,j) \in r} c_k(i, j) \in \mathbb{R}_+$ denote the value of a path r with respect to the objectives $k = 1, \ldots, p$. Hence, the vector $z(r) = (z_1(r), \ldots, z_p(r))$ represents the *performance vector* of path $r \in R_{s,t}$ in *the objective space* $Z = z(R_{s,t}) \subseteq \mathbb{R}_+^p$.

Let r^1, r^2 be two paths, and $z^1 = z(r^1), z^2 = z(r^2)$ the performance vectors. When all the objectives are to be minimized, z^1 *dominates* z^2 iff $z_k^1(r^1) \leq z_k^2(r^2)$, $k = 1, \ldots, p$, and $z^1 \neq z^2$. z is *non-dominated* iff $z \in Z$ and $\nexists z' \in Z$ such that z' dominates z. A path r^e is *efficient* iff $r^e \in R_{s,t}$ and $\nexists r \in R_{s,t}$ such that $z(r)$ dominates $z(r^e)$. When r^e is an efficient solution then $z(r^e)$ is *a non-dominated vector*.

7.2.1 Multiobjective Shortest Paths

The multiobjective shortest path problem (see Ehrgott and Gandibleux (2000) for an extensive survey) is a well-known MOCO problem. The version considered in this paper can be summarized as:

$$\text{" } \min_{r \in R_{s,t}} \text{ "}(z_1(r), \ldots, z_p(r)) \quad \forall t \in N \setminus \{s\} \tag{MOSP}$$

where each objective is a linear function. Let $E(R_{s,\bullet})$ denote the *maximal complete set* of efficient paths in $R_{s,\bullet}$ for a given source vertex s. In terms of complexity, the

---

[1] The terms "criterion" and "objective" are usual respectively in MCDA and in MOP. Even if they are not equivalent, they are considered as synonyms in this paper.

enumeration of all efficient paths in a MOSP may not be tractable in polynomial time (Hansen 1979). However, in practice the number of efficient paths is generally not exponential (Gandibleux et al. 2006).

Martins has introduced in 1984 (Martins 1984) a label setting algorithm which computes $E(R_{s,\bullet})$ when all the cost values are non negative (with at least one strict inequality holding for some values of k). This algorithm is a multiple objectives extension of the Dijkstra algorithm in which the 'min' operator is replaced by a dominance test. The main idea is quite simple. A label represents the performance of a path from source s to the current vertex i, plus information for building the corresponding path. At each iteration, for each vertex, there are two different sets of labels to qualify paths: *permanent* labels and *temporary* labels. The algorithm selects the lexicographically smallest label from all the sets of temporary labels, converts it to a permanent label, and propagates the information contained in this label to all the temporary labels of its successors. A temporary label is deleted when the dominance test is verified (a new temporary label is deleted if it is dominated by an another label of s; any temporary labels dominated by a new temporary label are deleted). The procedure stops when there are no more temporary labels. Each permanent label corresponds to a unique efficient path. The reader can refer to Martins (1984) for a more detailed description of this algorithm.

7.2.2 The Preference Model

A preference model mathematically expresses the subjective information provided by an expert on his preferences. We assume here that the set of p criteria is organized in a single level of aggregation. Each solution is represented by a set of attributes denoted $\Omega_i, i \in P$. For example, in the MOSP problem, $z_i(x)$ can be seen as an attribute of solution x on criterion i. According to the MultiAttribute Utility Theory (MAUT) (Figueira et al. 2005), attributes are made commensurate thanks to the introduction of partial utility functions $u_i : \Omega_i \rightarrow \xi$. The values returned by these functions indicate the level of satisfaction of the DM for each criterion independently. A solution a is characterized by a vector $(a_1, \ldots, a_p) \in \Omega = \Omega_1 \times \cdots \times \Omega_p$. The overall assessment of a is given by

$$U(a) = V(u_1(a_1), \ldots, u_p(a_p))$$

where $V : \xi^p \rightarrow \xi$ is the aggregation function. The overall preference relation $\succeq$ over Ω is then $a \succeq b \iff U(a) \geq U(b)$.

The most common aggregation function is the weighted sum function, but using it supposes that each criterion acts independently of the other criteria on the assessment of the solution. This limiting hypothesis can be avoided using the Choquet integral, which is able to model not only the importance of a criterion but also interactions between criteria (see example 1). An overview of the use of this function in MCDA is given in Grabisch and Labreuche (2010).

The definition of the Choquet integral is based on a capacity function that defines a weight for each subset of criteria.

Definition 1. (Capacity function Grabisch (1995)) Let $\mathscr{P}(P)$ be the power set of P. A capacity function $\mu : \mathscr{P}(P) \rightarrow [0, 1]$ is a set function satisfying (i) $\mu(\emptyset) = 0$, $\mu(P) = 1$ and (ii) $\forall A, B \subseteq P, A \subset B \Rightarrow \mu(A) \leq \mu(B)$.

A capacity function can be defined using the MYRIAD software (Labreuche and Lehuédé 2005) or the KAPPALAB (Grabisch et al. 2008) library. If $\forall A, B \subset P$, $\mu(A \cup B) + \mu(A \cap B) \leq \mu(A) + \mu(B)$ then the capacity function is called *submodular* (Grabisch 1995). Two indicators, described in Figueira et al. (2005), are also useful to explain a capacity function: the Shapley value v_i measures the importance of criterion $i \in P$ and the Interaction index, denoted $I(A)$, evaluates the interaction between the criteria of a coalition $A \subseteq P$.

Definition 2. (Choquet integral Grabisch (1995)) Let μ be a capacity function on P. The Choquet integral $C_\mu : \xi^p \rightarrow \xi$ with respect to μ is defined by:

$$C_\mu(y) = \sum_{i=1}^{p} [\mu(Y_{(i)}) - \mu(Y_{(i+1)})] \times y_{(i)}$$

where $(.)$ is a permutation function such that $y_{(1)} \leq \cdots \leq y_{(p)}$, $Y_{(i)} = \{(i), \ldots, (p)\}$ and $Y_{(p+1)} = \emptyset$.

Another formulation of the Choquet integral is: $C_\mu(y) = \sum_{i=1}^{p} [y_{(i)} - y_{(i-1)}] \times \mu(Y_{(i)})$, with $y_{(0)} = 0$.

Example 1 Let μ be a capacity function such that: $\mu(\emptyset) = 0$, $\mu(\{1\}) = \mu(\{3\}) = 0.4$, $\mu(\{2\}) = 0.2$, $\mu(\{1, 2\}) = \mu(\{2, 3\}) = 0.8$, $\mu(\{1, 3\}) = 0.4$ and $\mu(\{1, 2, 3\}) = 1.0$. The Choquet integral of a vector $y = (30, 20, 10)$ with respect to μ is $C_\mu(y) = 10 \times (1.0 - 0.8) + 20 \times (0.8 - 0.4) + 30 \times 0.4 = 2.2$.

The importances of the criteria given by the Shapley index vector are $v = (0.3, 0.4, 0.3)$. There is a positive interaction between criteria 1-3 ($I(\{1, 3\}) = -0.4$) and negative interactions between criteria 1-2 ($I(\{1, 2\}) = 0.2$) and between criteria 2-3 ($I(\{2, 3\}) = 0.2$).

In this paper, this general model is modified in two ways: in order to focus our study on the Choquet integral, we consider that partial utility functions are identity functions and we remain in the minimization paradigm of the MOSP problem. Thus, for all $i \in \{1, \ldots, p\}$, $\Omega_i = \xi = \mathbb{R}_+$, for a path $r \in R_{s,t}$, $u_i(z_i(r)) = z_i(r)$ and the Choquet integral should be minimized.

7.2.3 The Choquet-Optimal Path Problem

As mentioned before, the only integration of a preference model based on the Choquet integral in a MOSP algorithm has been done by Galand et al. (2007; 2010) to find balanced solutions in a robust optimization context (the capacity function is submodular). Regarding this integration, the main difficulty is that the Choquet integral does not verify the Bellman principle (a Choquet-optimal path is not made of Choquet-optimal sub-paths). In the general case, finding an optimal solution with respect to a given Choquet integral in a MOSP problem has been proved NP-Hard (Galand and Perny 2007).

Galand and Perny (2007) propose a lower bound of the Choquet integral that allows to prune sub-optimal sub-paths in shortest path algorithms. The lower bound is based on the definition of a weighted sum that is inferior to the Choquet integral for any solution. When dealing with sum objective functions, aggregating objectives with a weighted sum is equivalent to aggregating costs on arcs. The problem is then reduced to a standard shortest path problem that can be solved very efficiently, providing a lower bound of the Choquet integral for any partial solution.

Our generalization of Galand and Perny work relies on the definition of a lower bound that is valid for any capacity function and not only when it is submodular. To this end, we provide a more general definition of the weighted sum function that bounds the Choquet integral.

7.3 The Choquet Integral Within Martins' Algorithm

7.3.1 Lower Bound Definition

For the MOSP problem, considering costs on the edges of the graph are non-negative, a weighted sum that can be used to produce a lower bound of the Choquet integral can be defined as follows:

Definition 3. Let μ be a capacity function and $H_\lambda(y) = \sum_{i=1}^{p} \lambda_i \times y_i$ be a weighted sum function. H_λ provides a lower bound for the Choquet integral C_μ if it verifies the constraints: $\forall y \in \mathbb{R}_+^p$, $H_\lambda(y) \leq C_\mu(y)$.

Finding a solution to $\{H_\lambda(y) \leq C_\mu(y), \forall y \in \mathbb{R}_+^p\}$ is not trivial because this set is not finite. We propose an equivalent finite set of constraints that can be used in a linear problem in order to find a valid vector of weights.

Theorem 1. Let μ be a capacity function and $\lambda \in \mathbb{R}_+^p$ be a vector of weights, then:

$$\forall y \in \mathbb{R}_+^p, \ H_\lambda(y) \leq C_\mu(y) \Leftrightarrow \forall A \subseteq P, \ \sum_{i \in A} \lambda_i \leq \mu(A)$$

Proof. 1 *The two sides of the equivalence are demonstrated as follows:*

($\Rightarrow$) We suppose that $\forall y \in \mathbb{R}_+^p$, $H_\lambda(y) \leq C_\mu(y)$. $\forall A \subseteq P$ we define $y^A \in \mathbb{R}_+^p$ such that $\forall i \in A, y_i^A = 1$ and $\forall j \in P \setminus A, \ y_j^A = 0$. According to the definition of the Choquet integral, $C_\mu(y^A) = \mu(A)$. In addition, $H_\lambda(y^A) = \sum_{i \in A} \lambda_i \times y_i^A$. As $\forall A \subseteq P, H_\lambda(y^A) \leq C_\mu(y^A)$ then $\forall A \subseteq P, \sum_{i \in A} \lambda_i \leq \mu(A)$.

($\Leftarrow$) *Let* $\lambda \in \mathbb{R}^p_+$ *such that* $\forall A \subseteq P, \sum_{i \in A} \lambda_i \leq \mu(A)$. $\forall y \in \mathbb{R}^p_+$ *let us define (.) a permutation of indexes* $1, \ldots, p$ *such that* $0 = y_{(0)} \leq y_{(1)} \leq \cdots \leq y_{(p)}$. *According to this notation,* $H_\lambda(y) = \sum_{i=1}^{p} \lambda_{(i)} \times y_{(i)}$. *Therefore* $H_\lambda(y)$ $= \sum_{i=1}^{p} [\sum_{j=i}^{p} \lambda_{(j)} - \sum_{j=i+1}^{p} \lambda_{(j)}] \times y_{(i)}$. *As* $y_{(0)} = 0$, *we obtain* $H_\lambda(y) = \sum_{i=1}^{p} [y_{(i)} - y_{(i-1)}] \times \sum_{j=i}^{p} \lambda_{(j)}$. *According to the Definition 2 of the Choquet integral and the definition of* λ *(see above) :* $\forall y \in \mathbb{R}^p_+$, $\sum_{i=1}^{p} [y_{(i)} - y_{(i-1)}] \times$ $\sum_{j=i}^{p} \lambda_{(j)} \leq \sum_{i=1}^{p} [y_{(i)} - y_{(i-1)}] \times \mu(Y_{(i)}) = C_\mu(y)$.

Therefore $\forall y \in \mathbb{R}^p_+$, $H_\lambda(y) \leq C_\mu(y)$. $\square$

Among the feasible sets of weights defined by these constraints, we must select a vector that provides the best lower bound for our problem. Supposing that this is achieved by maximizing a function f (discussed in Sect. 7.3.2) we come to the following proposal.

Proposal 1 *According to Theorem 1, a vector of weights* λ *can be defined to compute a lower bound of the Choquet integral by solving linear program* (7.1):

$$
\begin{aligned}
\max \ & f(\lambda) \\
s.t. \ & \sum_{i \in A} \lambda_i \leq \mu(A) \ , \forall A \subseteq P \ (a) \\
& \lambda_i \in [0, 1] \qquad \quad , \forall i \in P \ (b)
\end{aligned}
\tag{7.1}
$$

7.3.2 Definition of Objective Functions

The constraints of linear program (7.1) restrict the domain of definition of λ but clearly, all vectors in this domain are not equivalent. First, the bound provided by optimizing H_λ should be as high as possible. Thus, a dominance relation exists between vectors. It can be ensured that the solution of linear program (7.1) is not dominated if f is strictly increasing. Second, the value of H_λ for a solution should be as close as possible to the value of C_μ. Hence, we will evaluate the use of information from μ to define λ.

In the following we present three functions f that have been evaluated. To illustrate the differences between these functions, the solution of (7.1) is given for a capacity function μ defined on three criteria by $\mu(\{1\}) = 0.3$, $\mu(\{2\}) = \mu(\{3\}) = 0.2$, $\mu(\{1, 2\}) = 0.3$, $\mu(\{1, 3\}) = 0.5$ and $\mu(\{2, 3\}) = 0.4$.

- (sum) The sum of weights: $f(\lambda) = \sum_{i=1}^{p} \lambda_i$. The sum function is used as a reference.
  The vector of weights obtained for μ with this function is $\lambda^a = (0.3, 0.0, 0.2)$. Hence, although the sum has been maximized, criterion 2 will not be taken into account on this example.
- (min) A min function plus a marginal sum: $f(\lambda) = \min_{i \in P} \lambda_i + \epsilon \times \sum_{i=1}^{p} \lambda_i$, where $\epsilon > 0$ is a small positive value that weight the sum part of this function and makes it strictly increasing.

The min function builds balanced vector of weights. In particular it ensures that, if it is possible, no weight is left to zero. This is observed on the solution of (7.1) for μ: $\lambda^b = (0.15, 0.15, 0.2)$.

- (sh) A min aggregator using a Shapley index plus a marginal sum: $f(\lambda) = \min_{i \in P}(\lambda_i - v_i) + \epsilon \times \sum_{i=1}^{p} \lambda_i$, where $\epsilon > 0$ is a small positive value that weights the sum as for (min).

  This function uses the Shapley values that represent the individual importances of each criterion in the capacity function μ. The impact of this function is similar to (min) but it takes into account that more important criteria should have greater weights to build a weighted sum that is as close as possible to the Choquet integral. On our example, the Shapley index vector of μ is $v = (0.36, 0.26, 0.36)$. The resulting vector $\lambda^c = (0.2, 0.1, 0.2)$ represents better these relative importances than λ^a and λ^b.

7.3.3   Integration Within Martins' Algorithm

The proposed lower bound has been integrated in the dominance test of the Martins' algorithm to delete labels that cannot lead to a Choquet-optimal solution. The resulting algorithm is denoted Choquet Optimal Path Algorithm (COPA) in the following.

7.4   Numerical Results

The objective of this numerical evaluation is twofold. First, to compare the performance of COPA with respect to the computation of the maximal complete set of efficient paths with Martins' algorithm (the time needed for the a posteriori choice of the preferred solution is considered negligible). Second, to evaluate the impact of the objective functions presented in Sect. 7.3.2, the experimentation are based on 18 sets of four graphs defined for three and five criteria by their number of nodes n (1,000 or 3,000 or 6,000) and their number of edges m (m is given relatively to n and can be $5 \times n$, $50 \times n$ or $500 \times n$). Four capacity functions denoted $\mu^1, \ldots, \mu^4$ have been defined as follows: μ^1 has only (strong) negative interactions, μ^2 has only (strong) positive interactions and μ^3 and μ^4 have both positive and negative interactions. The capacity functions $\mu^1, \ldots, \mu^3$ are defined on three criteria and μ^4 is defined on five criteria. Table 7.1 reports experiments for each set of graphs for COPA (for $\mu^1, \ldots, \mu^4$ and with each objective function defined in Sect. 7.3.2) as well as for Martins' algorithm. For a given capacity function and a given objective function, the deviation columns aggregate run-time differences (in percentage) between COPA with (sum), (min) and (sh) and the best of these three versions of the algorithm. The maximum and average deviation over each set of graphs are reported.

Table 7.1 CPU times for the search of a Choquet-optimal path using COPA and Martins

Preferences		CPU times (seconds)									Deviation (%)	
		$l = 5 \times n$			$l = 50 \times n$			$l = 500 \times n$				
Capacity function	Objective function	1,000	3,000	6,000	1,000	3,000	6,000	1,000	3,000	6,000	Max.	Avg.
μ^1	(sum)	0.086	0.261	3.62	0.09	1.23	4.15	1.78	5.05	22.14	1	0
	(min)	0.087	0.261	3.61	0.09	1.22	4.15	1.78	5.04	22.05	1	0
	(sh)	0.087	0.263	3.66	0.09	1.23	4.14	1.79	5.10	22.12	1	1
μ^2	(sum)	0.015	0.051	0.14	0.15	1.60	4.58	2.94	6.54	27.58	630	203
	(min)	0.008	0.032	0.09	0.08	0.27	0.62	0.95	3.91	11.06	0	0
	(sh)	0.009	0.035	0.10	0.08	0.27	0.63	0.95	3.91	11.09	11	1
μ^3	(sum)	0.047	0.101	0.79	0.08	0.30	1.25	1.26	4.92	11.46	4	1
	(min)	0.048	0.101	0.77	0.08	0.30	1.26	1.27	4.91	11.45	2	1
	(sh)	0.047	0.100	0.76	0.08	0.31	1.25	1.27	5.05	11.64	4	1
Martins (3)		0.466	4.657	19.00	2.35	26.54	99.26	9.80	58.63	204.18	—	—
μ^4	(sum)	0.018	0.062	0.14	0.10	0.34	0.76	1.15	4.73	13.65	9	1
	(min)	0.019	0.057	0.14	0.10	0.33	0.75	1.15	4.72	13.64	5	1
	(sh)	0.019	0.058	0.14	0.10	0.34	0.76	1.15	4.74	13.70	5	1
Martins (5)		1.224	12.808	56.14	19.48	171.79	765.58	234.04	2.10^3	1.10^4	—	—

The first comment is that COPA clearly outperforms the Martins' algorithm for all density, size of graphs and capacity functions. The difference between the two algorithms increases exponentially as the number of criteria gets higher. Regarding the objective functions (sh), (min) and (sum), no significant difference between the three functions is underlined by these results. The only impact is shown for μ^2 where a deviation of 200% in average is observed between (sum) and (min), which provides the best results for this capacity function. More generally, the performance of the algorithm slightly decreases when interactions are strongly negative (μ^1).

Note that, for the capacity functions class considered by Galand and Perny (2007), the run-times of COPA are similar to their results.

7.5   Conclusion and Future Work

This paper develops an approach to integrate preferences expressed over multiple criteria in a MOCO algorithm. Preferences are represented using a MCDA model based on the Choquet integral. We define a lower bound of this function that is integrated in the Martins' algorithm to solve MOSP problems. This lower bound generalizes some results of Galand and Perny in the context of robust optimization and allows to integrate the Choquet integral for any capacity function. Numerical experiments clearly show the interest of integrating preferences within the Martins' algorithm. The low CPU times observed validate the use of this proposal to solve real time optimization problems.

Several works are ongoing. The combinatorial structure of the MOSP problem could be better exploited in the pruning test. In addition, the integration of elaborated partial utility functions should be investigated. Finally, we are applying this approach to an industrial case, previously introduced in Gandibleux et al. (2006), and Randriamasy et al. (2004).

Acknowledgements   The authors would like to thank the regional council of Pays de la Loire (France), MILES project, for their support of this research.

References

J. Branke, K. Deb, K. Miettinen, and R. Slowinski. *Multiobjective Optimization: Interactive and Evolutionary Approaches*, volume 5252 of *Lecture Notes in Computer Science*. Springer, 2008. 470 p.

M. Ehrgott and X. Gandibleux. A survey and annoted bibliography of multiobjective combinatorial optimization. *OR Spektrum*, 22:425–460, 2000.

G. Evans. An overview of techniques for solving multiobjective mathematical problems. *Management Science*, 30(11):1268–1282, 1984.

J. Figueira, S. Greco, and M. Ehrgott. *Multiple Criteria Decision Analysis: State of the Art Surveys*. Springer Verlag, Boston, Dordrecht, London, 2005. 1045 p.

L. Galand and P. Perny. Search for Choquet-optimal paths under uncertainty. In *23rd conference on Uncertainty in Artificial Intelligence*, pages 125–132, Vancouver, 7 2007. AAAI Press.

L. Galand, P. Perny, and O. Spanjaard. Choquet-based optimisation in multiobjective shortest path and spanning tree problems. *European Journal of Operational Research*, 204(2):303–315, 2010.

L. Galand and O. Spanjaard. OWA-based search in state space graphs with multiple cost functions. In *20th International Florida Artificial Intelligence Research Society Conference*, pages 86–91. AAAI Press, 2007.

X. Gandibleux, F. Beugnies, and S. Randriamasy. Martins' algorithm revisited for multi-objective shortest path problems with a maxmin cost function. *4OR: A Quarterly Journal of Operations Research*, 4(1):47–59, 2006.

M. Grabisch. Fuzzy integral in multicriteria decision making. *Fuzzy Sets and Systems*, 69:279–298, 1995.

M. Grabisch, I. Kojadinovic, and P. Meyer. A review of capacity identification methods for Choquet integral based multi-attribute utility theory – applications of the kappalab R package. *European Journal of Operational Research*, 186(2):766–785, 2008.

M. Grabisch and C. Labreuche. A decade of application of the Choquet and Sugeno integrals in multi-criteria decision aid. *Annals of Operations Research*, 175:247–286, 2010.

P. Hansen. Bicriterion path problems. In G. Fandel and T. Gal, editors, *Multiple Criteria Decision Making Theory and Application*, volume 177 of *Lecture Notes in Economics and Mathematical Systems*, pages 109–127. Springer Verlag, 1979.

P. Kouvelis and G. Yu. *Robust Discrete Optimization and Its Applications*, volume 14 of *Nonconvex Optimization and its Applications*. Kluwer Academic Publishers, Dordrecht, 1997. 356 p.

C. Labreuche and F. Lehuédé. MYRIAD: a tool suite for MCDA. In *Proceedings of EUSFLAT'05*, Barcelona, September 7-9, 2005.

F. Lehuédé, M. Grabisch, C. Labreuche, and P. Savéant. Integration and propagation of a multi-criteria decision making model in constraint programming. *Journal of Heuristics*, 12(4-5):329–346, September 2006.

E.Q.V. Martins. On a multicriteria shortest path problem. *European Journal of Operational Research*, 16(2):236–245, 1984.

P. Perny and O. Spanjaard. A preference-based approach to spanning trees and shortest paths problems. *European Journal of Operational Research*, 162(3):584–601, 2005.

A. Przybylski, X. Gandibleux, and M. Ehrgott. Two phase algorithms for the bi-objective assignment problem. *European Journal of Operational Research*, 185(2):509–533, 2008.

S. Randriamasy, X. Gandibleux, J. Figueira, and P. Thomin. Device and a method for determining routing paths in a communication network in the presence of selection attributes. Patent 11/25/04. #20040233850. Washington, DC, USA.

Chapter 8
Penalty Rules in Multicriteria Genetic Search

Grzegorz Koloch and Tomasz Szapiro

Abstract In the paper, by means of numerical experiments conducted on artificially constructed problem instances, we test penalty rules for constrained genetic optimization of the Capacitated Heterogeneous Vehicle Routing Problem with Time-Windows in a bi-objective framework. Optimized criteria are cost minimization and capacity utilization maximization. Two approaches are employed – scalarization of objectives and dominance-based evaluation of solutions. We show that it is possible to handle infeasibility in such a way, that this risk of divergence to regions of infeasibility is acceptable. The most secure penalty rule among the tested ones turns out to be the rule which explicitly controls the proportion of infeasible solutions in the population. This rule, along with the rule which accounts only the notion of solutions distance from the feasible set, outperforms rules based on time-penalties and best to best-feasible solution comparison over considered case studies.

8.1 Introduction

Applied optimization problems involve both multiple criteria and feasibility constraints, which can be of various degree of complexity. For NP-hard problems, for which time efficient deterministic optimization techniques, if any, have not yet been found, a handful of stochastic, but efficient optimizers is available. These techniques include Genetic Algorithms (Holland 1975), Simulated Annealing (Kirkpatrick et al. 1984), Tabu Search (Glover and Laguna 1997) or Ant-Colony Optimization (Dorgio 1992). Out of these methods, Genetic Algorithms, as a population based method, was successfully adapted to analysis of multiobjective problems.[1]

---

[1] These extensions include, among others, the Vector Evaluated GA (Schaffer 1985), Multiple-Objective GA (Fonseca and Fleming 1993), (Narayanan and Azarm 1999) and the Nondominated Sorting GA (Srinivas and Deb 1994).

G. Koloch (✉) and T. Szapiro
Warsaw School of Economics, Al. Niepodleglosci 164, 02-554 Warsaw, Poland
e-mail: gkoloch@gmail.com, tszapiro@sgh.waw.pl

Y. Shi et al. (eds.), *New State of MCDM in the 21st Century*, Lecture Notes
in Economics and Mathematical Systems 648, DOI 10.1007/978-3-642-19695-9_8,
© Springer-Verlag Berlin Heidelberg 2011

Genetic Algorithms (GAs) for multiple objectives constituted originally an unconstrained optimization method. In order to handle constrained problems, GA formulation must have been extended so that it deals also with solutions which do not satisfy required constraints. Literature provides a range of approaches to handling infeasibility of solutions in the GA framework, see e.g. Kurpati et al. (2002). From the meta-level perspective, however, most of them consist in one of the following [2]:

1. Restricting infeasible solutions
2. Employing repair operators
3. Adjusting objective functions by imposing penalties for infeasibility

The first approach is straightforward to implement when it is easy to find genetic operators that render feasible offsprings from feasible parents and when it is easy to construct feasible solutions for the initial population. If so, a search which starts from a feasible population ends up within such. The drawback of this approach is twofold. First, for highly constrained combinatorial optimization problems[3] it is difficult to construct feasible solution from scratch, and second, genetic search is limited to feasible regions of solution space, which can result in inferior outcomes in terms of quality. The second approach is similar to the first one, with the difference, that original genetic operators are allowed to yield infeasible offsprings, but feasibility is restored after having repaired them by means of a suitable procedure. The third approach constitutes the most common one, see Coello (1999). Its rationale is intuitively supported by the theory of Lagrange relaxation technique which successfully drives constrained optimization in mathematical analysis. The penalty method consists of a range of penalty rules. It provides the GA with the possibility of search space exploration through infeasible regions, which comes, however, at a cost of risk of divergence or can result in longer convergence. To avoid divergence problems, and to make the search as efficient as possible, different penalty rules were analyzed and enhanced from their baseline specification as e.g. in Goldberg (1989).

In the paper we contribute to the analysis of penalty rules performance in a multiple objective framework by running simulation experiments for a multiple objective version of a Heterogeneous Capacitated Vehicle Routing Problem with Time Windows (VRP, see e.g. Toth and Vigo (2002) or Beham (2007)). Motivation for such an analysis comes from practice. More specifically, the need for comparison of penalty rules efficiency in case of multiple objective problem formulation comes from the transportation industry. Routing problems are formulated in such a way, that multiple objectives emerge in a natural way. The VRP we study here

---

[2] A survey of constraints handling methods is e.g. Coello (1999).

[3] Real life Multiple Criteria Capacitated Vehicle Routing Problem with Time Windows which is considered in this paper can serve as an example.

constitutes a practically important instance[4] of an NP-hard and highly constrained combinatorial optimization problem, for which GAs can successfully be applied. Problem formulation involves two criteria. The first criterion is distance traveled by all the vehicles in the fleet. The second criterion is capacity utilization of employed vehicles and it helps to construct an efficient fleet composition. It is so, because we assume that fleet size is unlimited, i.e. there is no limit on the number of vehicles available within each vehicle type. Hence, introducing the second, auxiliary, criterion, results in the fact, that the algorithm not only minimizes distance traveled for a given fleet of vehicles, but also enables the decision maker to optimize fleet composition. We run a GA implementation and report convergence properties under six different penalty rules. Furthermore, two alternative approaches to multiple criteria GA implementation are considered. The first one is based on objectives scalarization and the second is based on dominance structure of solutions populations.

Remainder of the paper is constructed as follows. The following Sect. 8.2 outlines the bicriteria Vehicle Routing Problem with Time Windows used for numerical simulations and the GA employed to solve it. Section 8.3 presents investigated penalty methods and Sect. 8.4 discusses results of numerical simulations. Final section concludes.

8.2 The Problem and the Algorithm

VRP constitutes a combinatorial optimization problem that consists in construction of an optimal transportation plan for a heterogeneous fleet of vehicles which capacities are limited. The transportation plan is evaluated according to two criteria – cost of shipment – measured as the total distance traveled by vehicles, which is minimized, and vehicles' capacity utilization, which is maximized. The first criterion is a standard criterion in the literature (Jozefowicz et al. 2008), whereas the second one is motivated by practitioners and helps to construct an optimal fleet composition.[5]

There are $m \geq 1$ clients who place total of $n \geq 1$ orders. Let $C = \{c_i, i \in \{1, 2, \ldots, m\}\}$ denote a set of clients and $O = \{o_i, i \in \{1, 2, \ldots, n\}\}$ a set of orders placed. Every order $o \in O$ is characterized by a client $c(o) \in C$ who placed it and by the volume of demanded cargo $\mu(o) \geq 0$. Vehicles which are to be routed to execute orders in O are located in the base. There are $k \geq 1$ vehicle types and let

---

[4] For a survey on multiple criteria VRPs, see Jozefowicz et al. (2008). For some recent applications of genetic algorithms in the domain of multiobjective VRPs see e.g. Chand et al. (2007) or Tan and Chew (2006).

[5] Standard perception of VRPs is that they help practitioners to construct an optimal transportation plan *given* available fleet of vehicles. In this respect capacity utilization maximization is purposeful, for it helps reducing the cost *per* unit of transported goods. On the other hand, this criterion can be exploited when one wants to answer the question what a fleet should be constructed to best serve existing needs. The optimization routine indicates which vehicles should be used, and maximization of capacity utilization helps composing a fleet that minimizes waste of free space in containers.

$V = \{v_i : i \in \{1, 2, \ldots, k\}\}$ denote a set of available vehicles, each of one type. We assume that the number of available vehicles is unlimited by allowing that each vehicle can be chosen arbitrary number of times. Vehicles' $v \in V$ capacity will be denoted by $\mu(v) \geq 0$.

Let Γ denote a generic transportation plan. A generic transportation plan Γ consists of $|\Gamma| \geq 1$ routes: $\Gamma = \{x_1, x_2, \ldots, x_{|\Gamma|}\}$. A generic route $x \in \Gamma$ constitutes a series of $|x| \geq 1$ orders, $x = (o_{k_1}, o_{k_2}, \ldots, o_{k_{|x|}})$, $o_{k_i} \in O, i = 1, 2, \ldots, |x|$. The volume of cargo transported along x equals $\mu(x) = \sum_{o \in x} \mu(o)$. Route x starts in the base, executes orders as they appear in x and finishes in the base. A vehicle assigned to route x will be denoted by $v(x) \in V$. For the final solution it must be the case that $\mu(v(x)) \geq \mu(x)$ for every route x, since otherwise assignment $v(x)$ is infeasible and cannot be a part of the final solution. One vehicle can be assigned to more than one route.

VRP consists in constructing an optimal transportation plan Γ for a fleet V, so that all orders in O are executed and have vehicles assigned. Also time-windows constraints must be satisfied.

Let $\delta(o) = (\underline{\delta}(o), \bar{\delta}(o))$, $\underline{\delta}(o), \bar{\delta}(o) \geq 0$ denote a time window associated with order $o \in O$. Time window of o is a time interval opening at time $\underline{\delta}(o)$ and closing at time $\bar{\delta}(o)$, during which commodities associated with o must be delivered to clients' $c(o)$ location.

Consider a generic route $\Gamma \ni x = (o_1, o_2, \ldots, o_n)$. Denote by $t_{c(o_i)c(o_j)}$ the time needed to travel between locations of customers $c(o_i)$ and $c(o_j)$. Vehicle $v(x)$ leaves the base at time $t(0) = 0$ and arrives at location of $c(o_1)$ at time $t(o_1) = t_{0c(o_1)}$. If $t(o_1) > \bar{\delta}(o_1)$, time window violation due to order o_1 equals $\bar{\phi}(o_1) = t(o_1) - \bar{\delta}(o_1)$. Otherwise $\bar{\phi}(o_1) = 0$. If $t(o_1) \leq \underline{\delta}(o_1)$, vehicle v waits $\underline{\phi}(o_1) = \underline{\delta}(o_1) - t(o_1)$ units of time for the time window $\delta(o_1)$ to open. Otherwise $\underline{\phi}(o_1) = 0$. Next, v arrives in the location of $c(o_2)$ at time $t(o_2) = t(o_1) + \phi(o_1) + t_{c(o_1)c(o_2)}$. Generally, for $2 \leq i \leq n$, we have $t(o_i) = t(o_{i-1}) + \phi(o_{i-1}) + t_{c(o_{i-1})c(o_i)}$, $\underline{\phi}(o_i) = \max(\underline{\delta}(o_i) - t(o_i), 0)$ and $\bar{\phi}(o_i) = \max(t(o_i) - \bar{\delta}(o_i), 0)$. Time windows violation along route x equals $\phi(x) = \sum_{i=1}^{n} \bar{\phi}(o_i)$ and total time windows violation in solution Γ equals $\phi(\Gamma) = \sum_{x \in \Gamma} \phi(x)$. If $\phi(x) > 0$, route x is infeasible for it violates at least one of the time windows. If $\phi(\Gamma) > 0$, solution Γ is infeasible for at least one of its routes is infeasible due to violation of time windows constraints.

The same applies to capacity constraints. Let us define overload of route x by:

$$l(x) = \max(\mu(x) - \mu(v(x)), 0) \tag{8.1}$$

and the overload of solution Γ by $l(\Gamma) = \sum_{x \in \Gamma} l(x)$. If $l(x) > 0$, route x is infeasible for it violates at least one of capacity constraints. If $l(\Gamma) > 0$, solution Γ is infeasible for at least one of its routes is infeasible due to violation of the capacity constraint. If $\phi(\Gamma) = l(\Gamma) = 0$, transportation plan Γ is feasible and can constitute a final solution of the problem.

Denote by $d(c(o_i), c(o_j))$ the distance between locations of customers $c(o_i)$ and $c(o_j)$. By index 0 we will denote the base, so $d(0, c(o))$ is a distance of $c(o)$ location to base. Notice that several orders can be placed at the same location (in such a case their distance is 0). Using this notation we can calculate the distance traveled along route $x = (o_{k_1}, o_{k_2}, \ldots, o_{k_{|x|}})$, $|x| \geq 1$, as:

$$d(x) = d(0, c(o_{k_1})) + \sum_{j=1}^{|x|-1} d(c(o_{k_j}), c(o_{k_{j+1}})) + d(c(o_{k_{|x|}}), 0) \qquad (8.2)$$

and total distance traveled on transportation plan as $d(\Gamma) = \sum_{x \in \Gamma} d(x)$. We also calculate capacity utilization along route x as:

$$u(x) = \frac{\mu(x)}{\mu(v(x))} \qquad (8.3)$$

and solutions Γ capacity utilization as $\mu(\Gamma) = \min_{x \in \Gamma} u(x)$. For feasible assignments we have $u(x), u(\Gamma) \in [0, 1]$.

First optimization criterion is distance $d(\Gamma)$ minimization and the second one is maximization of capacity utilization $u(\Gamma)$. They are both optimized subject to two types of constraints. First constraint is a technical one and states that each order is handled along exactly one route which has assigned a unique vehicle capable of handling it with respect to capacity constraints. The second constraint says time windows of orders are satisfied. The transportation plan of the form of Γ is evaluated according to $f : \Gamma \mapsto (f_1(\Gamma), f_2(\Gamma)) \in R^2$ for $f_1(\Gamma) = \sum_{x \in \Gamma} d(x)$ and for $f_2(\Gamma) = -u(\Gamma)$. The problem is therefore formulated as follows:

$$\min_{\Gamma : \phi(\Gamma) = l(\Gamma) = 0} f(\Gamma) \qquad (8.4)$$

Now we discuss briefly GA representation of a generic transportation plan of the form of Γ. For this purpose, orders and vehicles are represented by integers $O = \{1, 2, \ldots, n\}$, $V = \{1, 2, \ldots, k\}$. Solution Γ is represented by a pair of sequences, σ and ξ, and by a function $v : X \ni x \rightarrow v(x) \in V$, i.e. we identify it with a triple $\Gamma = \{\sigma, \xi, v\}$. Sequence $\sigma = \sigma(1, 2, \ldots, n)$ constitutes a permutation of orders. Sequence ξ is a sequence of pointers, which indicate separate routes along σ. Let, for example, $n = 9$, i.e. $O = \{1, 2, \ldots, 9\}$, $\sigma = (3, 6, 5, 4, 1, 2, 9, 8, 7)$ and $p = (1, 4, 8)$. There are $|p| = 3$ routes. These routes are: $x_1 = (3, 6, 5)$, $x_2 = (4, 1, 2, 9)$ and $x_3 = (8, 7)$. Route x_1 starts in base, goes to clients $c(3)$ location, clients $c(6)$ location, clients $c(5)$ location, and ends in the base. Let $k = 5$. For $v(x_1) = 3$, route x_1 is handled by vehicle $v = 3$.

We compare two alternative formulations of multiple criteria GA implementation. In the first one solutions are evaluated according to scalarized objectives: $\tilde{f}(\Gamma) = < \alpha, f(\Gamma) >$.[6] The second approach evaluates solutions according to the number of solutions they dominate in the population:

---

[6] Elements of α are nonnegative and sum up to unity. In the numerical simulations section we perform sensitivity analysis of results with respect to α. In practice elements of α have to be elicited from the decision maker.

$$\tilde{f}(\Gamma) = \sum_{\gamma \in P: f_1(\gamma) > f_1(\Gamma) \wedge f_2(\gamma) < f_2(\Gamma)} 1 \qquad (8.5)$$

where P stands for a population of solutions.

Genetic operator employed to perform selection is tournament selection. Out of two solutions Γ_1 and Γ_2, tournament is won by the solution which has better evaluation. For parent solutions Γ_1 and Γ_2, and permutations $\sigma_1 \in \Gamma_1$ and $\sigma_2 \in \Gamma_2$, the crossover operator chooses at random two routes: x_1 in σ_1 and x_2 in σ_2. Let x_1 consist of n_1 and x_2 of n_2 orders. For x_1 and x_2, points $i_1, j_1 \in \{1, 2, \ldots, n_1\}$, $i_1 \leq j_1$ and $i_2, j_2 \in \{1, 2, \ldots, n_2\}$, $i_2 \leq j_1$ are drawn. Orders in $s_1 = \sigma_1(i_1 : j_2)$ are erased from σ_2 and orders in $s_2 = \sigma_2(i_2 : j_2)$ are erased from σ_1. Sequences s_1 and s_2 are then inserted into σ_2 and σ_1 respectively.[7] After insertion, vehicles are reassigned to routes which were changed[8] during crossover. Mutation is conducted by means of the same crossover procedure, but applied to a single solution.

8.3 Penalty Rules

A general multiple criteria constrained optimization problem can be formulated as follows:

$$\min_{x \in \Omega_X = X \cap \Omega} f(x) \qquad (8.6)$$

where X stands for the set of constraints that are easy to satisfy, while Ω represents constraints which are hard to satisfy. In our VRP formulation easy constraints are:

$$
\begin{aligned}
X = \{&\Gamma = \{\sigma, \xi, v\} : \\
&\sigma \in \sigma(\{o_1, o_2, \ldots, o_n\}), \\
&\xi(1) = 1, \\
&\forall_{i \in \{1, 2, \ldots, |\xi|-1\}} \ \xi(i) < \xi(i+1) \leq n, \\
&\forall_{x \in \Gamma} \exists_{v \in V} : v(x) = v, \\
&\forall_{x \in \Gamma} \ l(x) = 0\},
\end{aligned} \qquad (8.7)
$$

whereas hard one requires that:

$$\Omega = \{\Gamma : \phi(\Gamma) = 0\} \qquad (8.8)$$

Easy constraints assure that solution syntax represents a technically correct solution, i.e. a consistent transportation plan Γ that, at least hypothetically, could be executed by the fleet. First three constraints demand that σ constitutes a permutation

---

[7] A random number of possible insertion places is considered and the best one is chosen.

[8] Due to the fact that some of its orders were erased or due to the fact that sequence s_1 or s_2 was inserted in them. We use the rule, that a vehicle with minimal capacity, but able to handle a route is assigned to it.

of elements of the set of orders O and that pointers properly define routes[9] in σ.
Two last conditions assure that a vehicle is assigned to each route $x \in \Gamma$ and that
assigned vehicles are capable of handling orders along corresponding routes. The
hard constraint says that no time window is violated along routes in Γ.

We allow for infeasibility in the course of genetic search in two aspects. First, it
may be the case, that time-windows are violated, i.e. that $\phi(\Gamma) \neq 0$. Infeasibility is
then measured by total time of time windows violation in the solution, i.e. by $\phi(\Gamma)$.
Second, we allow for the capacity constraint to be violated, i.e. for $l(x) > 0$ for
some $x \in \Gamma$. In this case, infeasibility is measured by total overload in the solution,
i.e. by $l(\Gamma)$. If solution is infeasible, penalty is imposed on it.

Technically, penalty method adjusts the objective function $\tilde{f}$ according to the
measure of solutions infeasibility, which can be perceived as a notion of distance
from the set of feasible solutions, $\rho : X \rightarrow R$, transformed by a scaling function
$\epsilon : R \rightarrow R$:

$$\bar{f}(\Gamma) = \tilde{f}(\Gamma) + \epsilon(\rho(\Gamma, \Omega_X)) \tag{8.9}$$

In our case, as far as time windows are concerned, $\rho(\Gamma)$ would equal total time
windows violation along routes in Γ, i.e. $\phi(\Gamma)$, and, as far as capacity constraint is
concerned, $\rho(\Gamma)$ would equal total overload, i.e. $l(\Gamma)$ and ϵ scales ρ so that it has
an order of magnitude appropriate for $\tilde{f}$, i.e. $\epsilon(\rho) = \gamma\rho$ for some $\gamma > 0$. Equation
(8.9) defines static penalty rule, since penalty is time-invariant.

Dynamic penalty method introduces notion of time in the penalizing rule:

$$\bar{f}(\Gamma) = \tilde{f}(\Gamma) + \epsilon(\rho(\Gamma, \Omega_X), t) \tag{8.10}$$

where t stands for the number of current iteration. One way of taking advantage of t
is to make the penalty grow with time by imposing e.g. $\epsilon(\rho, t) = \gamma\rho\lambda^t$ for $\lambda > 1$. At
the beginning of the search infeasibility is not penalized severely which allows the
search to go through regions of infeasibility by crossing-over feasible and infeasible
solutions. Eventually, however, we want solutions to be feasible, so penalty grows
with time to make feasible solutions better than infeasible ones. This can work,
as long as up to this point the whole population have not become infeasible. We
experiment with time rule which increases the penalty in a linear way: $\epsilon(\rho, t) =
\gamma\rho\lambda t$. More sensitive dynamic penalty rules are adaptive rules, which explicitly take
into account characteristics of solutions in the current population:

$$\bar{f}(\Gamma) = \tilde{f}(\Gamma) + \epsilon(\rho(\Gamma, \Omega_X), t, P_t) \tag{8.11}$$

We experiment with both dynamic and adaptive penalty rules. We also implement
rules which explicitly control the proportion of infeasible solutions in the population. It turns out that such a rule, along with the rule of the form of (8.9), tends to be
the most effective one in case of the problem in question.

---

[9] There is at least one route in σ, the one that starts in the first element of σ.

8.4　Numerical Simulations

Numerical experiments were conducted on artificially constructed problem instances. Characteristics of problem instances[10] were drawn randomly from predefined probability distributions.[11] Results are reported for two classes of problems, i.e. for medium-sized problems (50 orders) and large-sized ones (150 orders). For each class 10 different solution instances were constructed.

Results are presented for the following penalty rules:

1. Solutions' distance from the feasible set (labeled as rule 1) – measured as weighted sum of scaled total time windows violation and total overload of the solution:

$$\epsilon(\rho(\Gamma, \Omega_X)) = \gamma(\theta_1 \phi(\Gamma) + \theta_2 l(\Gamma)) \tag{8.12}$$

   where $\theta_1, \theta_2 \geq 0$, $\theta_1 + \theta_2 = 1$, are calibrated experimentally.
2. Average solutions' distance from the feasible set in the population (labeled as rule 2):

$$\epsilon(\rho(\Gamma, \Omega_X)) = \gamma \frac{1}{|P_t|} \sum_{\Gamma \in P_t} (\theta_1 \phi(\Gamma) + \theta_2 l(\Gamma)) \tag{8.13}$$

   where $\theta_1, \theta_2 \geq 0$, $\theta_1 + \theta_2 = 1$, are calibrated experimentally.
3. Time (labeled as rule 3) – in which penalty increases linearly with time (with iterations):

$$\epsilon(\rho(\Gamma, \Omega_X), t) = \gamma(\theta_1 \phi(\Gamma) + \theta_2 l(\Gamma)) \lambda t \tag{8.14}$$

   where $\theta_1, \theta_2 \geq 0$, $\theta_1 + \theta_2 = 1$, and $\lambda > 1$ are calibrated experimentally.
4. Proportion of infeasible solutions in the current population (labeled as rule 4):

$$\frac{|\{\Gamma \in P_t : \phi(\Gamma) = l(\Gamma) = 0\}|}{|P_t|} \leq \frac{1}{q} \tag{8.15}$$

   where $q \in (0, 1)$ is calibrated experimentally.
5. Average weighted proportion of infeasible solutions in past populations (labeled as rule 5):

$$\sum_{i=0}^{K} \beta_i \frac{|\{\Gamma \in P_{t-i} : \phi(\Gamma) = l(\Gamma) = 0\}|}{|P_{t-i}|} \leq \frac{1}{q} \tag{8.16}$$

   where $q \in (0, 1)$, $K > 0$ and $\beta_i > 0$, $i = 1, 2, \ldots, K$, are calibrated experimentally.
6. Difference between the best and the best feasible solution found in the current population (labeled as rule 6):

---

[10] These characteristics are: topology of the transportation network, distribution of clients locations over the network, number of orders placed by each client, volume of goods ordered within each order, time windows of orders and sizes of available vehicle types.

[11] These probability distributions were uniform over appropriate intervals.

Table 8.1 Penalty rules performances over 100 simulation runs for each of 20 problem instances. Evaluation based on the scalarization of objectives. Medium problem size (50 orders) – *the upper panel*, large problem size (150 orders) – *the lower panel*

Penalty	f	f_1	f_2	Dominance (%)	Infeasible (%)
Time (1)	138	137	140	38	79
Distance (2)	100	100	100	69	37
Average distance (3)	119	109	129	54	35
Proportion (4)	104	103	104	59	_[a]
Average proportion (5)	110	115	105	61	_[a]
Difference (6)	129	125	132	46	49
Time (1)	152	139	165	16	66
Distance (2)	108	107	109	64	32
Average distance (3)	110	109	111	62	40
Proportion (4)	100	100	100	76	_[a]
Average proportion (5)	104	104	104	59	_[a]
Difference (6)	120	118	122	48	48

[a]Fraction of infeasible solutions explicitly controlled for.

Table 8.2 Penalty rules performances over 100 simulation runs for each of 20 problem instances. Dominance-based evaluation of solutions. Medium problem size (50 orders) – *the upper panel*, large problem size (150 orders) – *the lower panel*

Penalty	f	f_1	f_2	Dominance (%)	Infeasible (%)
Time (1)	139	142	136	20	68
Distance (2)	100	100	100	82	31
Average distance (3)	121	118	125	52	36
Proportion (4)	102	101	102	77	_[a]
Average proportion (5)	106	101	110	55	_[a]
Difference (6)	123	111	136	48	58
Time (1)	149	151	148	36	79
Distance (2)	115	102	129	72	48
Average distance (3)	109	109	109	81	36
Proportion (4)	100	100	100	86	_[a]
Average proportion (5)	105	109	102	57	_[a]
Difference (6)	130	134	125	51	56

[a]Fraction of infeasible solutions explicitly controlled for.

$$\epsilon(\rho(\Gamma, \Omega_X), P_t) = \gamma(\theta_1\phi(\Gamma) + \theta_2 l(\Gamma))(\tilde{f}(\Gamma^\star \in P_t) - \tilde{f}(\Gamma^\star \in P_t \cap \Omega_X))^\beta$$

(8.17)

where $\beta > 0$ is calibrated experimentally and $\Gamma^\star \in A$ denotes the best solution in set A.

Tables 8.1 and 8.2 present simulation results. Scalarized evaluation of the best solution in the final population is denoted by f. f_1 and f_2 decompose f into distance traveled and capacity utilization respectively. Dominance indicates a fraction of solutions in the final population which are dominated by the best solution and "% of infeasible" says what is the fraction of infeasible solutions in the final

Table 8.3 Penalty rules performances over 100 simulation runs for each of 20 problem instances. Results averaged over scalarization and dominance-based evaluation of solutions. Medium problem size (50 orders) – *the upper panel*, large problem size (150 orders) – *the lower panel*

	Rule (1)	Rule (2)	Rule (3)	Rule (4)	Rule (5)	Rule (6)
% of divergences	67	32	31	7	12	52
Due to time windows constraint	54	32	28	7	9	42
Due to capacity constraint	59	24	29	4	12	38
% of divergences	76	28	36	5	15	57
Due to time windows constraint	72	25	27	4	13	54
Due to capacity constraint	69	27	36	4	9	55

population.[12] Averaged results over 100 simulation runs for each of 10 problem instances are presented for a medium sized VRP (50 orders) and for a large size VRP (150 orders). Table 9.1 presents results for scalarization based evaluation of solutions, whereas Table 9.2 for dominance based evaluation. Notation is standardized so that the best solutions evaluation equals 100 and better solutions have smaller evaluations.

First of all, results suggest, that it is possible to handle solutions' infeasibility in such a way, that the considerable fraction of the final population consists of feasible solutions. We have, however, found a substantial (30%–80%) risk of divergence, especially for rules that do not explicitly control for the amount of infeasibility allowed to be introduced. Second, no matter which approach is taken to solutions evaluation, penalty rules which are based on the notion of solutions distance from the feasible set, i.e. rules (2) and (3), and on the proportion of infeasible solutions in the population, i.e. rules (4) and (5), turned out to outperform remaining ones.[13] Their relative performance seems to depend on the problem size. For smaller problems distance-based rule performs slightly better than the proportion rule and the other way round for larger problem instances. Evaluation of distance traveled (f_1) and of capacity utilization (f_2) changes uniformly with penalty rules, i.e. rules which perform better according to the first criterion, tend to do so also according to the second one, which enables practical applications. One can also see, that better performing rules have lower proportion of infeasible solutions in the final population. Purely dynamic rule (1) and difference rule (5) recorded worst performance over considered test cases.

Table 9.3 provides empirical probabilities of divergence, which is defined as a situation in which no feasible solution is found in the final population of solutions. Figures are averages over 100 simulation runs for each of 20 problem instances for scalarization and dominance-based approach to solutions evaluations.[14] It shows, that the choice of a penalty rule significantly influences risk of divergence, which

---

[12] For rules (4) and (5) this characteristic is not reported, for the fraction of infeasible solutions is explicitly controlled for.

[13] This was the case also for other rules for which results are not reported here.

[14] Results were similar for these two approaches.

is important for practical applications. Once again, distance and proportion based rules turned out to outperform other rules, but this time, the difference between these two is more visible to the advantage of proportion-based penalty rule. Second and third row in the upper and lower panel of Table 9.3 decomposes divergence probabilities into divergences caused by time-windows violation and capacity constraints violation. One can see, that divergence is caused almost uniformly by the two criteria.

8.5   Conclusions

Six penalty rules for genetic optimization were tested in the paper by means of simulation experiment conducted for the Capacitated Heterogeneous Vehicle Routing Problem with Time-Windows in a two-criteria environment. Such a problem formulation was taken from business practice. First criterion is a standard one – cost minimization, whereas the second one, capacity utilization maximization, helps the decision maker to construct an optimal fleet composition. Two approaches to multiple criteria genetic optimization were employed – scalarization of objectives and dominance-based evaluation. Obtained results seem to be robust over these approaches. We show, that, although there is a structural significant risk of divergence, it is possible to handle infeasibility in such a way, that this risk is acceptable by practitioners. It turns out, that most secure is a penalty rule which explicitly controls the proportion of infeasible solutions in the population. This rule, along with the rule which accounts only the notion of solutions distance from the feasible set, outperforms rules based on time-penalties and best to best-feasible solution comparison over considered case studies.

References

Beham A., *Parallel Tabu Search and the Multiobjective Capacitated Vehicle Routing Problem with Soft Time Windows*, in: Lecture Notes in Computer Science, Vol. 4739/2007, p. 829–836, Springer, 2007.

Chand P., Mishra B.S.P. and Dehuri, S., *A Multiobjective Genetic Algorithm for Solving Nehicle Routing Problem*, International Journal of Information Technology and Knowledge Management, Vol. 2, No. 2, p. 503–506, 2010.

Coello Coello, C.A. *A Survey of Constraint Handling Techniques Used fwith Evolutionary Algorithms*, Technical Report Lania-RI-99-04, Laboratorio Nacional de Informatica Avanzada, MExico, 1999.

M. Dorigo, *Optimization, Learning and Natural Algorithms*, Politecnico di Milano, Italy, 1992.

Fonseca, C.M. and Fleming, P.J., *Genetic Algorithms for Multiobjective Optimization: formulation, discussion and generalization*, in: Forrest, S. (ed.)*Proc. 5-th Int. Conf. on Generic Algorithms*, pp.416–423, 1993.

Narayanan, S. and Azarm, S., *On Improving Multiobjective Genetic Algorithms for Design Optimization*, Struct. Optim., pp. 146–155, 1999.

Glover, F. and M. Laguna. (1997). *Tabu Search*, Kluwer, Norwell.

Goldberg D. E., *Genetic Algorithms in Search, Optimization and Machine Learning*, Addison-Wesley Pub. Co., 1989.

Holland, J.,H., *Adaptation in Natural and ArtificialSystems*, University of MIchigan Press, 1975.

Jozefowiez N., F. Semet, G. Talibi, *Multi-objective vehicle routing problems*, European Journal of Operational Research, 189, p. 293–309, 2008.

Jozefowiez N., F. Semet. G. Talibi, *Enhancements of NSGA II and Its Application to the Vehicle Routing Problem with Route Balancing*, in: Lecture Notes in Computer Science, p. 131–142, Springer, 2006.

Kirkpatrick, S., C. D. Gelatt and M. P. Vecchi, *Optimization by Simulated Annealing*, Science. New Series 220, 1984.

Kurpati, A., Azarm, S. and Wu, J., *Constraint Handling Improvements for Multiobjective Genetic Algorithms*, Struct. Multidisc. Optim. 23, 204–213, Springer, 2002.

Schaffer, J.D., *Multiple Objective Optimization with VEctor Evaluated Genetic Algorithms* in: *Genetic Algorithms and their Applications*, Proc. 1-st Int. Conf on Genetc Algorithms, pp. 93–100, 1985.

Srinivas, N. and Deb, K., *Multiobjective Optimization Using Nondominated Sorting in Genetic Algorithms*, Evolutionary Computation 2, pp. 221–248, 1994.

Tan K.C., and Chew, Y.H. *A Hybrid Multiobjective Evolutionary Algorithm for Solving Vehicle Routing Problem with Time Windows*, Computational Optimization and Applications, Vol. 34, p. 115–151, 2006.

Toth, O. and D. Vigo (eds.), *The Vehicle Routing Problem*, Society for Industrial and Applied Mathematics, 2002.

Part III
MCDM Applications

Chapter 9
The Bi-Criterial Approach to Project Cost and Schedule Buffers Sizing

Paweł Błaszczyk, Tomasz Błaszczyk, and Maria B. Kania

Abstract The aim of this research was the trial of modelling and optimizing the time-cost trade-offs in project planning problem with taking into account the behavioral impact of performers' (or subcontractors') estimations of basic activity parameters. However, such a model must include quantitative measurements of budget and duration, so we proposed to quantify and minimize the apprehension of their underestimations. The base of the problem description contains both safe and reasonable amounts of work estimations and the influence factors matrix. We assumed also the pricing opportunity of performance improving. Theoretical considerations were examined in several examples solved in spreadsheet environment.

Keywords Buffer management · Project planning · Time-cost trade-off

9.1 Introduction

The time-cost trade-off analysis, allowing for establishment of such a project plan which satisfies the decision-maker's expectations for the soonest completion date with as low budget as possible, is one of the basic multicriterial problems in project planning. The first researches in this subject, conducted by Fulkerson et al. (1961) and Kelley et al. (1961), have been publicated in 1960s. Precise reviews of temporary results were widely described by several authors, for instance by Brucker et al. (1999). The aim of the follow-ing research is to consider the critical chain approach described by Goldratt (1997) in multiple-criteria environment. The primal description of the method was based on verbal language, rather than formal. The

P. Błaszczyk (✉) and M.B. Kania
Institute of Mathematics, University of Silesia, ul. Bankowa 14, 40-007 Katowice, Poland
e-mail: pblaszcz@math.us.edu.pl, mkania@math.us.edu.pl

T. Błaszczyk
University of Economics in Katowice, ul. 1 Maja 50, 40-287 Katowice, Poland
e-mail: tomasz.blaszczyk@ue.katowice.pl

Y. Shi et al. (eds.), *New State of MCDM in the 21st Century*, Lecture Notes
in Economics and Mathematical Systems 648, DOI 10.1007/978-3-642-19695-9_9,
© Springer-Verlag Berlin Heidelberg 2011

chain and time buffers quantification methods were the results of successive authors. One of the detailed approaches was formally described by Tukel et al. (2006). The issues of buffering some project characteristics, other than duration, were considered by Leach et al. (2003), Gonzalez et al. (2009), Błaszczyk and Nowak (2008). The general critical chain approach, widely discussed by various authors (compare Herroelen et al. (2001), Rogalska et al. (2008), Van de Vonder et al. (2005)), is not drawback-free. So that, the range of its practical implementation is not as wide as the regular CPM and PERT methods. However, the critical chain has an important advantage because of the behavioral aspects inclusion, what can make it more useful in the real-life planning problem descriptions. Thus, by including the impact of the human factor on measurable project features, we are capable of using it to improve these features in return for financial equivalent. An example of such a solution, with using the extraordinary premium fund, was described by Błaszczyk and Nowak (2008). The following part of the paper is the consequence of continuing this research on buffering different project features. Here we took into consideration the duration and budget expectations by modelling the project with time and cost buffers. Apart from temporary results in the described procedure, we introduced buffers on overestimated amounts of labor which are given by employees or subcontractors. The model we are proposing assumes the opportunity to motivate them to participate in the risk of delays and budget overrunning in return for probable profits, in case of faster and cheaper realisation. The theoretical conception is illustrated by the numerical example terminated with spreadsheet solver.

9.2 Mathematical Model

We consider project which consist $x_1, \ldots, x_n$ activities characterized by cost and time criteria. We assume that only q factors has any influence on the cost and the time of the project. Let us consider the following matrix X:

$$X = \begin{bmatrix} x_{11} & \cdots & x_{1q} \\ \vdots & \ddots & \vdots \\ x_{n1} & \cdots & x_{nq} \end{bmatrix} \tag{9.1}$$

Elements of the matrix X equals 0 or 1. If x_{ij} equals 1 it means that factor j has influence on the completion of activity x_i. In the other case there is no influence of factor j on activity x_i. The matrix X we will call the *factor's matrix*. Let $K = [k_{ij}]_{i=1,\ldots,n;j=1,\ldots,q}$ to be the matrix of cost's ratios of all q factors for all activities and $W^m = [w_1^m, \ldots, w_n^m]$ to be the vector of minimal amounts of work for the activities $x_1, \ldots, x_n$. On the basis of matrix X and vector W^m for activity x_i we can calculate the total amount of work w_i by:

$$w_i = f_{w_i}(x_{i1}, \ldots, x_{iq}, w_i^m) \tag{9.2}$$

where f_{w_i} is a work assigning function. Moreover we assume that there is vector $R = [r_1, \ldots, r_q]$ describing the restrictions of accessibility of factors for whole project. Let $T = [t_{ij}]_{i=1,\ldots,n; j=1,\ldots,q}$ be the matrix of amounts of work for each factor in each activity. On the basis of the matrix X, T and K we calculate the cost and the duration of each activity by:

$$k_i = f_{i_k}(x_{i1}, \ldots, x_{iq}, t_{i1}, \ldots, t_{iq}, k_{i1}, \ldots, k_{iq}) \tag{9.3}$$

and

$$t_i = f_{i_t}(x_{i1}, \ldots, x_{iq}, t_{i1}, \ldots, t_{iq}) \tag{9.4}$$

where f_{i_k} and f_{i_t} are some functions. We called this functions the *cost* and the *time* functions, respectively. Thus the total cost and the total duration of the project are given by

$$K_c = \sum_{i=1}^{n} k_i \tag{9.5}$$

and

$$T_c = \max_{i=1,\ldots,n} (ES_i + t_i) \tag{9.6}$$

where ES_i is the earliest start of activity x_i. Under the following assumptions we minimize total cost of the project. It leads to find the optimal work assignments for every factor in each activities. From the set of alternate optimal solutions we choose this one, for which the total duration of project is minimal. In this way we obtain the optimal solution in safe case. According to the contractors' safe estimations the amount of work could be overestimated. It leads up to overestimations of the activities' cost and duration expected values and afterwards the total cost and the total duration of the whole project. That means

$$k_i = k_i^e + k_i^B \tag{9.7}$$

and

$$t_i = t_i^e + t_i^B \tag{9.8}$$

where k_i^e, t_i^e are the reasonable cost and reasonable duration for activity x_i and k_i^B, t_i^B are the buffers of budget and time for activity x_i, respectively. Therefore we can write the total cost and total duration of project by

$$K_c = K^e + K^B \tag{9.9}$$

and

$$T_c = T^e + T^B \tag{9.10}$$

where K^e, T^e are the reasonable cost and reasonable duration of the project and K^B, T^B are the buffers of budget and time, respectively. To set the buffers K^B, T^B up we must estimate the most probable amounts of work. We do that by changing appropriate elements x_{ij} in matrix X from 1 to 0 or vice versa. It means that some factors which had influence on activity x_i in safe estimation case does not have it in real estimation case and vice versa. Than we using the function w_i for each activity x_i. In this way we get the new factor's matrix X^* and the new vector of amounts of work W^*. Then we execute the same procedure for the most probable amount of work but under additional condition $t_{ij} \geq t_{ij}^*$ for $i = 1, \ldots, n; j = 1, \ldots, q$, where $T^* = \left[t_{ij}^* \right]$ is the matrix of amounts of work for each factor in each activity calculated for the new data. Since that is unlikelihood that all factors will occur, we can reduce the buffers for project by:

$$K_r^B = \alpha K^B \tag{9.11}$$

and

$$T_r^B = \beta T^B \tag{9.12}$$

where $\alpha, \beta \in [0, 1]$ are the ratios revising amount of buffers.

$$K^P = K^e + K_r^B \tag{9.13}$$

and

$$T^P = T^e + T_r^B \tag{9.14}$$

Part of saved money can generate bonus pool B and be divided between the factors. Let us introduce the weight of importance of activities $S = [s_i]_{i=1,\ldots,n}$, where $s_i \in [0, 1]$. To share the bonus pool we define function which depends on saved amount of work, importance of activity x_i and if the activity is critical or not and on the reduced buffers of cost and time. In the general case that factor i can receive the amount of money b_i

$$b_i = f_{b_i}(s_i, D_i^W, c, D_B^K, D_B^T) \tag{9.15}$$

where s_i is the importance of activity x_i, D_i^W is the saved amount of work for activity x_i, $c = 1$ if the activity is on critical path or $c = 0$ if is not on the critical path, D_B^K is the amount of saved cost, D_B^T is the amount of saved time and f_{b_i} is some function. In our example we used the following function

$$b_i = \begin{cases} \dfrac{s_j}{s^1} \dfrac{D_j^W}{D^1} \gamma_1 B & \text{if } x_i \text{ is on critical path} \\[3mm] \dfrac{s_j}{s^2} \dfrac{D_j^W}{D^2} \gamma_2 B & \text{else} \end{cases} \qquad (9.16)$$

where B is the bonus pool $\gamma_2 < \gamma_1$, $\gamma_1 + \gamma_2 = 1$, s^1 is the sum of importances of activities which is on critical path, s^2 is the sum of importances of activities which is not on critical path, D_j^W is the sum of saved amounts of work for activity x_i, D_i^1 is the saved amounts of work for activities which are critical and D_i^2 is the sum saved amounts of work for activities which are beside any critical path.

9.3 Example

Let us consider the project with seven activities: $A_1, A_2, \ldots, A_7$. Its Activity on Arc network is represented on Fig. 9.1: In the first step of the procedure we should ask potential performers (in this case we made an assumption that they are our internal employees) for their estimation of the work required to complete this project. The data we obtained represents the safe estimation of minimal amounts of labor in matrix W given in Table 9.1. The total effort required for the whole project completion is a sum of amounts of labor for all activities, equal $2,200$ man-hours. There were 5 employees assigned to work on this project. Their potential participation in completing of several activities is described by the influence matrix X in the table below (Table 9.2):

Table 9.3 includes the cost matrix K representing the elementary cost of single man-hour for employees in several activities:

The upper limits of accessibility R of employees are given in Table 9.4:

To improve the calculation process we transferred the project model to spreadsheet environment. In this case we have used the Microsoft EXCEL with its regular Solver (Fig. 9.2). After using the routine procedure we obtained the matrix with

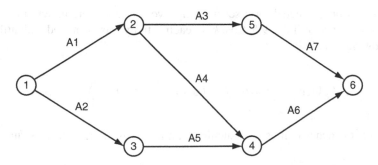

Fig. 9.1 The AoA project network

Table 9.1 Minimal amounts of labor in project activities: employees estimation

Activity	Minimal effort
A_1	200
A_2	240
A_3	150
A_4	400
A_5	340
A_6	200
A_7	690

Table 9.2 The resources influence matrix

Activity	Employee 1	Employee 2	Employee 3	Employee 4	Employee 5
A_1	0	0	1	1	0
A_2	1	1	0	0	0
A_3	0	0	0	0	1
A_4	0	0	1	1	0
A_5	1	1	0	0	0
A_6	0	1	0	1	0
A_7	1	0	1	0	1

Table 9.3 The cost matrix

Activity	Employee 1	Employee 2	Employee 3	Employee 4	Employee 5
A_1	50	60	33	35	28
A_2	45	50	52	48	35
A_3	32	40	30	68	43
A_4	67	55	63	57	47
A_5	55	60	45	54	51
A_6	45	42	50	50	38
A_7	50	50	45	57	49

Table 9.4 Accessibility limits

Employee 1	Employee 2	Employee 3	Employee 4	Employee 5
600	450	650	200	350

amounts of work expected form several employees to complete in activities. This matrix is described by Table 9.5. Cost k_i of each activity was estimated with utilising the following function:

$$k_i = f_{i_k}(x_{i1}, \ldots, x_{iq}, t_{i1}, \ldots, t_{iq}, k_{i1}, \ldots, k_{iq}) = \sum_{j=1}^{q} x_{ij} k_{ij} t_{ij} \qquad (9.17)$$

Duration t_i of each activities was calculated on the basis of the following function:

$$t_i = f_{i_t}(x_{i1}, \ldots, x_{iq}, t_{i1}, \ldots, t_{iq}) = \max_{1 \leq j \leq q} \{x_{iq} t_{iq}\} \qquad (9.18)$$

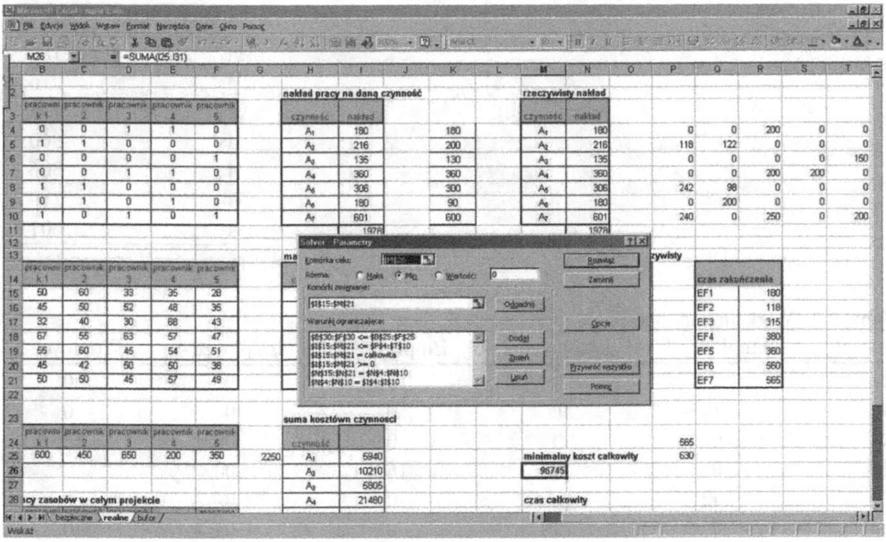

Fig. 9.2   The optimization model for spreadsheet solver

Table 9.5   Work amount matrix

Activity	Employee 1	Employee 2	Employee 3	Employee 4	Employee 5
A_1	0	0	200	0	0
A_2	118	122	0	0	0
A_3	0	0	0	0	150
A_4	0	0	200	200	0
A_5	242	98	0	0	0
A_6	0	200	0	0	0
A_7	240	0	250	0	200

This way we obtained the safe cost and duration estimations. According to the work
distribution in Table 9.5 we can calculate the total project cost K_c. On this moment
$K_c = 109100$ monetary units (e.g.$), and the total project duration $T_c = 600$ time
units (e.g. Hours). The numbers calculated above are probably overestimated and
includes hidden safety margins to protect their authors against delays and unex-
pected occurrences. In the next step we propose to analyse the required amounts of
labor within more optimistic assumptions. In this example we set up new estimations
of labor amounts given by vector W^*, in Table 9.6.   On the basis of the realistic
estimations we used the model in Microsoft EXCEL again. This way we obtained
the new distribution of labor for several employees and activities. New results are
shown in the matrix T^* in Table 9.7. With such a labor distribution we obtain the
total cost of the project $K_e = 96,745$$, and the total duration $T_e = 565$ h. Cost
savings, calculated as a difference between the total costs in safe and realistic dura-
tions – $K^B = 12,355$$. The difference between durations – $T^B = 35$ h. Here we
can see the profits we should achieve if the project is completed in line with realistic

Table 9.6 Minimal amounts
of labor: realistic (employer's
estimation)

Activity	Effort
A_1	180
A_2	216
A_3	135
A_4	360
A_5	306
A_6	180
A_7	601

Table 9.7 Work amount matrix

Activity	Employee 1	Employee 2	Employee 3	Employee 4	Employee 5
A_1	0	0	180	0	0
A_2	118	98	0	0	0
A_3	0	0	0	0	135
A_4	0	0	160	200	0
A_5	242	64	0	0	0
A_6	0	180	0	0	0
A_7	151	0	250	0	200

Table 9.8 Importance of
activities

Activity	Importance $\langle 0, 1 \rangle$
A_1	0.7
A_2	0.3
A_3	0.4
A_4	0.7
A_5	0.4
A_6	0.7
A_7	0.5

schedule and budget. But on the other hand, the realistic estimation are usually not acceptable by employees responsible for the activities completion. In our proposal we introduce the negotiated buffer sizes, calculated with declining factors. For the cost buffer we took $\alpha = 0.5$ and $\beta = 0.6$ for the time buffer. So here we obtain the reduced cost buffer $K_r^B = 6177.5\$$ and $T_r^B = 21$ h. When we include these buffers into schedule and budget plan we obtain a new goals equal $K^P = 102,922.5\$$ and $T^P = 586$ h. That means we have to solve the same work distribution model with new cost and duration limits. The part of the remaining estimated project cost between K^P and K in the safe estimation can be set up as a premium fund B. This fund will be distributed among project performers according to the diversified importance of activities. In this case we received the importance vector given in Table 9.8: In this case we used the following premium fund distribution function:

Table 9.9 Savings on amounts of labor, cost and duration

Activity	Effort	Required cost	Required duration
A_1	20	660	20
A_2	24	1,200	4
A_3	25	645	35
A_4	40	2,520	20
A_5	34	2,040	4
A_6	20	840	40
A_7	89	4,450	35
sum	242	12355	158

Table 9.10 Distribution of the premium fund among responsible employees

Activity	Value
A_1	411, 83
A_2	34, 32
A_3	28, 60
A_4	823, 67
A_5	64, 83
A_6	411, 83
A_7	212, 11

$$b_i = \begin{cases} \dfrac{s_j}{s^1}\dfrac{D_j^W}{D^1}\gamma_1 B & \text{if } x_i \text{ is on critical path} \\[2em] \dfrac{s_j}{s^2}\dfrac{D_j^W}{D^2}\gamma_2 B & \text{else} \end{cases}$$

where $\gamma_1 = 0.8$ and $\gamma_2 = 0.2$. Factors D^1, D^2, s^1, s^2 are respectively equal $D^1 - 80, D^2 = 162, s^1 = 2.1, s^2 = 1.6$. Now we are starting the same optimisation procedure in spreadsheet Solver with the objective function minimizing the total project cost with direct labor cost and premium fund utilisation and additional limitations on the duration and cost buffers consumption. In the final solution on the critical path we have three activities: A_1, A_4, A_6 with the total duration equals 630 h. Saved amounts of labor D_j^W, duration D_j^T, and cost D_j^K are represented by the Table 9.9:

With the assumptions above we obtained following success fees (Table 9.10): The premium fund will be distributed among responsible employees or their teams proportionally to their commission in activities execution and savings achieved towards base plans.

9.4 Summary

According to the authors of the paper, in the project planning issues it is possible to extract the safety buffers hidden in schedule estimations. The results of prior researches indicate that this mechanism is useful in project budgeting processes.

The main thesis of our study, stating the existence of required labor overestimations, seems to be justified as well. The theoretical consideration is compliant with the project cost buffering approach, described in Błaszczyk and Nowak (2008) in terms of the procedure of buffers sizing and profits distributing. Another extension of the prior approach was done with including the influence matrix describing the hypothetical dependence of resources on several time and cost drivers. The advantage of this model was described by the numerical example. It has to be highlighted, though, that proving its efficiency requires further empirical study in real-life conditions. It will be a subject of the next stage of this research.

References

Błaszczyk T, Nowak B, (2008) Szacowanie kosztów projektu w oparciu o metodę łańcucha krytycznego, Trzaskalik T. (ed.): Modelowanie Preferencji a Ryzyko '08, Akademia Ekonomiczna w Katowicach, Katowice

Brucker P, Drexl A, Möhring R, Neumann K, Pesch E et al. (1999) Resource-constrained project scheduling: Notation, classification, models, and methods. European Journal of Operational Research 112:3–41

Fulkerson D R et al. (1961) A network flow computation for project cost curves. Management Science 7:167–178

Goldratt E (1997) Critical Chain. North River Press

Gonzalez V, Alarcon L F, Molenaar K et al. (2009) Multiobjective design of Work-In-Process buffer for scheduling repetitive projects. Automation in Construction 18:95–108

Herroelen W, Leus R et al. (2001) On the merits and pitfalls of critical chain scheduling. Journal of Operations Management 19:559–577

Kelley J E et al. (1961) Critical-path planning and scheduling: Mathematical basis. Operations Research 9:296–320

Leach L et al. (2003) Schedule and cost buffer sizing: how account for the bias between project performance and your model. Project Management Journal 34(2):34–47

Rogalska M, Bożejko W, Hejducki Z et al. (2008) Time/cost optimization using hybrid evolutionary algorithm in construction project scheduling. Automation in Construction 18:24–31

Tukel O I, Rom W O, Eksioglu S D et al. (2006) An investigation of buffer sizing techniques in critical chain scheduling. European Journal of Operational Research 172:401–416

Van de Vonder S, Demeulemeester E, Herroelen W, Leus R et al. (2005) The use of buffers in project management: The trade-off between stability and makespan. International Journal of Production Economics 97:227–240

Chapter 10
The Multi-Objective Alternative Assets Investment Optimization Model on Sovereign Wealth Funds Based on Risk Control

Jing Yu, Bin Xu, and Yong Shi

Abstract This paper presents a new bi-objective stochastic chance-constrained 0-1 integer programming model to reflect the alternative assets allocation of SWFs, which can be modeled as multi-project and multi-item investment combination including profit-pursued objective and risk-avoided objective which can be measured from the perspective of negative entropy and real options or their integration, the constraint condition maps the relationship between demanded cash flow and supported cash flow among the whole process of operating projects. Then the Pareto solution set can be gotten by a modified DE proposed in this paper. In the last, a comparison will show that the performance of DE with random flexing factor has some advantage over that of flexing factor.

Keywords Alternative assets · Modified DE · Multi-project-multiple-item · Real option · Sovereign Wealth Funds · Stochastic chance-constrained

J. Yu (✉)
Research Center of Fictitious Economy and Data Science, Chinese Academy of Sciences, Beijing 100190, China
and
School of International Auditing, Nanjing Audit University, 211815, Nanjing, China
e-mail: yujing3721@163.com

B. Xu
School of Accountancy, Central University of Finance and Economic, Beijing 100081, China
e-mail: zhuohongxubin@163.com

Y. Shi
Research Center of Fictitious Economy and Data Science, Chinese Academy of Sciences, Beijing 100190, China
and
College of Information Science and Technology, University of Nebraska at Omaha, Omaha, NE 68182, USA
e-mail: yshi@gucas.ac.cn

Y. Shi et al. (eds.), *New State of MCDM in the 21st Century*, Lecture Notes in Economics and Mathematical Systems 648, DOI 10.1007/978-3-642-19695-9_10, © Springer-Verlag Berlin Heidelberg 2011

10.1 Introduction

Sovereign wealth funds (SWFs) are financial vehicles owned by states which hold, manage or administer public funds, which can be invested in a wider range of assets of various kinds. Their funds are mainly derived from excess liquidity in the public sector stemming from government fiscal surpluses or from official reserves at central banks. SWFs can be categorized into two types of funds according to their primary purpose. On the one hand, so-called stabilization funds aim to even out the budgetary and fiscal policies of a country via separating them from short-term budgetary or reserve developments which may be caused by price changes in the underlying markets, i.e. in oil or minerals, but also in foreign exchange conditions. On the other hand, savings or intergenerational funds create a store of wealth for future generations by using the assets they are allocated to spread the returns on a country's natural resources across generations in an equitable manner. Due primarily to high commodity prices, SWF are estimated to control assets in excess of $3 trillion, which could be seen that the holdings can rise to $12–15 trillion by 2015.

In thinking about how the investment combination of Sovereign Wealth Funds (SWFs) could evolve in the coming years. SWFs can be expected to adopt a long-term approach to their investment and spending decisions, differ from traditional institutional investors such as investment and pension funds or insurance companies. SWFs are observed to be invested to substantially broader, including public and private debt securities, equity, private equity, real estate and the use of derivative instruments. Morgan Stanley believes it is useful to consider the portfolios of established Sovereign Pension Funds (SPFs) as "model portfolios", in terms of their asset structure. Their judgment is that 25% bonds, 45% equities, and 30% alternative investments are a likely targeted portfolio structure for many SWFs. Norges Bank's GPF is a good example. As it has matured, it has raised its exposure to equities and alternative investments. The growing size and the long-term nature of their investment permit the NBIM to try to capitalize on the liquidity premium by entering into less liquid, but higher return investments. Other SWFs will follow the same path. So the alternative assets, such as infrastructure, real estate, private equity, commodity and hedge funds, will become more and more important in SWFs.

Just as any investment project management, many efforts have been directed to optimum models. These models, in general, are based on the objective of profit-pursued-type or risk-avoided-type, to maximize profit value and minimize the risk cost. In order to solve the problem, two key tasks must be faced, one is how to model the alternative assets investment, the other is how to measure the profit value and risk cost. Obviously, the coefficients in the developed model will be uncertain numbers because any forecasting approach can't get the precise future data. The paper will develop a new stochastic chance-constrained optimization programming model to model SWFs investment combination problem. In the proposed model, two objectives are taken into account, including risk-avoided objective and profit-pursued objective. The coefficients in the proposed model are generally uncertain to approximate practice.

The paper is organized as follows. In Sect. 10.2 some preliminary analyses will be provided and some notations will be also defined for the convenience of studying SWFs. The chance-constrained optimum 0–1 integer programming model will be developed in Sect. 10.2. Sections 10.3 and 10.4 will present a differential evolution algorithm to get the Pareto solution set with a small modification of DE, and a simulation numerical example will also be offered to illustrate the application of the model. Finally, Sect. 10.5 will conclude this paper and propose some feasible research directions for future study.

10.2 Preliminary Analyses and Notations

The SWFs can invest globally to look for the suitable mainly specified investment products of high profit companied with high risk, which must be evaluated based on two mainly criterions including profit evaluation and risk cost evaluation after a fixed period, then decide which will be held continuously or not. The above analyses mean that the SWFs investment management is just the same with that of project investment combination as each suitable specified investment product can be taken as one project. As each project must be evaluated after a fixed period, each project can be partitioned into many items corresponding to each fixed period holding project. Thus SWFs alternative assets management problem can be modeled as multiproject and multi-item optimization investment combination optimization problem.

Unlike our recent study in (Xu et al. 2009) with assuming fuzzy coefficients, all coefficients in this proposed model are assumed to be continuous stochastic numbers which can be simply narrated as follows. Suppose that there are mainly N projects of SWFs denoted as symbol $X_i (i = 1, 2, \ldots, N)$. Each project X_i can be partitioned into n_i items corresponding to each evaluation after a fixed period, which are sequentially represented by $U_{i,1}, U_{i,2}, \ldots, U_{i,n_i}$, which last for $a_{i,1}, a_{i,2}, \ldots, a_{i,n_i}$ years respectively.

Firstly, we analyze the output and input of cash flow at the end of each year in the process of the items, the minimal demanded cash at the beginning of each item can be described by Fig. 10.1.

In Fig. 10.1, $\xi_{i,j} (i = 1, 2, \ldots, N, j = 1, 2, \ldots, n_1, \ldots, n_N)$ denotes the minimal demanded cash of the item $U_{i,j}$ of project X_i at the beginning of the item $U_{i,j}$. On the other hand, the net cash flow produced at the end of each year among the process the items shown in Fig. 10.1 can be described as Fig. 10.2.

$$X_1 : \xi_{1,1}, \xi_{1,2}, \xi_{1,3}, \ldots\ldots\ldots, \xi_{1,n_1}$$
$$X_2 : \xi_{1,1}, \xi_{1,2}, \xi_{1,3}, \ldots\ldots\ldots, \xi_{1,n_2}$$
$$\ldots\ldots\ldots\ldots\ldots\ldots\ldots\ldots\ldots$$
$$X_N : \xi_{N,1}, \xi_{N,2}, \xi_{N,3}, \ldots\ldots\ldots, \xi_{N,n_N}$$

Fig. 10.1 Minimal demanded cash at the beginning of each item

$$X_1 : \eta_{1,0} - - \eta_{1,a_{1,1}}, \eta_{1,a_{1,1}+1}, - - \eta_{1,a_{1,2}+a_{1,1}}, \ldots\ldots\ldots\ldots, \eta_{1,\sum_{m=1}^{n_1-1} a_{1,m}+1}, - - \eta_{1,\sum_{m=1}^{n_1} a_{1,m}}$$

$$X_2 : \eta_{2,0} - - \eta_{2,a_{2,1}}, \eta_{2,a_{2,1}+1}, - - \eta_{2,a_{2,2}+a_{2,1}}, \ldots\ldots\ldots\ldots, \eta_{2,\sum_{m=1}^{n_2-1} a_{2,m}+1}, - - \eta_{2,\sum_{m=1}^{n_2} a_{2,m}}$$

$$\ldots\ldots\ldots\ldots\ldots\ldots\ldots\ldots\ldots\ldots\ldots\ldots\ldots\ldots\ldots\ldots\ldots\ldots$$

$$X_N : \eta_{N,0} - - \eta_{N,a_{1,1}}, \eta_{N,a_{1,1}+1}, - - \eta_{N,a_{1,2}+a_{1,1}}, \ldots\ldots\ldots, \eta_{N,\sum_{m=1}^{n_N-1} a_{N,m}+1}, - - \eta_{N,\sum_{m=1}^{n_N} a_{N,m}}$$

Fig. 10.2 The net cash flow produced at the end of each year

Where $\eta_{1,0}, \ldots, \eta_{1,a_{11}}$ represent the net cash flow at the end of each year in the process of the item $U_{1,1}$ which lasts for $a_{1,1}$ years, and so are others. And some other imperative financial data will be offered in the following sections.

10.3 The Stochastic Chance-Constrained Optimization Model

10.3.1 The Bi-Objective Functions

Under the stochastic environment, the negative entropy (Qiu 2002; Benaroch 1996) can be used to measure the event risk. Without loss of generality, the continuous stochastic type will only be considered in this paper. Based on Fig. 10.2, the corresponding stochastic density function for each item can be expressed. To X_1 project, its items' density functions can be expressed as ($a_{i,0} = 0, 1 \leq i \leq N$) following:

$$f(\eta_{1,0}), \ldots, f(\eta_{1,a_{11}}), \quad f(\eta_{1,a_{11}+1}), \ldots, f(\eta_{1,a_{11}+a_{12}}), \ldots,$$
$$f(\eta_{1,\sum_{m=1}^{n_1-1} a_{1,m}+1}), \ldots, f(\eta_{1,\sum_{m=1}^{n_1-1} a_{1,m}}).$$

Though there are some approaches used to measure the risk, the entropy had been proved to be the suitable approach to measure risk (Maasoumi and Racine 2002), thereby the corresponding negative entropy H can be calculated based on the probability density function $f(\eta)$ by the following formulation (Qiu 2002)

$$H = - \int f(\eta) \ln f(\eta) d\eta.$$

So the corresponding negative entropy can be derived. To X_1 project, its items' negative entropy can be expressed as:

$$H(\eta_{1,0}), \ldots, H(\eta_{1,a_{11}}), \quad H(\eta_{1,a_{11}+1}), \ldots, H(\eta_{1,a_{11}+a_{12}}), \ldots,$$
$$H(\eta_{1,\sum_{m=1}^{n_1-1} a_{1,m}+1}), \ldots, H(\eta_{1,\sum_{m=1}^{n_1-1} a_{1,m}}).$$

And so are other projects. The risk value r_r at the end of each year in the process of each item can be determined by negative entropy $H:r_r = cH$.

Where $c(0 \leq c \leq 1)$ denotes the risk coefficient which can be adjusted according to practical situation. Thus, the risk value at the end of each year in the process of the item $U_{1,1}$ can be expressed as:

$$c_{11}H_{11}, c_{12}H_{12}, \ldots, c_{1,a_{11}}H_{1,a_{11}} \quad (0 \leq c_{11}, c_{12}, \ldots, c_{1,a_{11}} \leq 1).$$

The whole risk r can be calculated by the formulation $r = r_r + r_f$, where r_f denotes the interest rate without risk, and the discounted rate k at the end of each year in the process of item can be formulated by $k = r = r_r + r_f$. For example, the discounted rate at the end of each year in the process of the item $U_{1,1}$ can be represented as:

$$r_f + c_{1,1}H_{1,1}, \quad r_f + c_{1,2}H_{1,2}, \quad \ldots\ldots\ldots\ldots, \quad r_f + c_{1,a1,1}H_{1,a1,1}.$$

Just like (Xu et al. 2009), the Net Present Value of Risk Value (NPVR for short) can be calculated by following formulation. Let $\psi_{i,j}$ denotes $NPVR_{i,j}$ of the item $U_{i,j}$, we have following formula (1):

$$\psi_{i,j} = \sum_{w=ai,j-1}^{ai,j-1+ai,j} \left(c_{i,w}H_{i,w} / \left(\prod_{l=1}^{w}(1+rf+c_{i,l}H_{i,l}) \right. \right.$$
$$\left. \left. \times \prod_{m=1}^{ai,1+ai,2+\ldots+ai,j-1} (1+rf+c_{i,m}H_{i,m}) \right) \right).$$

In (Xu et al. 2009), any item can only be evaluated by classical NPV model, let $\xi_{i,j}$ be NPV of the item $U_{i,j}$, then we can have following formula (2):

$$\zeta_{i,j} = \left(-\xi_{i,j} + \sum_{w=1}^{ai,j}(\eta_{\underset{m=1}{(\sum}ai,m)+w}^{j-1}) / \prod_{l=1}^{w}(1+rf+c_{i,l}H_{i,l}) \right) /$$
$$\times \prod_{m=1}^{ai,1+ai,2+\ldots+ai,j-1} (1 = rf+c_{i,m}H_{i,m})$$

In addition, the value of any item had only be evaluated by classical NPV model whereas the real option has be worldwide applied to evaluating item (Schütz et al. 2008; Pantelous 2008; Kumbaroğlu2008 et al. 2008; Scheuenstuhl and Zagst 2008), which means any item holder can have the right to continue or abolish (Benaroch 1996; Meng 2008; Nishihara 2008; Botteron and Chesney 2003), so the real option can't be neglected, and it can be evaluated by Black-Scoles (1988) (B-S for short) as follows:

$$\pi(S, t, K, r, \sigma) = S_t N(d_1) - K e^{-rt} N(d_2) \tag{10.1}$$

$$d_1 = [\ln(S_t/K) + (r + \sigma^2/2)\tau]/(\sigma\sqrt{\tau}) \tag{10.2}$$

$$d_2 = d_1 - \sigma\sqrt{\tau} \tag{10.3}$$

Where the symbol S_t denotes the value of target enterprise which can be decided by NPV model, K denotes the exercise price of call option, r denotes the interest without risk in the light of compound interest, T denotes expiry date, t denotes the present price date, $\tau = T - t$ denotes the distance between expiry date and the present price date, which is measured by unit year, σ denotes the fluctuation rate of enterprise value, $N(\bullet)$ denotes the accumulated distribution function of standard normal variable.

To item Ui, j, its real option can be formulated as:

$$\pi_{i,j}(S, t, K, r, \sigma) = \zeta_{i,j} N(d_1^{i,j}) - \xi_{i,j} e^{-r_f a_{i,j}} N(d_2^{i,j}) \tag{10.4}$$

$$d_1^{i,j} = [\ln(\zeta_{i,j}/\xi_{i,j}) + (r_f + (c_{i,j} H_{i,j})^2/2)a_{i,j}]/(c_{i,j} H_{i,j} \sqrt{a_{i,j}}) \tag{10.5}$$

$$d_2^{i,j} = d_1^{i,j} - c_{i,j} H_{i,j} \sqrt{a_{i,j}} \tag{10.6}$$

Easy to know, the objective functions must be both profit-oriented and risk-avoided, so the stochastic-chance optimization functions (Charnes and Cooper 1959; Liu 2002) can be expressed as ($0 \le \alpha1 \le 1, 0 \le \alpha2 \le 1$):

$$Obj : \begin{cases} Min\{NPVRH | NPVRH = \sum_{i=1}^{N} \sum_{j=1}^{n_i} \psi_{i,j}\} \\ Max\{V | \Pr\{\sum_{i=1}^{N} Xi \sum_{j=1}^{nj} Ui, j(\zeta i, j + \pi_{i,j}) \ge V\} \ge \alpha1\} \end{cases} \tag{10.7}$$

Where $Xi = 0$ means that the project Xi has not been selected; $Xi = 1$ means that the project. Xi has been selected; $Ui, j = 0$ means that the item Ui, j of project Xi has not been selected; $Ui, j = 1$ means that the item Ui, j of project Xi has been selected. V is the maximization of minimum $\sum_{i=1}^{N} Xi \sum_{j=1}^{nj} Ui, j(\zeta i, j + \pi i, j)$ when the minimum of $Pr\{.\}$ is $\alpha1$, $NPVRH$ is minimum $\sum_{i=1}^{N} \sum_{j=1}^{n_i} \psi_{i,j}$. The same meanings will be held in the next section.

10.3.2 The Stochastic Chance-Constrained Condition Functions

Just discussion in (Xu et al. 2009), the main condition is mapping a relationship between the demanded cash and supplied cash, the former couldn't be more than the latter. The supplied monetary resource at the beginning of any items is composed of the monetary resource raised by the item itself and the remained monetary resource of the previous items. For example, we can construct the condition functions when $j = 2$ by two steps, the first step doesn't consider the produced cash and interests whereas it will be considered in the whole process of projects, and their corresponding stochastic chance condition functions can be expressed as (10.5) and (10.6) respectively.

$$\Pr\left\{\sum_{i=1}^{N} X_i U_{i,2}\xi_{i,2} \leq \vartheta_2 + \left(\vartheta_1 - \sum_{i=1}^{N} X_i U_{i,1}\xi_{i,1}\right)\right\} \geq \beta_2 \qquad (10.8)$$

$$\Pr\left\{\sum_{i=1}^{N} X_i U_{i,2}\xi_{i,2} \leq \vartheta_2 + \Delta\vartheta_1(1+k)^{a_{11}} + \sum_{i=1}^{N}\sum_{m=1}^{a_{11}} \eta_{i,m}(1+k)^{a_{11}-m} U_{i,1}X_i\right\} \geq \beta_2$$
$$(10.9)$$

Where ϑ_2 represents the own raised monetary resource at the beginning of the items $U_{1,2}, U_{2,2}, \ldots, U_{N,2}$, and so is $\vartheta_1 . \vartheta_1 - \sum_{i=1}^{N} X_i U_{i,1}\xi_{i,1}$ represents the remained monetary resource of the previous items, $k_{i,w}$ ($1 \leq i \leq N$, $1 \leq w \leq a_{11}$) represents the interest rate of each year in the whole process, $\Delta\vartheta_1(1+k)^{a_{11}}$ represents the sum of the remained monetary resource and its corresponding interests, $\sum_{i=1}^{N}\sum_{m=1}^{a_{11}} \eta_{i,m}(1+k)^{a_{11}-m} U_{i,1}X_i$ represents the sum of the net cash flow $\eta_{i,m}$ produced by the items $U_{1,1}, U_{2,1}, \ldots, U_{N,1}$ and their corresponding interests at the mth year. Both (10.7) and (10.8) implicate the fact that the possibility of the demanded monetary resource not exceeding the sum of the owned monetary resource and the remained monetary resource of the previous items should not be less than β_2.

For the sake of simplicity, we use the following notation to express the conditions among the whole process of all projects.

$$\Pr\left\{\sum_{i=1}^{N} X_i U_{i,j}\xi_{i,j} \leq \vartheta_j + \Delta\vartheta_{j-1}\right\} \geq \beta_j, \quad j = 1, 2, \ldots, n_1, \ldots, n_N \quad (10.10)$$

where $\Delta\vartheta_{j-1} = \sum_{k=2}^{j} (\vartheta_{k-1} - \sum_{i=1}^{N} X_i U_{i,k-1}\xi_{i,k-1})$ denotes the previous remained cash. Obviously, there are at most n_N conditions.

10.4 The Solution to Optimum Model with Modified DE

10.4.1 The Modified DE Approach

How to solve the multi-objective optimum model composed of (10.5) and (10.9) to get its non-dominated Pareto solutions is the main task in this section. This paper intends to use Differential Evolution (DE) to solve the optimum model. DE were proposed by Storn and Price (1995, 1997) which only operated in continuous space. In this paper, a modified DE will be proposed to get Pareto solution set by absorbing the elite idea of NSGA-II (Deb et al. 2002, 1999a,b) which is composed of three main phases such as DE arithmetic operator, elite replication tactic, group evolution process. It is worth to point out that the constraint handing rule to sort the non-dominated solutions in NSGA-II is based on the distance of violating the constraint condition between left side and right side of constraint condition, which is not suitable for cash constraint handing rule of investment combination optimization problem. Because any litter violation of distance of cash constraint condition will cause the project operating process ceasing, the suitable constraint handing rule to sort the non-dominated solutions is in accordance with the number of violating constraint conditions, and in fact the proposed rule can reflect the nature of investment combination. The designed modified DE algorithm can be narrated simply as following.

Step 1: Initialization: Order symbol $X_i (i = 1, 2, \ldots, N)$ denotes the oversea target market, $X_i = 0$ means that any item of project X_i will not be selected whereas $X_i = 1$ means the project X_i will be selected. In fact any project X_i must be in the scope of all selected projects and the corresponding items $U_{i,j} (i = 1, 2, \ldots, N, j = 1, 2, \ldots, n_1, \ldots, n_N)$ must be evaluated at a fixed interval, so any project X_i under the scope of consideration must be selected, the only initialization task is initialize the item set $\{U_{i,j} | i = 1, 2, \ldots, N, j = 1, 2, \ldots, n_1, \ldots, n_N\}$. The random number $rand()/RAND\_MAX$ which lies in [0,1] can be used, the size of population which can be denoted as $U_1, U_2, \ldots\ldots, U_{pop}$. The define rule to initialize items $U_{i,j}$ can be expressed as following:

IF $rand()/RAND\_MAX \geq 0.5$ THEN $U_{i,j} = 1$ Else $U_{i,j} = 0$

Step 2: DE arithmetic operator:

(1) Mutation : The DE arithmetic operator handling aims at any individual solution, and assume the current evolution generation is t with the maximization generation T. Select randomly an individual $U_p(t)$ ($p = 1, 2, \ldots, pop, t \leq T$), and three individuals $U_{p1}(t) U_{p2}(t) U_{p3}(t)$ ($p \neq p1 \neq p2 \neq p3$, $p1, p2, p3 = 1, 2, \ldots, pop$), then the new individual $V_p(t + 1)$ can be gotten after mutation operator: $V_p(t + 1) = U_{p1}(t) + F (U_{p2}(t) - U_{p3}(t))$ with corresponding individual variables denoted as $\{V_{i,j}(t + 1) | i = 1, 2, \ldots, N, j = 1, 2, \ldots, n_1, \ldots, n_N\}$, where $F \in [0, 2]$ denotes flexing factor which aims to control differential variable. The rule of any individual variable of $V_p(t + 1)$ can be defined as:

IF sigmoid $(V_{i,j}(t + 1)) \geq 0.5$ THEN $V_{i,j}(t + 1) = 1$ ELSE $V_{i,j}(t + 1) = 0$

Where the function sigmoid(x) denotes activation function $sigmod(x) = 1/(1 + e^{-x})$

(2) Crossover : The discrete crossover arithmetic operator will be operated between the mutated individual $V_p(t + 1)$ and current individual $U_p(t)$, then the new trial individual $W_p(t + 1)$ will be produced, and its variables decided rule is as following:

IF $rand()/RAND\_MAX \leq CR$ THEN $W_{i,j}(t+1) = V_{i,j}(t+1)$ ELSE $W_{i,j}(t+1) = U_{i,j}(t)$

Where the symbol CR denotes crossover probability. The bigger the CR is, the bigger the contribution of crossed individual to trial individual will be.

(3) Selection : Select optimum individual greedily between trial individual $W_p(t + 1)$ and current evolution individual $U_p(t)$. To bi-objective Pareto set problem, use the non-dominated sorting approach to decide which individual be preserved to be one individual $U_p(t + 1)$ in the next generation, and the detail process can be seen in NSGA-II (Charnes and Cooper 1959; Storn and Price 1995).

Step 3: Elite copying tactic

The idea of the tactic can be illustrated as following: When the evolution operator ends at each generation, incorporate the new evolution population into old population, eliminate the repeated individual in the mixed population, copy the selected individual of mixed population orderly from small rank of non-dominated solution to high rank of non-dominated solution to next generation population. If the size of copied population with same rank exceeds maximum size, copy each individual to next evolution generation based on the distance between the individual and any other one with same rank according to the sparseness preferred rule until the size of new evolution population reaches the prescribed size. By the way the detail process can be seen form Ruifeng SHI's research literature (Shi and Zhou 2007).

10.4.2   Simulation Example

Suppose that the SWF management corporation wants to investment 10 mainly investment projects $N(N = 10)$, we assume that any investment project must be evaluated at 4 years to decide which one will be continued to hold or not in the next 4 years and each project will be repeated for 10 times during the whole plan period, thus the whole duration of each project is $40(4 \times 10)$ years. Each 4-year project among the whole project is taken as an item and there are at most 10 items to each project. Based on the above narration in Sects. 10.2 and 10.3, there are 10 different projects and there are 10 items to each project, thus the total amount of all items is $40(4 \times 10)$.If the constrained-resources can support all items to operate well, all items will be selected. Unfortunately, the amount of constrained-resource is limited enough to satisfy the demands of all items, and our aim is to select some items among all items (40 items) by optimizing our objectives. That means the items of each project will be decided whether to be selected or not whereas all projects must be selected according to the corporation's completion strategy. Because of uncertainty of investment projects, we can not forecast each item's cost, each item's input cash flow and output cash flow precisely. Thus the stochastic method is a feasible approach to deal with these data, and the developed model in this paper can reflect the optimization problem (Avinash and Pindyck 1994).

So we can have the following data:

$$N = 10, \quad a_{i,j} = 4, \quad n_1 = n_2 = \ldots = n_N = 10 \quad (i, j = 1, 2, \ldots, 10).$$

Because the columns for each row in Fig. 10.1, Fig. 10.2 are same, we can describe them with matrixes. Also we assume that the own raised cash $\vartheta_{i,j}$ is of normal distribution, and its expected value and deviation are as follows:

$$[E\vartheta_{i,j}^{)}|(D\vartheta_{i,j}^{)}]1 \times 10 = [300, 80, 83, 88, 51, 63, 85, 81, 70, 64|315, 95, 98, 103, 66, 78, 100, 96, 85, 79]$$

The demanded cash $\xi_{i,j}$ is of uniform distribution and its left boundary and right boundary are as follows:

$$[(a\xi_{i,j})|(b\xi_{i,j})]\,10 \times 10 = \begin{bmatrix} 10, 15, 20, 18, 25, 23, 24, 30, 37, 13 & 15, 20, 25, 23, 30, 28, 29, 35, 42, 18 \\ 20, 23, 24, 25, 30, 40, 35, 20, 25, 28 & 25, 28, 29, 30, 35, 45, 40, 25, 30, 33 \\ 30, 35, 40, 45, 40, 38, 37, 20, 27, 30 & 35, 40, 45, 50, 45, 43, 42, 25, 32, 35 \\ 08, 10, 12, 06, 15, 14, 18, 10, 08, 10 & 13, 15, 17, 11, 20, 19, 23, 15, 13, 15 \\ 15, 20, 25, 30, 15, 24, 28, 15, 18, 20 & 20, 25, 30, 35, 20, 29, 33, 20, 23, 25 \\ 18, 25, 27, 20, 25, 20, 19, 30, 24, 23 & 23, 30, 32, 25, 30, 25, 24, 35, 29, 28 \\ 25, 30, 35, 35, 40, 28, 32, 15, 18, 10 & 30, 45, 40, 40, 45, 33, 37, 20, 23, 15 \\ 40, 38, 40, 45, 55, 60, 37, 42, 25, 30 & 45, 53, 45, 50, 60, 65, 42, 47, 30, 35 \\ 35, 40, 45, 38, 37, 40, 38, 45, 50, 35 & 40, 45, 50, 43, 42, 45, 43, 50, 55, 40 \\ 30, 33, 38, 35, 48, 25, 27, 18, 20, 25 & 35, 38, 43, 40, 53, 30, 32, 23, 25, 30 \end{bmatrix}$$

The net cash flow $\eta_{i,j}$ is of normal distribution whose corresponding expected vale and deviation are as follows:

$$[E\eta_{i,j}, D\eta_{i,j}]10 \times 10 = \begin{bmatrix} 15, 18, 20, 28, 40, 28, 43, 35, 55, 44 & 3, 4, 5, 7, 9, 7, 8, 9, 9, 9 \\ 54, 28, 41, 35, 40, 50, 35, 36, 35, 45 & 8, 7, 9, 7, 9, 9, 9, 9, 2, 3 \\ 35, 43, 55, 56, 50, 58, 49, 49, 30, 48 & 7, 8, 9, 9, 9, 2, 3, 5, 2, 5 \\ 10, 15, 20, 10, 23, 19, 24, 17, 11, 23 & 2, 3, 5, 2, 5, 2, 5, 6, 9, 7 \\ 14, 25, 30, 40, 28, 40, 43, 20, 30, 40 & 2, 5, 6, 9, 7, 3, 5, 2, 5, 2 \\ 23, 30, 40, 30, 33, 25, 29, 40, 34, 34 & 3, 4, 5, 7, 9, 7, 8, 9, 9, 9 \\ 31, 38, 45, 45, 50, 40, 50, 30, 28, 20 & 8, 7, 9, 7, 9, 9, 9, 9, 2, 3 \\ 48, 50, 51, 56, 70, 75, 50, 55, 35, 45 & 7, 8, 9, 9, 9, 2, 3, 5, 2, 5 \\ 46, 49, 57, 45, 50, 48, 48, 58, 68, 50 & 2, 3, 5, 2, 5, 2, 5, 6, 9, 7 \\ 39, 40, 47, 45, 61, 36, 34, 30, 34, 35 & 2, 5, 6, 9, 7, 3, 5, 2, 5, 2 \end{bmatrix}$$

For simplicity, it is assumed that the cost occurs at the beginning of each item whereas the net cash flow happens at the end of each item and no other cash flow occurs in the process of all items.

10.4.3 The Simulation Results

Now we apply the developed model to get its Pareto-optimal solutions with modified DE, which is implemented by using C++, some parameters is as following: the size of population POP = 200, crossover probability CR = 0.4, flexing factor F = 0.5. In order to get its global Pareto solution, 100 successful runs are operated, the 580

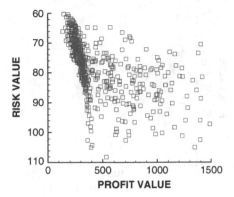

Fig. 10.3 All solution set

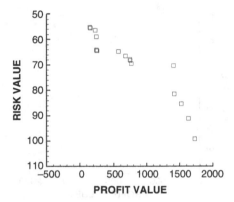

Fig. 10.4 Global pareto solution set

initial Pareto solutions can be gotten and the 17 global Pareto solutions can finally be gotten. Finally the following Figs. 10.3 and 10.4 can show the above two Pareto solution sets respectively, where the x-axis denotes the value including classical NPV and its real option, y-axis denotes risk value.

In order to test the impact of the choice of fixed flexing factor to global Pareto solution set, the flexing factor will be produced randomly at closed interval [0,2] corresponding the evolution generation of DE with other same parameters as the above, then 100 successful runs are operated, 582 initial solutions can be gotten and the 15 global Pareto solutions can finally be gotten. In last, the following Figs. 10.5 and 10.6 can be drawn to reflect them respectively.

Of course, the incorporated initial 1,162 solutions can be gotten based on the above two initial solution set, and 15 global Pareto solutions can be finally gotten which can be shown in Fig. 10.7 and the following Fig. 10.8 shows the three global solution sets sequentially, which are orderly named as ZONE1, ZONE2 and ZONE3 respectively, and obviously the performance of ZONE3 is advantage over that of ZONE2 which is advantage over than that of ZONE1.

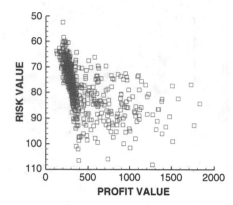

Fig. 10.5 All solution set

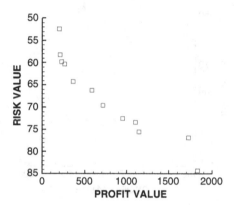

Fig. 10.6 Global pareto solution set

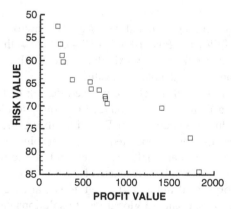

Fig. 10.7 Incorporated global pareto solution

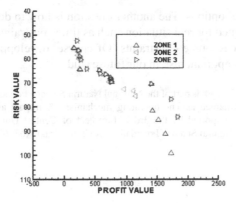

Fig. 10.8 Performance comparison

In addition, we can apply index C proposed by Zitzler (1999) to Fig. 10.8 to evaluate the performance of the above Pareto solution sets, which is defined as:

$$C(A, B) := |\{b \in B | \exists a \in A : a \succ B\}|/|B|$$

Where A and B are non-domination sets of two algorithms, and index C is defined in interval [0,1] to show the performance of sets a and A. $C(A, B) = 1$ means that there is at least one solution a in set A, which dominates any solution b in set B. $C(A, B) = 0$ means that there is no single solution a in set A that dominates any solution b in set B. $0 < C(A, B) < 1$ means that there is at least one solution a in set A that dominates any solution b in a part of set B. Based on the same aforementioned concept, the same conclusion for non-domination sets of corresponding algorithms can also be deduced. Based on our experimental results, the index C can be calculated as follows:

$$C(ZONE1, ZONE2) = 0, \quad C(ZONE2, ZONE1) = 0.1334$$
$$C(ZONE1, ZONE3) = 0, \quad C(ZONE3, ZONE1) = 0.567$$
$$C(ZONE2, ZONE3) = 0, \quad C(ZONE3, ZONE2) = 0.4317$$

10.5 Conclusion

This paper has developed a 0–1 integer stochastic chance constrained programming model to solve multiproject and multi-item investment combination which can reflect the SWF alternative assets management problem, which including risk-avoided objective and value-pursued objective. The risk-avoided value has been measured by negative entropy; the item value has been evaluated by classical NPV model based on the perspective of real option. But how to measure the item value precisely is an important problem because of uncertain surroundings which including some kinds of real options. The another question is how to develop the realistic constraints to be adapted for real situation such as time constraints, human resource constraints and other resource constraints. Of course, developing a fast effective algorithm is forever important task in our future study.

Acknowledgements This work is part of the National Natural Science Foundation of China (Grant No.70840010), which is named as The operating mechanism & impact analyses of Sovereign Wealth Funds, and also supported by the 3rd 211 project of Central University of Finance & Economics and National Natural Science Foundation of China Grant No70621001, No70531040.

References

L. Schütz, A. Stougie, P. Tomasgard: Preview Stochastic facility location with general long-run costs and convex short-run costs, Computers & Operations Research, 35(9) (2008)

T.A. Pantelous: Preview Dynamic risk management of the lending rate policy of an interacted portfolio of loans via an investment strategy into a discrete stochastic framework, Economic Modelling, 25 (4) (2008)

G. Kumbaroğlu2008, R. Madlener, M. Demirel: Preview A real options evaluation model for the diffusion prospects of new renewable power generation technologies, Energy Economics, 30 (4) (2008)

G. Scheuenstuhl, R. Zagst, Preview Integrated portfolio management with options, European Journal of Operational Research, 185(3) (2008)

B. Xu, W.G. Fang, R.F. Shi, J. Yu, L. Liu: Three objective fuzzy chance-constrained programming model for multiproject and multi-item investment combination, Information Science, 179 (5) (2009)

W.H. Qiu: Management and Applied Entropy. Mechanics Industrial Press, Beijing, China, 2002

M. Benaroch: A technique for qualitatively synthesizing the structure of risk management vehicles, Information Sciences, 90(1–4) (1996)

R.J. Meng: A patent race in a real options setting: Investment strategy, valuation, CAPM, beta, and return volatility, Journal of Economic Dynamics and Control, 32(10) (2008)

M. Nishihara, M. Fukushima: Evaluation of firm's loss due to incomplete information in real investment decision, European Journal of Operational Research, 188 (2) (2008)

F. Black, M. Scoles, The Pricing of Options and Corporate Liability, Journal of Political Economy, 81 (1988)

A. Charnes, W.W. Cooper: Chance-constrained programming. Management Science 6(1) (1959)

R. Storn, K. Price: Differential Evolution–A Simple and Efficient Adaptive Scheme for Global Optimization over Continuous Spaces. University of California, Berkeley ICSI, 1995.

R. Storn, K. Price: Differential Evolution–A Simple and Efficient Heuristic for Global Optimization over Continuous Spaces. Journal of Global Optimization (S0925–5001) 11(4) (1997)

K. Deb, A. Pratap, S. Agarwal, et al: A fast and elitist multiobjective genetic algorithm: NSGA-II IEEE Transaction on Evolutionary Computation, 6(2) (2002)

K. Deb: Multiobjective genetic algorithms: problem difficulties and construction of test functions. IEEE Transaction on Evolutionary Computation, 7 (1999a)

K. Deb: Multiobjective optimization and multiple constraint handling with evolutionary algorithms—Part I: A unified formulation. IEEE Transaction on Systems, Man and Cybernetics–Part A, (28) (1999b)

B. Liu: Theory and Practice of Uncertainty Programming, Heidelberg, Physica Verlag, 2002

P. Botteron, M. Chesney, R.G. Asner: Analyzing firms' strategic investment decisions in a real options' framework. Journal of International Financial Markets, Institutions and Money, 13(5) (2003)

K.D. Avinash, R.S. Pindyck, Investment under Uncertainty, 1994

E. Maasoumi, J. Racine: Entropy and predictability of stock market returns Journal of Econometrics, 10(7) (2002)

R.F. Shi, H. Zhou, Escalating evolutionary algorithm with application to bi-objective flow shop scheduling problems, Journal of Management Sciences in China, 10(5) (2007)

E. Zitzler: Evolutionary algorithms for multiobjective optimization: Methods and applications Switzerland: Swiss Federal Institute of Technology, 1999

Chapter 11
A New Tool for Feature Extraction and Its Application to Credit Risk Analysis

Paweł Błaszczyk

Abstract The aim of this paper is to present a new feature extraction method. Our method is an extension of the classical Partial Least Squares (PLS) algorithm. However, a new weighted separation criterion is applied which is based on the within and between scatter matrices. In order to compare the performance of the classification the economical datasets are used.

Keywords Classification · Credit risk · Feature extraction · Partial Least Square · Separation criterion

11.1 Introduction

The basic methods used to analyze and interpret economical data are feature extraction and classification. Economical datasets contains vectors of features, belonging to certain classes. These vectors are called samples. However, in some cases the number of samples could be much more smaller than the number of features. In this situation it is impossible to estimate the classifier parameters properly and the classification results may, therefore, be inadequate. In literature this phenomenon is known as the Curse of Dimensionality. In this case it is important to decrease the dimension of the feature space. This can be done either by feature selection or feature extraction. In this paper we introduce a feature extraction and classification method which can be used also in the situation when number of samples is smaller than number of features. Let us assume that we have the L-classes classification problem and let $(x_i, y_i) \in X \times \{C_1, \ldots, C_L\}, x \in \mathbb{R}^p$ where matrix of sample vectors X and response matrix Y are given by the following formulas:

P. Błaszczyk
Institute of Mathematics, University of Silesia, 14 Bankowa Street, 40-007 Katowice, Poland
e-mail: pblaszcz@math.us.edu.pl

Y. Shi et al. (eds.), *New State of MCDM in the 21st Century*, Lecture Notes
in Economics and Mathematical Systems 648, DOI 10.1007/978-3-642-19695-9_11,
© Springer-Verlag Berlin Heidelberg 2011

$$X = \begin{bmatrix} x_{11} \; \ldots \; x_{1p} \\ \vdots \;\; \ddots \;\; \vdots \\ x_{n1} \; \ldots \; x_{np} \end{bmatrix}, \quad Y = \begin{bmatrix} 1 \; 0 \ldots \ldots 0 \\ \vdots \;\;\;\;\;\;\;\;\; \vdots \\ 0 \; 0 \ldots \; 0 \; 1 \end{bmatrix}. \tag{11.1}$$

Each row of the matrix Y contain 1 in a position denoting the class label. One of the commonly used feature extraction methods is the Partial Least Squares (PLS) Method (Wold 1975; Garthwaite et al. 1994; Höskuldsson et al. 1988). PLS makes use of the least squares regression method (Gren 1987) in the calculation of loadings, scores and regression coefficients. The idea behind the classic PLS is to optimize the objective function:

$$(w_k, q_k) = \arg \max_{w^T w = 1; q^T q = 1} \text{cov} \left(X_{k-1} w, Y_{k-1} q \right) \tag{11.2}$$

under conditions:

$$w_k^T w_k = q_k q_k^T = 1 \quad \text{for } 1 \leq k \leq d, \tag{11.3}$$

$$t_k^T t_j = w_k^T X_{k-1}^T X_{j-1} w_j = 0 \text{ for } k \neq j, \tag{11.4}$$

where $\text{cov}\, (X_{k-1} w, Y_{k-1} q)$ is a covariance matrix between $X_{k-1} w$ and $Y_{k-1} q$, vector t_k is the kth extracted component, w_k is the vector of weights for kth component, d denotes the number of extracted components, X_k, Y_k arise from X_{k-1}, Y_{k-1} by removing the kth component by the following formulas:

$$X_{(k+1)} = X_k - t_k t_k^T X_k \tag{11.5}$$

$$Y_{(k+1)} = Y_k - t_k t_k^T Y_k. \tag{11.6}$$

This is the so called deflation technique. One can proof that the extracted vector w_k corresponds to the eigenvector connected with the largest eigenvalue of the following eigenproblem:

$$X_{k-1}^T Y_{k-1} Y_{k-1}^T X_{k-1} w_k = \lambda w_k. \tag{11.7}$$

Let S_B denote the between scatter matrix and S_W within scatter matrix respectively. It means that they are given by:

$$S_B = \sum_{i=1}^{L} p_i \, (M_i - M_0) \, (M_i - M_0)^T, \tag{11.8}$$

$$S_W = \sum_{i=1}^{L} p_i E \left[(X - M_i) \, (X - M_i)^T \, |C_i \right] = \sum_{i=1}^{L} p_i S_i, \tag{11.9}$$

where S_i is the covariance matrix, p_i is a-priori probability of the appearance of the ith class, M_i is the mean vector for the ith class and M_0 is given by:

$$M_0 = \sum_{i=1}^{L} p_i M_i. \tag{11.10}$$

These matrices are often used to define separation criteria. By separation criteria we mean the nonparametric function for evaluating and optimizing the separation between classes. For the PLS maximizing a separation criterion is used to find such vectors of weights that provide an optimal separation between classes in the projected space.

Theorem 1. *For the matrix Y and the normalized input data matrix X the following property:*

$$X^T Y Y^T X = \sum_{i=1}^{L} n_i^2 (M_i - M_0)(M_i - M_0)^T \tag{11.11}$$

holds.

So we can say that for PLS the matrix $X^T Y Y^T X$ is almost identical with the between class scatter matrix S_B. These eigenvector are used as a vectors of weight for providing the appropriate separation. Hence we can say that the separation criterion in the PLS method is only based on the between scatter matrix. The disadvantage of the classic PLS method is that it does not give a proper separation between classes, particularly when the dataset is nonlinearly separated and the features are highly correlated. To provide a better separation between classes we propose a new weighted separation criterion. The new weighted separation criterion is used to design an extraction algorithm, based on the classic PLS method.

In the next section we present methods used in this paper. In Sect. 11.2.1 we introduced a new weighted separation criterion and the algorithm for the estimation parameter in the separation criterion. The linear and nonlinear version of the new extraction algorithm is described in Sect. 11.2.2. The decision rule used to classify samples into classes is presented in Sect. 11.2.3. Section 11.3 focused on the datasets as well as on the experimental scheme and the results obtained. The final conclusions are drawn in Sect. 11.4.

11.2   Methods

11.2.1   The New Weighted Separation Criterion

Let us assume that we want to find a coefficient w which separates classes the best. The existing separation criteria described in literature have some disadvantages. Some criteria can not be applied if the within scatter matrix is singular due to a small number of samples. For others the computational cost is high. In practice there are situations in which the distance between classes is small. In this case it is more important to increase the distance between classes than to decrease the distance between samples within a class, hence the influence of components denoting between and within scatters for classes is important. In this paper we propose a new weighted separation criterion, which we call the Weighted Criterion of Difference Scatter Matrices (WCDSM). Our new criterion is denoted by:

$$J = \text{tr}(\gamma S_B - (1 - \gamma)S_W) \tag{11.12}$$

where γ is a parameter, S_B and S_W are between scatter matrix and within scatter matrix respectively. Applying a linear transformation criterion, condition (11.12) can be rewritten in the following form:

$$J(w) = \text{tr}\left(w^T (\gamma S_B - (1 - \gamma)S_W) w\right) \tag{11.13}$$

which is more suitable for optimization. Next we optimize the criterion:

$$\max_{w_k} \sum_{k=1}^{d} w_k^T (\gamma S_B - (1 - \gamma)S_W) w_k, \tag{11.14}$$

under the conditions:

$$w_k^T w_k = 1 \quad \text{for } 1 \le k \le p. \tag{11.15}$$

Theorem 2. *Under the conditions (11.15) for the optimization problem (11.14) the solution is defined by eigenvector connected with the largest eigenvalue for the following eigenproblem:*

$$(\gamma S_B - (1 - \gamma)S_W) w_k = \alpha w_k. \tag{11.16}$$

Proof. The solution to this problem can be found with the use of the Lagrange multipliers method. Let

$$L(w_k, \alpha) = \sum_{k=1}^{p} w_k^T (\gamma S_B - (1 - \gamma)S_W) w_k - \alpha_k \left(w_k^T w_k - 1\right),$$

be the Lagrangian function where $\alpha = [\alpha_1, \ldots, \alpha_p]$ is the vector of Lagrange multipliers connected with the conditions (11.15). For such defined optimization task we maximize function L with respect to w. This problem can be solved by maximization of the function L by providing the following conditions:

$$\frac{\partial L(w_k, \alpha)}{\partial w_k} = 0 \quad \text{for } 1 \le k \le p \tag{11.17}$$

$$\alpha_k \ge 0 \quad \text{for } 1 \le k \le p.$$

Calculating the partial derivative of L with respect to w_k we obtain:

$$\frac{\partial L}{\partial w_k} = 2\left(\gamma S_B - (1-\gamma)S_W\right)w_k - 2\alpha w_k.$$

Then, from (11.17), we get:

$$(\gamma S_B - (1-\gamma)S_W)\,w_k = \alpha w_k.$$

This completes the proof.   □

To find the correct value of the parameter γ we used the following metric:

$$\rho(C_1, C_2) = \min_{c_1 \in C_1, c_2 \in C_2} \rho(c_1, c_2), \tag{11.18}$$

where C_i is the ith class, for $i \in \{1, 2\}$. The value of the parameter γ was chosen by the using the following formula:

$$\gamma = \frac{\min_{i,j=1,\ldots,L,i\neq j}\left\{\rho(C_i, C_j)\right\}}{1 + \min_{i,j=1,\ldots,L,i\neq j}\left\{\rho(C_i, C_j)\right\}}. \tag{11.19}$$

Such a parameter γ equals 0 if and only if certain i and j classes exist for which $\rho(C_i, C_j) = 0$. This means that at least one sample which belongs to classes C_i and C_j exist. If distance between classes increase, the value of γ also increases. Therefore the importance of the component S_W becomes greater.

11.2.2   The New Extraction Method

In this section we will apply a new weighted separation criterion to design a new extraction algorithm based on PLS. Let us recall that the vector of weights in the PLS corresponds to the eigenvector connected with the largest eigenvalue of the eigenproblem (11.7) and the matrix (11.11) is almost identical to the between scatter matrix. To improve separation between classes we replace the matrix (11.11) with the matrix from our new separation criterion (11.13). The idea of the new extraction algorithm is to optimize the objective criterion

$$w_k = \arg\max_w \left(w^T(\gamma S_B - (1-\gamma)S_W)w\right), \tag{11.20}$$

under the following conditions:

$$w_k^T w_k = 1 \quad \text{for } 1 \leq k \leq d \tag{11.21}$$

$$t_k^T t_j = w_k^T X_{k-1}^T X_{j-1} w_j = 0 \quad \text{for } k \neq j. \tag{11.22}$$

We shall call this extraction algorithm – Extraction by applying Weighted Criterion of Difference Scatter Matrices (EWCDSM).

Theorem 3. *For the input matrices X and Y the extracted vector w_k corresponds to the eigenvector connected with the largest eigenvalue for the following eigenproblem:*

$$(\gamma S_B - (1 - \gamma)S_W)w = \lambda w. \tag{11.23}$$

Also, the kth component t_k corresponds to the eigenvector related to the largest eigenvalue for the following eigenproblem:

$$X_{k-1}X_{k-1}^T (D - (1 - \gamma)I) t_k = \lambda t_k. \tag{11.24}$$

Matrix $D = [D_j]$ is an $n \times n$ block-diagonal matrix, where D_j is a matrix in which all elements equals $1/nn_j$, where n_j is the number of samples in the jth class.

Proof. From the definition of the between scatter matrix we have

$$S_B = X^T DX, \tag{11.25}$$

where $D = [D_j]$ is an $n \times n$ block-diagonal matrix, where D_j is a matrix in which all elements equals $1/nn_j$, where n_j is the number of samples in the jth class. Also we know that covariance matrix S_T has the following form

$$S_T = X^T X. \tag{11.26}$$

Using (11.25) and (11.26) we obtain

$$S_B - (1 - \gamma)S_T = X^T DX - (1 - \gamma)X^T X = X^T (D - (1 - \gamma)I) X, \tag{11.27}$$

where I is identity matrix. In the EWCDSM the criterion WCDSM is used. So because of Theorem 2 we have that in the EWCDSM algorithm in kth step we extract kth component by calculate the eigenvector connected with the biggest eigenvalue for the following eigenproblem

$$(\gamma S_B - (1 - \gamma)S_W)w = \lambda w.$$

Using (11.27) we get

$$X_{k-1}^T (D - (1 - \gamma)I) X_{k-1}w = \lambda w.$$

Then we calculate the kth component t_k as a linear combination of features of the matrix X

$$t_k = X_{k-1}w_k.$$

After extraction we delete the extracted component from the matrix X and Y using the so called "deflation technique". The new matrix X and Y we can write as follow:

$$X_{k+1} = X_k - t_k p_k^T, \qquad Y_{k+1} = Y_k - t_k c_k^T,$$

where

$$p_k = (X^T t_k)\backslash(t_k^T t_k), \qquad c_k = (Y_{k-1}^T t_k)\backslash(t_k^T t_k).$$

From the above we infer that eigenproblem for extraction component t_k has formula:

$$X_{k-1} X_{k-1}^T (D - (1 - \gamma)I) X_{k-1} w_k = \lambda X_{k-1} w_k,$$

what is equivalent to

$$X_{k-1} X_{k-1}^T (D - (1 - \gamma)I) t_k = \lambda t_k.$$

This completes the proof.   □

Above we design linear version of the extraction algorithm but it can not be used for nonlinear case. A proper features extraction for nonlinear separable is difficult and could be inaccurate. Hence, for this problem we design a nonlinear version of our extraction algorithm. We use the following nonlinear function $\Phi : x_i \in \mathbb{R}^N \rightarrow \Phi(x_i) \in F$ which transforms the input vector into a vector into a new, higher dimensional feature space F. Our aim is to find an EWCDSM component in F.

Theorem 4. *In the dual feature space* F, *vectors* w_k *and* t_k *are given by the following formulas:*

$$w_k = w_k^\star = (D - (1 - \gamma)I)\mathbf{K}_k w_k^\star \tag{11.28}$$
$$t_k = \mathbf{K}_k w_k^\star \tag{11.29}$$

where $\mathbf{K}_k = \Phi_k \Phi_k^T$.

Proof. Because the vector w_i lies in the primary space we must transform them into the dual space. Like for kernel PLS method (Shawe-Taylor and Cristianini 2004) we use formula:

$$\beta_k w_k = \Phi_k^T w_k^\star, \tag{11.30}$$

where w_k is a weight vector in primary space, whereas vector $w_k^\star$ is weight vector in the dual space. For the nonlinear version of extraction algorithm we implement the deflation of the matrix D. Let D_k denote the matrix D in $k + 1$ step. Using (11.30) into $w_k = X^T (D - (1 - \gamma)I)X w_{k-1}$ we get the recursive form of the vector $w_k^\star$:

$$w^\star_{k,l} = (D_k - (1 - \gamma)I)\, \Phi_k \Phi^T_k w^\star_{k,l-1}.$$ (11.31)

Next we normalize the vector $w^\star_{k,l}$ i.e.

$$w^\star_{k,l} = (w^\star_{k,l})\backslash(\|w^\star_{k,l}\|).$$ (11.32)

We repeat this procedure for the vector $w^\star_{k,l}$ until the convergence. Finally, we get that vector $w^\star_{k,l}$ correspond to the vector $w^\star$ in the dual space, which is the rescaled version of the vector w_k. Therefore in the dual space the components t_k are given by the formula:

$$t_k = \beta_k \Phi_k \Phi^T_k w^\star_k.$$ (11.33)

Let $\mathbf{K}_k = \Phi_k \Phi^T_k$. We have:

$$w^\star_k = (D - (1 - \gamma)I)\mathbf{K}_k w^\star_k$$ (11.34)

$$t_k = \mathbf{K}_k w^\star_k.$$ (11.35)

This completes the proof.   □

We called the matrix $\mathbf{K}$ the kernel matrix. From the definition of the kernel matrix $\mathbf{K}$ we have that:

$$\Phi\Phi^T_{(k+1)} = \left(\Phi_k - tp^T\right)\left(\Phi_k - tp^T\right)^T = \mathbf{K}_{k+1} = \left(I - t_k t^T_k\right)\mathbf{K}_k\left(I - t_k t^T_k\right)$$

Theorem 5. *In the dual space F the extracted vector w_k corresponds to the eigenvector connected with the largest eigenvalue for eigenproblem:*

$$(D_k - (1 - \gamma)I)\, \Phi_k \Phi^T_k w^\star_k = \lambda w^\star_k.$$ (11.36)

Also, the kth component t_k corresponds to the eigenvector connected with largest eigenvalue for the following eigenproblem:

$$\mathbf{K}_{k-1}(D_{k-1} - (1 - \gamma)I)t = \lambda t,$$ (11.37)

11.2.3 Classification

Let us assume that X_{train} and X_{test} are the realizations of the matrix X for train and test datasets respectively. The idea of a training step is to extract vectors of weights w_k and components t_k by using the train matrix X_{train} and to store them as a column in matrices W and T respectively. In order to classify samples into classes we use train matrix X_{train} to compute the regression coefficients by using the least squares method (Gren 1987) given by:

$$Q = X^T U \left(P^T X^T U \right)^{-1} U^T, \qquad (11.38)$$

where $U = Y Y^T T \left(T^T T \right)^{-1}, P = X^T T \left(T^T T \right)^{-1}$. Then we multiply test matrix X_{test} by coefficients of the matrix Q. In order to classify samples, corresponding to the Y_{test} matrix, we use decision rule:

$$y_i = \arg\max_{j=1,\ldots,L} Y_{test}(i, j). \qquad (11.39)$$

11.3 Experiments

11.3.1 Dataset

We applied the new extraction method to commonly accessible economical datasets: Australian Credit Approval and German Credit Data. We compared our method with PLS on the basis of the Australian Credit Approval available at[1]. The Australian Credit Approval (Quinlan 1987, 1993) contains information from credit card application form divided into two classes denoted as 0 and 1. Class 1 contains information from application form for people which have positive decision about credit cards. In this dataset there are 690 samples, where 307 samples are those taken from class 0. The others 383 samples belong to class 1. Each sample is represented by 14 features. The second dataset German Credit Data (see footnote 1) contains 1,000 samples divided into two class: 0, 1 and represented by 30 features. In both datasets there are some nonnumerical features. In order to apply extraction algorithm into those datasets relabeling is needed. We assign natural number as a new values of nonnumerical features.

11.3.2 Experimental Scheme and Results

In order to examine the classification performance of EWCDSM for economical data, we use the following experimental scheme. First, we randomly divide each dataset into validation, train and test sets. Then each dataset is normalized. We use the jackknife method (Duda and Hart 2000) and validation dataset to find the proper value of parameter d which denotes the number of extracted components. Classification performance is computed by dividing the number of samples classified properly by the total number of samples. This rate is known as a standard

---

[1] http://archive.ics.uci.edu/ml/

Table 11.1 Classification performance (percent) for economical datasets

	EWCDSM	PLS	LibSVM	BPN
German credit data	98.50	83.78	94.00	83.86
Australian credit approval	92.17	63.91	44.83	77.83

error rate (Duda and Hart 2000). Appropriate values of parameter d are 10 for *Australian Credit Approval* and 5 for *German Credit Data* datasets. The result for both economical datasets are presented in the Table 11.1.

For the German Credit Data classification performance of the EWCDSM algorithm equaled 0.9850. It means that 5 samples from class 1 were badly classify into class 0. Classification performance for classic PLS method was not so high. We noted best result for 14 components. Then classification performance equaled 0.8378. In these case 54 samples from class 0 and 6 samples from class 1 was classify improperly. For the Australian Credit Approval we noted best classification performance for 10 components. Then classification performance equaled 0.9217, what means that 18 samples from class 1 were classified improperly. For the classic PLS method the best results were noted also for 10 components and equaled 0.6391. It means that 83 samples from class 1 were classify improperly. The performance of PLS and EWCDSM was compared with LibSVM[2] and Back Propagation Neural Network (BPN) (see Yu et al. 2009).

11.4 Conclusions

We have introduced a new linear and nonlinear version of an algorithm for feature extraction. Our algorithm uses a new weighted separation criterion to find the weights vector which allows for the scatter between the classes to be maximal and for the scatter within the class to be minimal. On comparing the new criterion with the other well known ones, it can be seen that the new one can be used in a situation where the number of samples is small and the costs of computation are lowered. The new extraction algorithm can distinguish between high-risk and low-risk samples for two different economical datasets. Moreover, we have shown that the classification performance of the proposed algorithm was significantly higher for our method than for classical methods. The presented method performs well in solving classification problems. However, to draw some more general conclusions further experiments with the use of other economical datasets are necessary.

References

Duda R, Hart P (2000) Pattern Classification. John Wiley & Sons, New York
Garthwaite P H et al (1994) An interpretation of Partial Least Squares. Journal of the American Statistical Association 89:122–127

---

[2] http://www.csie.ntu.edu.tw/~cjlin/libsvm

Höskuldsson A et al (1988) PLS Regression methods. J. Chemometrics 2:211–228

Gren J. (1987) Mathematical Statistic. PWN, Warsaw

Quinlan J R (1987) Simplifying decision trees. Int. J. Man-Machine Studies 27:221–234

Quinlan J R (1993) C4.5: Programs for Machine Learning. Morgan Kaufmann

Shawe-Taylor J, Cristianini N (2004) Kernel Methods for Pattern Analysis., Cambridge Univ. Press, Cambridge

Wold H (1975) Soft Modeling by Latent Variables: The Non-Linear Iterative Partial Least Squares (NIPALS). Approach Perspectives in Probability and Statistics. Papers in Honour of M.S. Bartlett, 117–142

Yu L, Wang S, Cao J et al (2009) A Modified Least Squares SVM Classifier With Application To Credit Risk Analysis, Int J Inform Tech Decis Making 8:697–710

Chapter 12
Algorithm for MCDM in Intelligent Braking Diagnostics System of Railway Transport

Anatoly Levchenkov, Mikhail Gorobetz, Leonids Ribickis, and Peteris Balckars

Abstract The purpose of this research is to prevent railway accidents by reducing the human factor. In this paper the algorithm for multiple criteria decision making (MCDM) intelligent agent system of railway transport diagnostics task is proposed. The multiple criteria decision making target function for the rolling stock and railway system control is described by three criteria: the dangerous level of the current state of the system; the comfort level of passengers; the consumption of the energy. Computer simulation of the developed algorithm is used to test its workability. The functional prototype of the train emergency braking device is proposed to stop the train in case of the emergency or dangerous situation to prevent the accident.

12.1 Introduction

Nowadays human factor (Hasegawa et al. 2009) plays a significant role in control of railway system as a whole and a rolling stock in particular. The task of this research is to prevent railway accidents by reducing the human factor. The control of railway braking system is concerned with a large quantity of parameters, such as temperature, pressure, mass, acceleration, velocity etc., to be monitored and optimized. For this reason multiple criteria decision making (MCDM) algorithm is necessary.

In this paper the algorithm for multiple criteria decision making intelligent agent system of railway transport diagnostics task is proposed. Physically intelligent agent system is presented as a network of the programmable controllers, which have interface to work in global network and wireless networks and are programmed to use methods of the artificial intelligence (Russel and Norvig 2006) and methods of MCDM (Yi and Kou 2009). In this paper artificial neural network

A. Levchenkov (✉), M. Gorobetz, L. Ribickis, and P. Balckars
Riga Technical Universiy, 1, Kalku Street, Riga, 1658, Latvia
e-mail: anatolijs.levcenkovs@rtu.lv, mihails.gorobecs@rtu.lv, leonids.ribickis@rtu.lv, peteris@dzti.edu.lv

Y. Shi et al. (eds.), *New State of MCDM in the 21st Century*, Lecture Notes in Economics and Mathematical Systems 648, DOI 10.1007/978-3-642-19695-9_12, © Springer-Verlag Berlin Heidelberg 2011

(Haykin 2006) controller, mathematical models and clustering algorithm for task solution is proposed.

The multiple criteria decision making target function for the rolling stock and railway system control is described by three criteria: the dangerous level of the current state of the system; the comfort level of passengers; the consumption of the energy.

Computer simulation (Luo and Zeng 2009) is used to test the proposed algorithm for task solution.

12.2   Problem Formulation

The primary purpose of research is to diagnose the current state of the railway system and the algorithm for multiple criteria decision making is used to stop the train in case of emergency and to prevent the accidents.

Therefore, various system elements should be controlled and monitored permanently. Practically, the definite time intervals are necessary to get the state of the process for analysis and control, i.e. analog process should be digitized.

For this reason the distributed intelligent agent system is necessary to analyze to state and condition of each system element. The results of analysis of each system elements should be collected for final multiple criteria decision making about the dangerous level, comfort level and optimal energy consumption.

The secondary task is to find out an optimal time interval for process digitizing and monitoring. Too short time interval needs a lot of CPU resources for analysis and disk space for storage, but too long time interval may be dangerous. Time interval has minimum and maximum limits. Minimum is limited by all sensors response time, because the data from all the sensors are necessary for analysis. Maximum is limited by safety level criterion.

The authors propose to use clustering analysis for intelligent devices of diagnostics system to increase safety level in railway systems and special grid function for optimizing monitoring time interval.

12.3   Structure of the Railway System

Following objects may be defined in railway system: rail ways R; points P; stations ST; block-sections CP; signalisation, centralisation and interlocking system SCB; dispatching centre DC; traffic lights G; rolling stocks RS; locomotives L; wagons V.

Figure 12.1 shows the functional connections between objects of railway system. Solid lines mean strong and permanent functional dependencies. Dashed lines mean usage of rail ways for signal transmitting from traffic light to the locomotive on the sections that are equipped with automatic interlocking. On the stations and on the

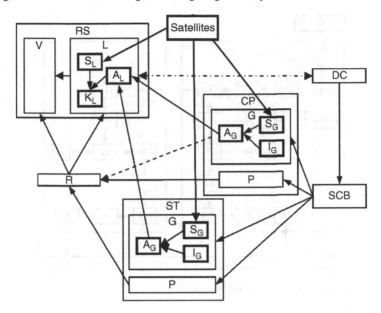

Fig. 12.1 Proposed structure of interaction of railway system objects

sections with half-automatic interlocking automatic locomotive signalisation is not working.

Authors propose to add following objects to the existing system:

- Satellite navigation receivers of traffic lights S_G and locomotives S_L (GPS, GALILEO,...).
- Wireless signal transmitting antennas of traffic lights A_G and locomotives A_L (GSM-R,...).
- Device for signal generation of the traffic light I_G.
- Device of braking system control of the locomotive K_L.

Objects of braking system of rolling stock are: steel rails – S, locomotive – L; wagon – V; steel wheels – R; brake pads – K; brake cylinder – BC, stopping transmission levers – PS; air splitter – G; stock air tank – KR; main reservoir – GR; air pipe with fittings – GV; compressor – LK; brake control devices – BV; release valve – AV, automatic mode – AR.

Figure 12.2 presents structure of existing braking system improved with new devices for diagnostics of braking system:

- DK – diagnostics controller.
- DV – sensors, that measures current state of the braking system.
- SAT – receiver of satellite navigation signals.

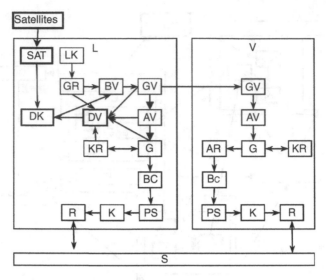

Fig. 12.2 Proposed structure of train braking system

12.4 Mathematical Model

The paper proposes mathematical model of the whole railway transport system including electromechanical model of traction and braking system of rolling stock.

12.4.1 Model of Railway Tracks and Points

Rail ways may be represented as graph $R = \{C, S\}$, where rails are divided into sections S, and each section $s \in S$ connected with each other by two connectors $s = < c_i, c_j >$.

Each section $s \in S$ has constant length l_s, curve a_s, and speed limit $v*_s$.

Each point $p \in C$ connecting set W of three or more sections and set of possible states of point D_p, where $d_p^n = < s_i, s_j >$ means opened both directions from s_i to s_j and from s_j to s_i is following for different point types:

- Single point: $D_p = \{< s_i, s_j >, < s_i, s_k >\}$.
- Dual point: $D_p = \{< s_i, s_j >, < s_i, s_k >, < s_i, s_m >\}$.
- Cross point: $D_p = \{< s_i, s_j >, < s_i, s_k >, < s_m, s_j >, < s_m, s_k >\}$.

Each state of point $d_p \in D_p$ has speed limit $v*_{d_p}$; maximal switching time for each point $d_p \in D_p - t_{d_p}$.

12.4.2   Model of Railway Signals

Railway signal G is an object with fixed coordinates x0, y0 connected to fixed position on the track. Type of signal: Each signal $g \in G$ has the following states of signals $L_g \subseteq \{R, Y, YG, G, V, W\}$, where "R" – red, and rolling stock must stop before the signal; "Y" – yellow, can move and be ready to stop, next signal is red; "YG" – yellow and green, next two sections are free; "G" – green, "V" – violet, "W" – moonlight white.

Each signal sets up the speed limits for the next block-section: v_{def} – maximal predefined speed on the section, v_0 – 0 kmh, stop; v_1 – < 50 kmh, movement on turnouts 1/9 and 1/11 types; v_2 – < 80 kmh for movement on turnout 1/18 type; v_3 – < 120 kmh for movement on turnout 1/22 type.

12.4.3   Rolling Stock Model

The following parameters of system's electromechanical elements are proposed for mathematical model.

The following parameters of system's electromechanical elements are proposed for mathematical model: U – railway contact net voltage; E – counter-electromotive force of the drive of the train; I_a – armature current of the drive of the train; R_a – armature resistance of the drive of the train; L_a – armature inductance of the drive of the train; I_f – field current of the drive of the train; R_a – field resistance of the drive of the train; L_a – field inductance of the drive of the train; L_{af} – mutual field-armature inductance of the drive of the train; K_E – voltage constant; K_T – torque constant; T_e – electrical torque of the drive; T_L – torque load; R_b – braking resistance; m – mass of rolling stock; g – gear box ratio; F – friction force; B – mechanical braking force; J – inertia of the drive; B_m – viscous friction coefficient of the drive; T_f – Coulomb friction torque of the drive; ω_1 – angular velocity of the motor; ω_2 – angular velocity of output shaft of transmission; T_2 – torque on the output shaft of transmission; P_1 – power on the input shaft of transmission; P_2 – power on the output shaft of transmission; r – wheel radius; F – force on the wheel periphery; v – linear velocity on the wheel periphery; t – time.

Functional dependencies of electromechanical part are the following: $E = K_E\omega$; $K_E = L_{af} \cdot I_f$; $T_e = K_T I_a$; $K_T = K_E$; $T_e, TL > 0$ – generator mode; $T_e, TL < 0$ – motor mode; $J\frac{d\omega}{dt} = T_e - sgn(\omega) \cdot T_L - B_m \cdot \omega - T_f$; $\omega_1 = g \cdot \omega_2$; $T_2 = g \cdot T_e$; $P_1 = \omega_1 \cdot T_1$; $P_2 = -\omega_2 \cdot T_2$; $v = r \cdot \omega_2$; $F = m\frac{dv}{dt}$; $T = r \cdot F$.

12.4.4   Neural Network Model for Accident Prevention

Control part of rolling stock is represented as neural network mathematical model:

- Input data set: $X = \{x_1, x_2, \ldots, x_n\}$
- Weights: $W = \{w_1, w_2, \ldots, wn, w_{n+1}\}$

- Fitness function: $F = x_1^* w_1 + x_2^* w_2 + \cdots + x_n^* w_n + w_n + 1$
- Result classes: $C = \{c_1, c_2, \ldots, c_m\}$
- Set of states: $I = \{i_1, i_2, \ldots\}$
- Set of properties: $E_i = \{x_1, x_2, \ldots, x_n\}$
- Set of clusters $C = \{c_1, c_2, \ldots\}$
- Members of cluster: $Mc = \{m_1, m_2, \ldots\}$
- Prototype-vectors: $Pc = \{p_1, p_2, \ldots, p_n\}$
- Sum vector: $S_m = P_c \cap E_m = \{s_1, s_2, \ldots, s_n\}$
- Vigilance: $\rho(0 < \rho \leq 1)$.

This model is proposed to detect dangerous state of the braking system, when a breakdown or crash is possible.

12.4.5 Multiple Criteria Target Function for Optimal Braking Control Task

Multiple criteria target function for braking system:

$$
\begin{cases}
F^{br}(DL, CL, EL) \to \min \\
DL = \Delta s \to 0 \\
CL = a(t) \to a* \\
EL = \frac{da}{dt} = const
\end{cases}
\tag{12.1}
$$

where Δs – distance between closed section and rolling stock – danger level criteria (DL):

- $a(t)$ – deceleration of rolling stock
- $a*$ – optimal deceleration for passengers – comfort level criteria (CL)
- da/dt – changes of deceleration and braking torque – optimal energy consumption criteria (EL)
- F^{br} – function for braking process optimization

12.4.6 Target Function for Routing and Scheduling Task of the Rolling Stock

Routing task for accident prevention consists of generating of new route and schedule for rolling stocks V moving on points P.

Target function for scheduling and routing is to arrange points for each train to reach a destination and assigning of time moments t to each train and each point:

- Train's schedule: $\sigma_v : P \to \{t_{v1}, t_{v2}, \ldots, t_{vs}\} \subset \Re$
- Point's schedule: $\sigma_{p1} : V \to \{t_{p1}, t_{p2}, \ldots, t_{pm}\} \subset \Re$

12.5 Algorithm for Task Solution

Clustering analysis is based on artificial neural network model. Clustering is one of adaptation methods. It gives self-training possibilities to the intelligent agents and allows classifying unorganized input data. This way, clustering give possibility to create new neurons on the output layer of the neural network. Clustering analysis is used when output classes are not predefined. Mathematical model for clustering consists of the following elements: set of input objects; set of attribute vectors for each object; dynamic set of clusters with variable size – at the beginning of analysis it is empty; dynamic set of prototype vectors for each cluster – attribute vector, which defines the class; set of cluster members for each cluster; set of sum vectors for each member – defines the correspondence of each member to prototype vector of the cluster; parameter of attentiveness – affects the precision of clustering analysis.

There are many algorithms for clustering analysis. The authors propose to use one of the adaptive resonance algorithms for intelligent agents. General algorithm consists of four main steps. The first step is the creation of the first prototype vector from the first input attribute vector. The second step is the beginning of the cycle, where a number of iterations depends on a number of objects. If this number is limited the number of iterations is finite. If objects are states of the process in mechatronic system, this number is unlimited, and clustering analysis is infinite. On the second step the next object is checked for membership of already created clusters. The step consists of three tests: test for attentiveness; comparing of attribute vector with prototype vector and attentiveness parameter; test for identity. If one of this tests failed a new cluster is created, otherwise the object gets membership in already existed clusters. The authors propose to use the clustering algorithm for state analysis of complicated processes in the mechatronic systems obtaining information from sensors.

- Step 1: The first prototype vector creation from the first property vector – $P_{c1} = E_{i1}$.
- Step 2: Cycle. Next object $i \in I$ is checked to be assigned to cluster from C.
- Step 2.1. Check for vigilance: $|P_c \cap E_i|/(\beta + |P_c|) > |E_i|/(\beta + n)$; False – Step 4.
- Step 2.2: Compare of with vigilance parameter: $|P_c \cap E_i|/|E_i| < \rho$; False – Step 4.
- Step 2.3. Check for identity: $|P_c| = |E_i|$?; False – Step 4.
- Step 3: Assign current object i to cluster members Mc (i = m ∈ Mc). Go to Step 2.
- Step 4: Create new prototype vector. Go to. Step 2.

Fig. 12.3 Input parameters
for experiment

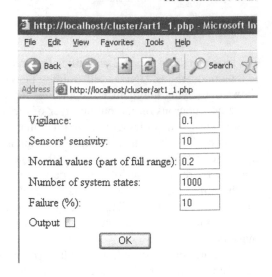

12.6 Computer Experiment

Experiment is devoted to test the workability of clustering algorithm for intelligent diagnostics system and using of special grid function to digitize data getting from sensors. The states of the mechatronic system are classified to separate dangerous or unusual situations. The authors propose to use the imitation modelling for the experiment.

The object of research is simplified to several abstract sensors of mechatronic system were taken for the experiment. The most important sensors of the research object are temperature and pressure sensors, 2 analog temperature sensors with different range, 1 pressure sensor and 2 binary sensors were selected.

The interface of the model with input parameters is presented in Fig. 12.3.

The railway model (Fig. 12.4) consists of 3 series block-sections; 2 rolling stocks of ER-2 type; 4 railway signals.

Each rolling stock and signal is equipped with receiving and transmitting devices that gives for possibility in multi-agent system.

Electrical part of the model consists of DC drive with characteristics of 8 DC motors, 1 switch to connect or disconnect electric drive to electric contact network. Two pairs of switches for acceleration and for breaking that changes direction of field current If flow. Braking branch contains braking resistance. Output of DC drive is electrical torque which handles mechanical part of rolling stock.

Mechanical part of rolling stock model gets electrical torque of electric drive as input transmitted to gears of rolling stock and wheels as well electrical and mechanical braking.

The control part of rolling stock (Fig. 12.5) contains two artificial neural network ANN controllers.

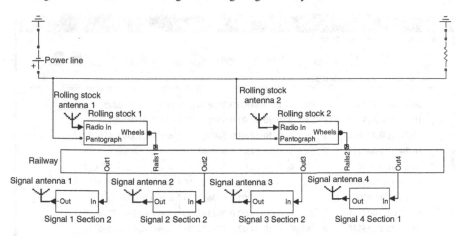

Fig. 12.4 Model of railway system

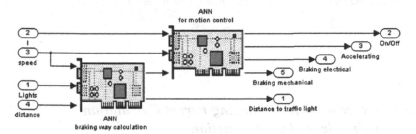

Fig. 12.5 Fragment of control part of computer model with ANN controllers

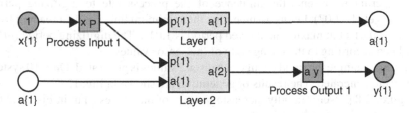

Fig. 12.6 Cascade-forward back-propagation neural network for braking way calculation

ANN controller (Balckars et al. 2008) for braking way calculation is trained to predict estimated distance of rolling stock which will be passed if braking process will begin at current speed. Input of this controller is wireless signal from railroad signal, current relative position of rolling stock and linear speed of rolling stock. Output of this controller is a distance to traffic light and braking way transmitted to motion controller of rolling stock. Cascade-forward back-propagation neural network (Fig. 12.6) is used for braking way calculation. It is trained using Levenberg–Marquardt algorithm.

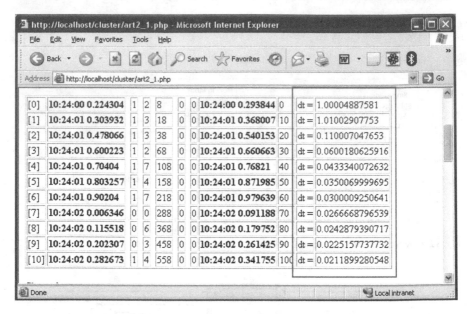

Fig. 12.7 Result of digitizing period calculation

12.6.1 Experiment for Digitizing Period Calculation Using Special Grid Function

This experiment presents the influence of the process rate to digitizing period (Greivulis et al. 2007). Let us assume, that the minimum time for data reading from sensors is 0.01 s but maximum allowed period is 1.01 s. The digitizing period (dt) is calculated according to the change rate of the sensor values.

For this example the rapid change of sensor 3 values is generated. Only 10 system states were generated. The results of generation are shown in Fig. 12.7.

Figure 12.8 presents rapidly increasing values of the process, but in Fig. 12.9 the changes of digitizing period are shown.

There are 6 clusters created by clustering algorithm. Cluster 0 contains regular values, but all others contain dangerous states of the system. The result of clustering is presented in Fig. 12.10.

12.6.2 Experiment of Clustering Algorithm with Special Grid Function

For this experiment 10,000 states have been generated.

According to the failure percent of all modelling situations, some values from the whole range are generated. Usually it is abnormal or dangerous state of the system

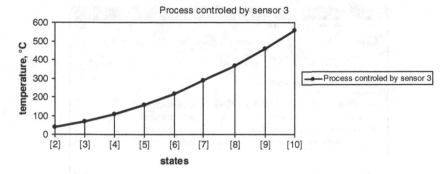

Fig. 12.8 The rapidly changing process

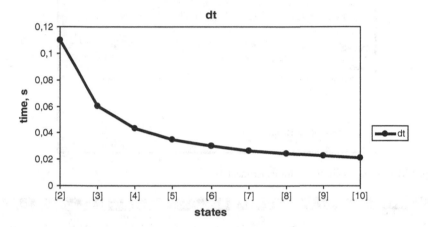

Fig. 12.9 Changes of digitizing period

process. In the case of unusual situation detection the intelligent diagnostics system warns user about this.

Data for the experiment are generated as uniformly distributed random values, which are the part of the sensor range (Fig. 12.11).

12.7 Experimental Device

The result of this work is train emergency braking device (Gorobetz et al. 2009). The invented device is proposed to increase safety on railway transport. It gives possibility to stop rolling stock automatically before closed signal timely.

In comparison with well-known devices that actuate braking only after the passing of closed signal, the invented device provides a train emergency braking and stopping before a closed section, even if it is not equipped with automatic

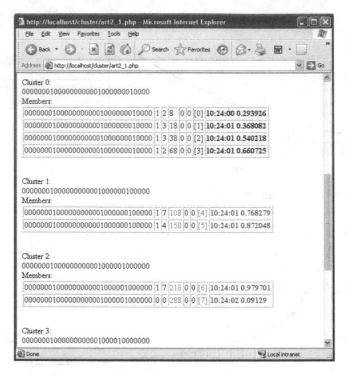

Fig. 12.10 Result of clustering for experiment 1

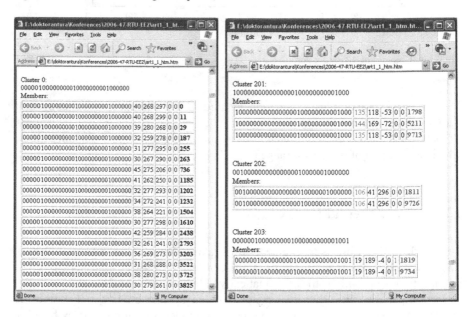

Fig. 12.11 Results of simulation of the clustering algorithm

Fig. 12.12 Functional prototype of train emergency braking device installed in the locomotive

locomotive signalling. The device also provides distance control and the emergency braking way calculation.

Figure 12.12 presents the functional prototype of the device, which can be installed on the trains. There are two traffic lights; the electric motor, sensors and wireless communication equipment are installed on the demonstrator.

According to the traffic light signal controller selects the appropriate engine speed. When burning a red light, the control system automatically stops the engine. In response to the light sensor, the control unit in addition to the fan is turned on and switches to another mode of operation.

Remote monitoring and control of the processes is possible using wireless communication. In real system, it could be dispatching control centres, from which it is possible to switch both signals and also take over control of the train speed.

12.8 Conclusions

Results of experiment show the possibility to use the proposed system as auxiliary safety device to prevent infringements of red signal crossing and crashes on the railway.

Technical efficiency of train emergency braking device is safety increasing of train movement on any railway section. Train emergency braking device allows stopping the train in time before the beginning of a closed block-section by automatic actuation of the emergency brake that prevents collision of trains.

The results show the ability of the proposed algorithm to classify dangerous and unusual states among the normal states. According to the failure percent of all modelling situations, some values from the whole range are generated. Usually it is abnormal or dangerous state of the system process. In case of unusual situation detection the intelligent diagnostics system warns user about this.

References

Hasegawa Y., Tsunashima H., Marumo Y., Kojima T. Detection of unusual braking behavior of train driver//In Proceedings of 21st International Symposium on Dynamics of Vehicles on Roads and Tracks(IAVSD09), 2009–166 pp.

S. J. Russel, P. Norvig. Artificial Intelligence. A Modern Approach, 2 edition. Prentice Hall, 2006, 1408 p.

Haykin S. Neural Networks. A Comprehensive Foundation. Second Edition, Prenctice Hall, 2006, 1104 p.

Luo R., Zeng J. Computer simulation of railway train braking and anti-sliding control. //In Proceedings of 21st International Symposium on Dynamics of Vehicles on Roads and Tracks (IAVSD'09), 2009–189 p.

M. Gorobetz, P. Balckars, A. Levchenkov, L. Ribickis, Modelling of Neural Network Controller for Scheduling Task in Intelligent Transport Systems //In Proceedings of 16th International Symposium "Towards more competitive European rail system", Zilina, Slovakia, 4–5 June 2008, 279–289 pp.

Greivulis J., Levchenkov A., Gorobetz M. Modelling of Clustering Analysis with Special Grid Function in Mechatronics Systems for Safety Tasks. //In Proceedings of 6th International Conference on Engineering for Rural Development, Jelgava, Latvia, 2007, 56–63 pp.

Yi Peng, Gang Kou. Perspective on Multi-Criteria Decision Analysis, 1985–2008. The 20th International Conference on Multiple Criteria Decision Making. Abstracts. Chengdu/Jiuzhaigou, China, 2009, p. 153.

M. Gorobetz, J. Greivulis, A. Levchenkov, P. Balckars, L. Ribickis, Patent Nr. LV13978. Train emergency braking device. 14.05.2009

Chapter 13
The Online Advertising Types of Choices Based on DEA Method

Xianglan Jiang, Yingjin Lu, and Wen-bo Yang

Abstract The evaluation criteria of online advertising types of choices are discussed under the background of China's current online advertising market continues to expand. With the development of Chinese economy and the Internet, more and more companies choose to advertise on the Internet. Because there are many online advertising types on the Internet and each of them has different function, some can make good profit and some not. Therefore, It's important for distributors and advertising agencies to make good choices by evaluating the efficiency of the online advertisement. In order to solve such problem, this paper establishes DEA model to evaluate the online advertising types of choices.

Keywords Data envelopment analysis · iAdTracker · Online advertising · Rich media advertising

13.1 Introduction

The market scale of China's online advertising is up to 10.6 billion yuan in 2007, increased by 75.3% compared with the last year. Appropriate advertising types can bring good result. Therefore, it has practical significance to research on the online advertising types of choices.

13.1.1 The Advantages of Online Advertising

The online advertising has a unique advantage compared with the three traditional media (newspapers, radio, television) and the outdoor advertising, which has been

X. Jiang (✉), Y. Lu, and W. Yang
School of Management and Economics, University of Electronic Science and Technology
of China, Chengdu, 610054, China
e-mail: xianglan196@yahoo.com.cn, luyingjin@uestc.edu.cn, yangwenbo76@163.com

Y. Shi et al. (eds.), *New State of MCDM in the 21st Century*, Lecture Notes
in Economics and Mathematical Systems 648, DOI 10.1007/978-3-642-19695-9_13,
© Springer-Verlag Berlin Heidelberg 2011

favored by people recently. It is an important part of implementing modern marketing media strategy. The unique advantages of Online advertising include six aspects.

1. Wide dissemination range
2. Strong interaction
3. Clear target
4. Accurate statistical of audience quantity
5. Flexible, low cost
6. Strong sense

13.1.2 The Characteristics of Online Advertising

Online advertising is applied most widely as online marketing. The following are some highlight characteristics of the online advertising:

1. Orientability
2. Traceability
3. Convenient and flexible operability
4. Interactivity

13.1.3 Types of Online Advertising

The main types of online advertising: horizontal banner, banner, button, vertical banner, square banner, couplet banner, floating button, network software ads, pop-up windows, interstitials rich media advertising, full screen ads, retractable rich media ads and video rich media ads.

There are so many types of online advertising and each has a certain effect. Therefore, the distributors are required to know which has the best effect, for the purpose of choosing better effect ads types in future advertising publicity and getting higher revenue later. When the distributors and advertising agencies choose accurate and reliable online advertising, they need to choose a method which is applicable to solve such problems. From the point of view of evaluation method, the decision-making problem of online advertising types of choices is a typical multi-objective decision-making problem. When there are many online advertising types competing for certain product or service, therefore, some online advertising propagandizer have good effect and some have bad effect. The main reason for distributors and advertising agencies to choose one rather than the overall online advertising is the evaluation criteria of online advertising types of choices. Through depth research and investigation, online advertising types of choices can make use of Data Envelopment Analysis (DEA) to evaluate their efficiency.

13.2 DEA Model

13.2.1 The Brief Introduction of DEA

The famous operations research experts A. Charnes, W.W. Cooper and E. Rhodes first presented a method called Data Envelopment Analysis (Charnes et al. 1978), referred to as DEA in 1978 to evaluate the relative effectiveness of inter-department (known as DEA effective). Their first model was named for the CCR model. From the perspective of production function, this model is an ideal and fruitful approach which is used to study "effective scale" and "technical efficiency" production department with multiple inputs especially with multiple outputs.

R.D. Banker, A. Charnes and W.W. Cooper proposed a model known as BCC in 1984.

Charnes, Cooper, B. Golany, L. Seiford, and J. Stutz presented another model (known as CCGSS model) in 1985. These two models are used to study "technology effective" between the production departments.

In 1986, for the purpose of further estimating the "efficient production frontier", Charnes, Cooper and Wei Quan-ling used the semi-infinite programming theory which first presented by Charnes, Cooper and K. Kortanek in 1962 to research the situation with infinitely multi decision-making units, and proposed a new data envelopment analysis model – CCW model (Charnes et al. 1986).

Charnes, Cooper, Wei Quanling and Huang Zhimin also presented the cone ratio data envelopment model – CCWH model in 1987 (Charnes et al. 1989). This model can be used to deal with the situation overmany inputs and outputs, and the choice of the cone can embody decision-makers' "Preferences". Flexible application of this model can use the DEA effective decision-making unit which identified by CCR model to classify or queue and so on.

Sebastian Lozano and Gabriel Villa proposed a model which can make each unit come to efficiency and make the total inputs of the whole decision-making units get the minimum while the total outputs do not decrease in 2004 (Lozano and Villa 2004). Tomoe Entani created interval DEA through evaluating decision making units from both optimistic and pessimistic evaluation perspectives (Entani et al. 2002). GR. Jahanshahloo presented a method to weigh the influence of inefficacy decision-making units after getting rid of an efficiency decision-making unit (Jahanshahloo et al. 2004).

These models as well as new models are being constantly improved and further developed.

Some of these models can be seen as the method of multi-objective decision-making problem which deals with multiple inputs (the smaller output the better) and multiple outputs (the greater input the better). It can prove that DEA effectiveness is equivalent to the multi-objective programming problem of pareto efficient solution (or non-dominated solutions). Data Envelopment Analysis (DEA) can be seen as a new method of statistical analysis. It estimates the efficient production frontier based on a set of input–output observations. In economics and econometrics, it often uses statistical regression and other statistical methods to estimate efficient production frontier. The production function estimated by these methods did not show the actual frontier, and in fact the function is non-effective. Since such estimates are from confusing effective decision-making unit with non-effective decision-making unit else. At the evaluation of the effectiveness, in addition to DEA method, there are other methods, but those methods are limited to nearly single-output situation. In contrast, DEA method has an absolute advantage over dealing with multi-input, especially multi-output problem. Moreover, DEA method not only can use linear programming to determine whether the corresponding point in decision-making unit is in the efficient production frontier level, but also can get much useful management information. Therefore, it is superior to some methods (including the use of statistical methods) and it is more useful. It is worth pointing out in particular that DEA method is purely technical and can be unrelated to the market (prices).

13.2.2 The Establish of Online Advertising DEA Model

In fact, for the online advertising, the smaller input index the better and the greater output index the better. In accordance with specific circumstances, it can choose the output index and input index separately to establish DEA model and resolve the evaluation problem of online advertising types of choices.

At present, there is no research on the evaluation problem of online advertising choices. Therefore, this paper can be seen as a new study in this aspect.

Make the online advertising types as Decision Making Unit (DMU), the total number is n, for decision making unit j, the smaller of the evaluation index x_{ji} ($i = 1, 2, \ldots, m$) the better(corresponding to the input index), the greater of the evaluation index y_{ji} ($i = 1, 2, \ldots, s$) the better (corresponding to the output index). Thus, DEA model can be established as follows:

$$(P1) \begin{cases} \max \quad \dfrac{u^T y_0 = y_{j_0} ms}{v^T x_0 = x_{j0}} \\ \text{s.t.} \quad \dfrac{u^T y_j}{v^T x_j} \leq 1, j = 1, 2, \ldots, n \\ v \geq 0 \\ u \geq 0 \end{cases}$$

Where $x_j = (x_{j1}, x_{j2}, \ldots, x_{jm}) y_j = (y_{j1}, y_{j2}, \ldots, y_{js})$, y_j = the output index of decision-making unit j (the greater the better); x_j = the input index of decision-making unit j (the smaller the better); u = the weight of y_j ; v = the weight of x_j; n = the number of decision-making units; m = the number of x_j index; s = the number of y_j index; $y_0 = y_{j0}$ expresses the evaluation index of the pending evaluation online advertising types; $x_0 = x_{j0}$ expresses the evaluation index of the pending evaluation decision-making units.

The model assumed that the constraint of the evaluation effectiveness is the effectiveness maximum of all online advertising is 1. It is from the principle that the maximum of the energy conversion efficiency is 1 in natural process. The main characteristic of the model is to make the weight u of the input index and the weight v of output index as the optimal variable to get pending evaluation decision-making unit j_0 effectiveness maximum. The effectiveness value of decision-making unit j_0 is equal to 1, or less than 1. The former expresses the decision-making unit is relatively effective, the latter expresses the decision-making unit is relatively ineffective. For the relative ineffective decision-making unit, the solution of the model can reflect the gap between the decision-making unit and effective decision-making unit. Solving the above model for the overall decision-making units in turn can get the relative efficiency of each decision-making unit. Generally speaking, different online advertising solutions are corresponding to different weights of evaluation index. The advantage of the weight choice method is that it is more objective than weight analysis method. Data envelopment analysis method, through the fine choice of the weight, makes the decision-making unit, which takes advantage over a few indexes but takes disadvantage over most indexes, be likely to be relative effective decision-making unit. Using this method, if the decision-making unit is appraised as relatively ineffective, it effectively shows that the decision-making unit has disadvantage over every index.

Fractional programming can be transformed into the following linear programming problem:

$$(P2) \begin{cases} \textbf{max} \quad u^T y_0 \\ \textbf{s.t.} \quad w^T x_j - \mu^T y_j \geq 0, j = 1, 2, \ldots, n \\ \quad\quad w^T x_0 = 1 \\ \quad\quad w \geq 0 \\ \quad\quad \mu \geq 0 \end{cases}$$

Through Charnes–Cooper transformation, the numerator part of the fractional objective function retained from the form and the value of the denominator transformed into 1. It became one part of the constraint condition. In this way, the fractional objective function became the linear objective function.

Definition 1. If the optimal solution of linear programming problem w^*, μ^* meets $\mu^T y_0 = 1$, the decision making unit DMU j_0 is weak DEA effective.

Definition 2. If the optimal solution of linear programming problem $w^* > 0$, $\mu^* > 0$ meets $\mu^T y_0 = 1$, the decision making unit DMU j_0 is DEA effective.

The evaluation indexes of the model are expressed by quantifying online advertising evaluation criteria. There are four main evaluation criteria of the online advertising: put number, running costs, click throughs, and revenue. Based on the guideline, the paper formulates the specific evaluation criteria which apply to the paper.

13.3 The Evaluation of Online Advertising Types of Choices

The major data refer to the evaluation criteria of online advertising are from iAdTracker. The data or estimate values are based on more than 100 Chinese mainstream online media brand graphics advertisement monitoring data statistics.

iAdTracker has monitored many network media long-term continuity for years through self-developed advertisement automatic monitoring system. It is the most authoritative and most comprehensive network monitoring system of China. It can help web marketers, advertising agencies and marketing staff of various product brands have better understanding of subtle changes of online advertising market development. At the same time, it has a more comprehensive control of the trend of the online advertising market at the first time. Therefore, it is of realistic significance of getting the research results by using its data.

Table 13.1 shows the data of put number, running costs, click throughs and revenue of the 13 major online advertising.

In Table 13.1, the put number x_1, expressed the put number of all kinds of online advertising every day; click throughs x_2 expressed the weighted average of advertisement browse, page browse, ads impression, ads click, click rate and ads display when Internet users see the online advertising; running costs x_3 expressed the costs expended on the online advertising publicity; the revenue expresses the profit of the online advertising publicity of the distributor, expressed by y_1. In the above – mentioned indexes, the smaller of the put number, click throughs and running costs the better, so they are rank in the input indexes of the evaluation model; the greater of the revenue the better, so it ranks in the output index of the evaluation model. The evaluation result is the relative effectiveness index of online advertising.

When evaluate the major online advertising, use the software DEA-Solver to run out the results of all types of online advertising data indexes, as shown in Table 13.2.

Table 13.1 The data index of the main online advertising types

Main online advertising types	Put number (time/day)	Click throughs (time/day)	Running cost (10,000 yuan)	Revenue (10,000 yuan)
Horizontal banner	64,272	61,672	13,474	29,884
Banner	26,881	25,653	7,485	20,453
Button	25,021	20,432	6,978	17,294
Vertical banner	12,885	10,281	2,582	10,837
Square banner	8,657	8,129	2,001	9,528
Couplet banner	1,753	1,354	1,880	8,256
Floating button	1,622	1,540	714	4,569
Network software ads	1,152	1,152	479	3,761
Pop-up winds	828	828	431	2,589
Interstitial rich media ads	704	651	336	2,697
Full screen ads	702	600	204	1,964
Retractable rich media ads	241	189	87	1,568
Video rich media ads	111	100	50	1,309

Table 13.2 DEA analysis results of the main online advertising types

No.	DMU	Score	Rank	Reference set (lambda)	
1	Horizontal banner	0.08472	13	F13	22.829641
2	Banner	0.10437	11	F13	15.624905
3	Button	0.09467	12	F13	13.211612
4	Vertical banner	0.16032	10	F13	8.2788388
5	Square banner	0.18188	9	F13	7.2788388
6	Couplet banner	0.46581	3	F13	6.3071047
7	Floating button	0.24443	8	F13	3.4904507
8	Network software ads	0.29991	6	F13	2.8731856
9	Pop-up winds	0.26515	7	F13	1.9778457
10	Interstitial rich media ads	0.32486	5	F13	2.0603514
11	Full screen ads	0.36774	4	F13	1.500382
12	Retractable rich media ads	0.68843	2	F13	1.197861
13	Vedia rich media ads	1.00000	1	F13	1

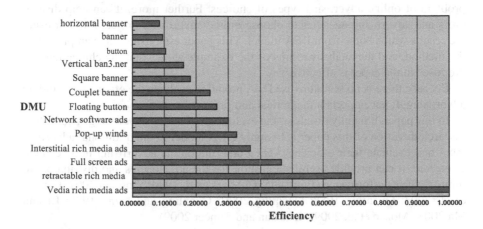

Fig. 13.1 DEA analysis results of the main Internet advertising type

Graph as shown in Fig. 13.1.

The Score in Table 13.2 is the evaluation results of DEA, from Table 13.2 and Fig. 13.1 can be seen that the relative efficiency 1 is video rich media advertising; the relative efficiency greater than 0.6 are retractable rich media ads and video rich media. Rich media ads mainly include interstitial rich media ads, retractable rich media ads, video rich media ads and so forth. By Fig. 13.1 can be seen the relative efficiency of rich media ads are greater than other online advertisements.

Therefore, we can know that in all types of online advertising, although, the input number and input costs of video rich media online advertising is not many at present, it is DEA effective. So when the distributors and advertising agencies choose the online advertising types, they can choose more video rich media online advertising. Or, more general, it is relatively good for enterprises to choose more rich media ads.

13.4 Conclusion

According to "the market share report of China's online advertising" which issued by iResearch, the rich media advertising continued to maintain rapid growth momentum in 2007 (iResearch 2007). Online advertising presented a rich media trend. "The explosive growth of network video ads becomes the direct cause of promoting the rapid development of rich media. The emergence of rich media ads and video advertisements integrates accurate audience matching with effective interaction. The marketing value of network media has been mined further. Rich media will become the development trend of future network ads and the proportion of rich media ads will also increase year by year. It expects the proportion of rich media advertising market will reach 10.1% in 2011."

Through introducing the basic concept of DEA and online advertising, this paper establishes DEA model of online advertising evaluation. On this basis, it researches on the evaluation efficiency of the online advertising types and solves the evaluation problem of online advertising types of choices. Further more, it can help distributors and advertising agencies to choose online advertising project through using the results which come from DEA model. This paper establishes an example to test the method, and the analysis results of the example shows that the choice method proposed in the paper is effective.

Because there is no literature use DEA model to evaluate the efficiency of online advertising. It has important theoretical and practical significance.

In this paper, it mainly discusses the evaluation of online advertising. The further research direction of this paper is to apply DEA model to the traditional advertisement and evaluate their efficiency. Then take the online advertising into account. Therefore, it can provide useful suggestion for the ad agencies and distributors to improve their performance (Jing 1995; Charnes et al. 1990; Yingjian 2004; Cooper et al. 2007; Quanling 1988; Quanling 2000; Quanling and Ming 1989; Li and Ma 2008; Alonso et al. 2009; Koksalan and Tuncer 2009).

Acknowledgements We thank the anonymous referee for useful comments. We also thank Gang Feng for his help.

References

Charnes A., Cooper W.W., Rhodes E. (1978) Measuring the Efficiency of Decision Making Units [J]. European Journal of Operational Research, 6 (2) , (1978) :429–444
He Jing (1995) Data Envelopment Analysis and Application with only Output(Input) [J]. Systems Engineering Journal 10 (2) :48–55
A. Charnes, W.W. Cooper, Z.M. Huang, D.B. Sun (1990) Polyhedral cone-ratio DEA models with an illustrative application to large commercial banks, Journal of Econometrics 46 (1990) 73–91
Charnes A., Cooper W.W., Wei Q.L. (1986) A Semi-infinite Multicriteria Programming Approach to Data Envelopment Analysis with Infinitely Many Decision Making Units[R].The University of Texas at Austin, Center for Cybernetic Studies Report CCS 551,1986

A. Charnes, W.W. Cooper, Q.L. Wei, Z.M. Huang (1989) Cone ratio data envelopment analysis and multi-objective programming, International Journal of Systems Science 20 (1989) 1099–1118

F. Yingjian (2004) Foundation and practice of network marketing [M]. Beijing: Tsinghua University Press 2004: 195–220

W.W. Cooper, L.M. Seiford, K. Tone (2007) Data Envelopment Analysis—A Comprehensive Text with Models, Applications, References and DEA-Solver Software[M]. Springer Science Business Media 2007:438–473

W. Quanling (1988) DEA Method of Evaluation Relative Effectiveness [M]. Beijingï£¡FRenmin University of China Press

W. Quanling (2000) Data Envelopment Analysis (DEA) [J]. Chinese Science Bulletin 45 (17):1493–1796

W. Quanling, Y. Ming (1989) DEA Introduction and CCR model – Data Envelopment Analysis (1) [J]. System Theory and Practice, 1989 (1) :58–69

iResearch. 2007 Chinese online advertising market share report. http://www.ecidea.net/ ecidea{_}article/b4/201.html

Sebastian Lozano, Gabriel Villa (2004) Centralized Resource Allocation Using Data Envelopment Analysis [J]. Productive Analysis, 22, (2004):143–16

Han-Lin Li, and Li-Ching Ma (2008) Ranking Decision Alternatives By Integrated Dea, Ahp And Gower Plot Techniques, International Journal Of Information Technology & Decision Making 2(2008): 241–258

Tomoe Entani, Yu Maeda, and Hideo Tanaka (2002) Dual model of interval DEA and its extension to interval data [J]. European Journal of Operational Research. 136 (2002):32–45

S. Alonso, E. Herrera-Viedma, F. Chiclana, and F. Herrera (2009) Individual And Social Strategies To Deal With Ignorance Situations In Multi-Person Decision Making, International Journal Of Information Technology & Decision Making 2(2009):313–333

G.R. Jahanshahloo, F. Hosseinzadeh, N. Shoja, G. Tohidi, S. Razavyan (2004) a method for detecting influectial observations in radial DEA models, Applied Mathematics and Computation 1(2004):415–421

Murat Koksalan, and Ceren Tuncer (2009) A Dea-Based Approach To Ranking Multi-Criteria Alternatives, International Journal Of Information Technology & Decision Making 1(2009): 29–54

Chapter 14
Examination of Decision Support Systems for Composite CBA and MCDA Assessments of Transport Infrastructure Projects

Michael Bruhn Barfod, Anders Vestergaard Jensen, and Steen Leleur

Abstract This paper examines decision support systems (DSS) for composite appraisals of transport infrastructure projects comprising both cost-benefit analysis (CBA) and multi-criteria decision analysis (MCDA). Two DSS, REMBRANDT and COSIMA, are in this context examined and compared using a case study dealing with alternatives for a new high-speed railway line in Sweden. The REMBRANDT system is based on multiplicative value functions and makes use of pair wise comparisons on both attribute and criteria level. The COSIMA system is based on additive value functions and makes use of the REMBRANDT technique using pair wise comparisons on attribute level and swing weights on criteria level. One difference between the two approaches is the focus the COSIMA system puts on combining the CBA and MCDA results influencing, among other things, the way that the final results are expressed. Finally, a recommendation for the use of DSS within transport infrastructure appraisals is set out.

Keywords COSIMA · Decision support systems · Multi-criteria decision analysis · REMBRANDT

14.1 Introduction

Two DSS, REMBRANDT[1] and COSIMA[2], are compared with the purpose of identifying the most appropriate DSS for transport infrastructure assessments including both CBA and MCDA. The first DSS examined, which is widely used and based on acknowledged methods, comprises the REMBRANDT technique (Lootsma 1992)

---

[1] Ratio Estimation in Magnitudes or deci-Bells to Rate Alternatives which are Non-DominaTed.
[2] Composite Model for Assessment.

M.B. Barfod (✉), A.V. Jensen, and S. Leleur
Department of Transport, Technical University of Denmark, Bygningstorvet 115, 2800 Kgs. Lyngby, Denmark
e-mail: mbb@transport.dtu.dk(MichaelBruhnBarfod)

Y. Shi et al. (eds.), *New State of MCDM in the 21st Century*, Lecture Notes in Economics and Mathematical Systems 648, DOI 10.1007/978-3-642-19695-9_14, © Springer-Verlag Berlin Heidelberg 2011

using pair wise comparisons for rating of the alternatives and determination of the criteria weights. The results of the CBA are in this system compared and included as an additional criterion in the MCDA. Hence, the result of the system is a relative weight-score for each alternative reflecting its performance in the composite appraisal.

The second DSS examined, the so-called COSIMA approach (Leleur 2000; Salling et al. 2007), provides a framework for adding value functions determined in a MCDA to impacts monetarily assessed in a CBA. The DSS comprises the REMBRANDT technique (Lootsma 1992) using pair wise comparisons for rating of the alternatives and swing weights (von Winterfeldt and Edwards 1986) for the determination of criteria weights. However, the COSIMA system does not convert the CBA into an additional MCDA criterion. Instead the value functions computed in the MCDA are added to the CBA results using a balance indicator assigning shadow prices to the MCDA criteria. Subsequently, the resulting total value is divided by the investment costs. Hence, the result is a total rate for each alternative reflecting its attractiveness in the appraisal as a function of the weight-set between the CBA and MCDA.

The input for the two DSS examined was generated using a case study. For this purpose a decision conference (Phillips 2006) was set up where various stakeholders and decision-makers under the guidance of a facilitator were producing input to the DSS in form of their preferences.

The purpose of the examination and comparison of the two DSS is to determine which is the most appropriate for conducting composite appraisals of transport infrastructure projects. The REMBRANDT system provides a conventional widely used and theoretical well founded framework, while the COSIMA framework is more recent and founded on a somewhat different set of axioms. However, the two systems provide the decision-makers with the same type of result, only expressed differently. The question treated in this context is hence if the COSIMA system provides the decision makers with some information that the REMBRANDT system does not provide and vice versa.

Finally, conclusions are drawn including a recommendation based on the case study for the most appropriate system for conducting composite appraisals of transport infrastructure projects, and research questions defining future work in the context of composite DSS and their use in decision making processes are set out.

14.2 Value Measurement

Value measurement theory is introduced in the following in order to underpin the theory behind the two DSS, which makes use of different types of value function methods and scales.

Value function methods basically produce the assessments of the performance of alternatives against individual criteria. This together with inter-criteria information reflecting the relative importance of the different criteria, w_j, makes it possible to

give an overall evaluation of each alternative indicative of the decision-makers preferences. The simplest and most widely used form of value function method, which
is used by the COSIMA system, is the additive model (Belton and Stewart 2002):

$$V(a) = \sum_{j=1}^{m} w_j v_j(a) \qquad (14.1)$$

Considerably more complicated in appearance, but as easy to use, is the multiplicative model which the REMBRANDT system makes use of (Ibid):

$$V(a) = \prod_{j=1}^{m} [v_j(a)]^{w_j} \qquad (14.2)$$

In its analytical expansion the multiplicative model seems prohibitive compared
to the additive model. However, it requires only the addition of a single parameter (w), which defines all interaction terms. Therefore, the type of interaction
it models is rather constrained (Von Winterfeldt and Edwards 1986). Moreover,
additive aggregation is the form that is most easily explained and understood by
decision-makers from a wide variety of backgrounds, while not placing any substantially greater restrictions on the preference structures than more complicated
aggregation formulae (Belton and Stewart 2002).

If the criteria are structured as a value tree (for details see for instance Goodwin
and Wright (2004)) then the alternatives must be scored against each of the bottom
level criteria. These values need to be assessed on an interval measurement scale,
i.e. a scale on which the difference between the points is the key factor. A ratio of
values will only be meaningful if the zero point on the scale is absolutely and unam-
biguously defined. Thus to construct a scale it is necessary to define two reference
points and to assign numerical values to these points. The minimum and maximum
points on the scale can be defined in a number of ways (here 0 and 100). However,
it is very important to distinguish between a local and a global scale.

A local scale is defined by the set of alternatives that are under consideration. The
alternative which performs best within a specific criterion is for instance assigned
the score 100 and the alternative which performs least well is assigned the score 0.
All other alternatives will then receive intermediate scores which reflect their performance relative to the end points. The use of local scales allows a relative fast
assessment of values and it can be very useful for preliminary "roughing out" of a
problem, or if operating under time constraints. However, some issues in the context
of local scales will be discussed later.

A global scale is defined by reference to a broader set of possibilities. The end
points may be defined by the ideal and the worst possible performance within the
particular criterion (extreme endpoints), or by the best and worst performance that
can realistically occur. The definition of a global scale requires more preparatory
work than a local scale. However, it has the advantages that it is more general than
a local scale and that it can be defined before consideration of specific alternatives.
This also means that it is possible to define criteria weights before consideration of
alternatives.

The important point is that subsequent analysis, including the assessment of the weights (w_j), must be consistent with the chosen scaling. Once the reference points of the scale have been determined consideration must be given to how other scores are to be assessed. In this paper it has been chosen to use direct rating of the alternatives using pair wise comparisons. The pair wise comparisons have shown to be a strong decision aid when making decisions in groups, and hence are appropriate for use at the decision conference in the treated case study.

14.3   The Case Study

The case study examined concerns an assessment of alternatives for a new high-speed railway line in Sweden named Ostlänken. More specific the case study considers a section between Bäckeby and Norrköping about 100 kilometres south of Stockholm. The work described in this paper was done as a part of a research project granted by the Swedish Research Council – VINNOVA.

Four alternatives describing different alignments were to be compared. These are in the following referred to as alternative R, BS, BL and G. A conventional cost-benefit analysis (CBA) in accordance with a national socio-economic manual was carried out at a preliminary stage. The calculations were carried out according to Swedish standards (Hiselius et al. 2009), and the outcome expressed as benefit-cost rates (BCR) are shown in Table 14.1.

The results clearly indicate that alternative R is the economically most feasible project. However, all four alternatives were beneficial seen from a CBA based point of view. The decision-makers decided to complement the assessment with some strategic (non-monetary) impacts as well, as they felt that the CBA did not cover all aspects of the decision problem. Hence, there was a need for a more comprehensive assessment. Eight different criteria were in this context defined describing what was lacking in the CBA. Effort was made to avoid double counting; however, the decision-makers were aware of the risk of this. The eight complementing criteria will in the following be referred to as C1 to C8.

Using a decision conference as proposed by Phillips (2006) the input needed for the two DSS were produced. The participants were experts with extensive knowledge within the respective criteria and each assessment made was documented in a protocol (developed for the purpose). This procedure makes it possible for decision makers as well as the general public to review each judgment made; thereby the decision process becomes more transparent.

Table 14.1 CBA information for the four alternatives

	R	BS	BL	G	Method	Unit
Costs	1,509	1,774	2,033	2,167	CBA	M SEK
Benefits	3,018	3,138	3,138	3,140	CBA	M SEK
BCR	2.00	1.77	1.54	1.45	CBA	

The following two sections describe the two DSS applied to the case study and their results are presented.

14.3.1   The REMBRANDT System

A systematic pair wise comparison approach is one of the cornerstones of the REMBRANDT system by Lootsma (1992). REMBRANDT makes use of a procedure for direct rating which requires the decision makers to consider all possible pairs of alternatives with respect to each criterion in turn, in order to determine which of the pair is preferred and to specify the strength of preference according to a semantic scale (or the associated numeric 0–8 scale). The approach is a further development of the Analytical Hierarchy Process (AHP) by Saaty (1977) and it proposes to overcome three issues regarding the theory behind AHP.

First, the direct rating in REMBRANDT is on a logarithmic scale (Lootsma 1988) which replaces Saaty's 1 – 9 fundamental scale. Second, the eigenvector method originally used in AHP is replaced by the geometric mean, which avoids potential rank reversal (Barzilai et al. 1987). Third, the aggregation of scores by arithmetic mean is replaced by the product of alternative relative scores weighted by the power of weights obtained from analysis of hierarchical elements above the alternatives (Olson 1996). The differences between AHP and REMBRANDT have been treated very thoroughly by Olson et al. (1995) and will for this reason not be treated any further in this paper.

In the REMBRANDT system the ratio value r_{jk} on the geometric scale is expressed as an exponential function of the difference between the echelons of value on the geometric scale δ_{jk}, as well as a scale parameter . Lootsma considers two alternative scale parameters γ to express preferences. For calculating the weight of criteria, $\gamma = \ln\sqrt{2} \approx 0.347$ is used. For calculating the weight of alternatives on each criterion, $\gamma = \ln 2 \approx 0.693$ is used.

The participants at the decision conference were using the REMBRANDT technique based on pair wise comparisons of the four alternatives within all eight criteria (C1 to C8). Moreover an additional economic efficiency criterion (C9), was added as the alternatives were also compared on the basis of their BCR. Then scores were calculated within all nine criteria (C1 to C9) using logarithmic regression and the geometric mean method. Finally, criteria weights were determined using pair wise comparisons as well, and aggregated values for the alternatives were calculated. The participants decided to test 3 different weight-sets at 0.85, 0.70 and 0.55 (derived by the pair wise comparisons) where the relative weight of the BCR-criterion was changed: This was done to test the robustness of the result, see Table 14.2.

The results in Table 14.2 depict BS as the most attractive alternative within the three weight-sets as this alternative obtain the highest relative values. However, if testing other weight-sets the resulting ranking could be different. The participants at the decision conference were confident that the total BCR-weight should be

Table 14.2 Results from REMBRANDT

Total BCR weight – relative value	0.85	0.70	0.55
R	0.316	0.246	0.184
BS	**0.319**	**0.354**	**0.380**
BL	0.214	0.267	0.322
G	0.151	0.133	0.114

somewhere within the investigated interval. Hence, BS proved to be a robust choice when combining the CBA and MCDA results in the REMBRANDT DSS.

14.3.2 The COSIMA System

The COSIMA system is based on adding non-monetary MCDA-criteria to the monetary CBA-impacts. The model uses the argument that the MCDA-criteria are additive to the CBA-impacts if proper value-functions for the MCDA-criteria are computed and assigned with shadow prices describing each criterion's importance.

COSIMA is developed with the purpose of handling a situation where criteria (strategic impacts) cannot be monetised in a comprehensive and transparent manner. This aspect is in COSIMA ensured through the determination of appropriate weights for the MCDA-criteria and appropriate value function scores for the alternatives. The COSIMA system has proven its worth for providing efficient decision support in various types of infrastructure projects; for example the Copenhagen-Ringsted railway line (Salling et al. 2008) and the Øresund fixed link (Salling et al. 2007). Unlike the REMBRANDT system the COSIMA system does not include the BCRs in the MCDA module. Instead, COSIMA "translates" the MCDA-part into a CBA-like 'language' keeping the economic information provided by the BCRs intact at all times. For readers interested in the specific calculations – not accounted for here – see Leleur (2008) or Hiselius et al. (2009).

COSIMA features several possible options for assigning scores to the alternatives and weights to the criteria. More or less any MCDA-technique can be applied to the system. For the case study it was, however, decided to apply the REM-BRANDT technique for the scoring of alternatives (similar to Sect. 14.3.1) and the swing weight technique (Von Winterfeldt and Edwards 1986) for the determination of criteria weights.

The resulting scores from the pair wise comparisons within the eight MCDA-criteria were consequently transformed into value function scores applying the previously mentioned local scale using a linear assumption, see Table 14.3.

The swing weight technique was used for the determination of criteria weights. The participants at the decision conference were asked to rank the criteria in order of importance and subsequently assess the value of the swing from best to worst

Table 14.3 Value function scores derived using the REMBRANDT technique

	C1	C2	C3	C4	C5	C6	C7	C8
R	1	0	35	0	0	11	0	39
BS	100	18	35	100	100	5	100	0
BL	70	25	100	51	100	0	100	0
G	0	100	0	15	55	100	2	100

Table 14.4 Swing weights for the eight criteria

Criteria	Swing weights	Normalised weights
C1	90	0.19
C2	80	0.17
C3	100	0.21
C4	60	0.12
C5	70	0.14
C6	20	0.04
C7	60	0.12
C8	5	0.01

performance within each criterion in turn compared to the swing from best to worst within the highest ranked criterion. The weights are shown in Table 14.4.

The participants had already decided to test 3 different weight-sets where the relative weight of the BCR compared to the MCDA-part was the varying parameter (see Sect. 14.3.1). The COSIMA DSS was consequently calibrated in accordance with the weights in Table 14.4 and the balance (trade-off) between MCDA and CBA. Summarising the calculations and the process concerning the case it can be noted that the analysis is based on the use of cost-benefit analysis (CBA) using a national manual and multi-criteria analysis (MCDA) using a decision conference. The CBA produces results that can be measured in monetary units – here million Swedish Kroner (M SEK). The MCDA on the other hand produces results that by comparison with the CBA results can be calibrated to 'assessment M SEK'. In order to obtain a total value for an examined alternative M SEK and 'assessment M SEK' is added. This mix between M SEK and the fictitious 'assessment M SEK' is expressed by the unit 'attractiveness M SEK'. The result can also be presented as a total rate of return (TRR), where the result in 'attractiveness M SEK' is divided by the investment costs, see Table 14.5. In this context it should be noted that the process based on input (scoring of alternatives, determination of criteria-weights and balancing the CBA and MCDA) makes it possible to provide a transparent evaluation process involving the decision-makers. Thus, the result of the COSIMA analysis is that it by use of stakeholder and decision-maker involvement is possible to add a value to the MCDA-criteria which can be compared to the monetary CBA values. Thereby, the result scheme in Table 14.5 indicates the 'gain' by choosing an alternative that performs well within the MCDA instead of the alternative that performs the worst. Thus, seen from a strategic point of view the decision-makers in the current case study would gain most from the investment by choosing the BS alternative.

Table 14.5 Result scheme from the COSIMA analysis with the CBA weight set to be 0.70

	R	BS	BL	G	Method	Unit
Costs	1,509	1,774	2,033	2,167	CBA	M SEK
Benefits	3,018	3,138	3,138	3,140	CBA	M SEK
B/C rate	2.00	1.77	1.54	1.45	CBA	
C1	7	555	387	0	MCDA	'Assessment M SEK'
C2	0	87	123	493	MCDA	'Assessment M SEK'
C3	215	215	616	0	MCDA	'Assessment M SEK'
C4	0	370	188	54	MCDA	'Assessment M SEK'
C5	0	431	431	236	MCDA	'Assessment M SEK'
C6	14	6	0	123	MCDA	'Assessment M SEK'
C7	0	370	370	8	MCDA	'Assessment M SEK'
C8	12	0	0	31	MCDA	'Assessment M SEK'
Total MCDA	248	2,033	2,114	945	MCDA	'Assessment M SEK'
Total value	3,266	5,171	5,252	4,058	CBA+MCDA	'Attractiveness M SEK'
Total rate	2.16	2.91	2.58	1.88		

Table 14.6 Rankings of the alternatives at different weight-sets

CBA weight	0.85		0.70		0.55	
	REMBRAND T	COSIM A	REMBRAND T	COSIM A	REMBRAND T	COSIM A
R	2	2	3	3	3	3
BS	1	1	1	1	1	1
BL	3	3	2	2	2	2
G	4	4	4	4	4	4

14.3.3 Comparison of the Two DSS

Two DSS have in this paper been applied to the same case study revealing the same results. In Table 14.6 the rankings of the alternatives at the different weight-sets are depicted for both DSS. This clearly shows that the two DSS also provide the same results on second and third level in the rankings.

The difference on the results of the two DSS, however, consists in the way they are expressed. The REMBRANDT DSS provides the decision-makers with weight-scores expressing the alternatives relative performance against each other. The COSIMA DSS on the other hand provides the decision-makers with a somewhat more informed result. The total rate (TRR) from COSIMA features both the CBA result and the MCDA result expressed in one single rate. The REMBRANDT system is a theoretical well founded system which have been applied to various decision problems, see e.g. (Van den Honert and Lootsma 2000), and on which other systems can be measured. Given that the COSIMA DSS provides the same result (in this case) as REMBRANDT the DSS seems most appropriate for use within transport infrastructure planning as the results provide the decision-makers with two-way information containing both an economic argument and a strategic argument. This makes the COSIMA results more useful especial when the results need to be transparent and defendable to the public.

However, the use of local scales within the COSIMA system arises some issues. Firstly, projects assessed using this scale cannot easily be compared with other projects as the scale presupposes a closed system. This way the endpoints within the assessment define the scale, in contradiction to a global scale which considers the extreme endpoints in defining the scale. If projects are not assessed using the same scale it is obvious that they cannot be compared to each other. Secondly, the segregation between the attributes within some criteria can in some cases almost be negligible. However, the use of a local scale will anyway imply large differences between these attributes. For example in a case where $a_1 = 0.33$, $a_2 = 0.33$ and $a_3 = 0.34$ the value function scores will be 0 for a_1 and a_2, but a_3 will obtain the score 100. This does not seem reasonable as the alternatives perform almost identical in the assessment of the criterion. A means to overcome this problem is to perform a check of all the criteria in the assessment using the swing weight method. If this check reveals some criteria where the swing from the best to the worst performing alternative almost does not exist (a lower boundary can be set by the decision-makers), the criteria should be removed from the analysis as they do not contribute to the segregation between the alternatives and therefore are without significance for the appraisal task in hand.

Furthermore, it is most likely that the weightings of the criteria will diverge dependent of the decision-maker or stakeholder that makes the judgments. Thus, this level of the assessment can be seen as more subjective than the attribute level where the issues are broken down into simple objective judgments within each criterion. Therefore, it can be beneficial to evaluate different stakeholder's preferences in order to obtain a broader perspective for the final decision making.

14.4 Conclusion and Perspective

This paper has compared the COSIMA and REMBRANDT DSS with the purpose of determining which of the techniques are most appropriate for decision making within transport infrastructure projects. Both systems seem well suited for decision making in groups, thus the differences between the systems relate to their procedural operations. COSIMA and REMBRANDT are both considered to be effective tools for aiding decision problems (especially in groups) faced with multiple criteria. However, for the use within transport planning the COSIMA DSS seems most appropriate. The COSIMA DSS provides the decision-makers with a more informed result as the TRR express both the feasibility using the BCR and the added value of the assessed MCDA-criteria.

The COSIMA DSS, moreover, provides the opportunity for using other MCDA techniques depending on the character of the assessment task. A future research task is in this respect to outline a framework of MCDA techniques that are appropriate to apply to COSIMA at different levels of complexity and at the same time be used by a decision conference.

References

Barzilai, J., Cook, W., Golany, B.: Consistent weights for judgement matrices of the relative importance for alternatives. Operations Research Letters **6: 3**, 131–134 (1987)

Belton, V., Stewart, T.J.: Multi Criteria Decision Analysis – An Integrated Approach. Kluwer (2002)

Goodwin, P., Wright, G.: Decision Analysis for Management Judgment. Wiley (2004)

Hiselius, L., Barfod, M.B., Leleur, S., Jeppesen, S.L., Jensen, A.V., Hjalte, K.: Helhetsorienterad Utvärdering av Kollektivtrafikåtgärder. University of Lund (2009)

Leleur, S.: Road Infrastructure Planning – A Decision Oriented Approach. Polyteknisk Press (2000)

Leleur, S.: Systemic Planning. Polyteknisk Press, pp. 169–197 (2008)

Lootsma, F.A.: Numerical scaling of human judgement in pairwise-comparison methods for fuzzy multi-criteria decision analysis. In: Mitra, G. (ed.), Mathematical Models for Decision Support, Springer-Verlag, pp. 57–88 (1988)

Lootsma, F.A.: The REMBRANDT system for multi-criteria decision analysis via pair wise comparisons or direct rating. Report 92–05, Faculteit der Technische Wiskunde en Informatica, Delft University of Technology, Netherlands (1992)

Olson, D.L.: Decision Aids for Selection Problems. Springer-Verlag (1996)

Olson, D.L., Fliedner, G., Currie, K.: Comparison of the REMBRANDT system with analytic hierarchy process. European Journal of Operational Research **82**, 522–539 (1995)

Phillips, L.D.: Decision Conferencing. A working paper LSEOR **06.85** (2006)

Saaty, T.L.: Scenarios and priorities in transport planning: Application to the Sudan. Transport Research **11**, 343–350 (1977)

Salling, K.B., Leleur, S., Jensen, A.V.: Modelling decision support and uncertainty for large infrastructure projects: The CLG-DSS Model of the Øresund fixed link. Decision Support Systems **43**, 1539–1547 (2007)

Salling, K.B., Landex, A., Barfod, M.B.: Appraisal of the railway line between Copenhagen and Ringsted by the use of a decision support model named COSIMA-DSS. Accepted for Journal of Advanced Transportation (2008)

Van den Honert, R.C., Lootsma, F.A.: Assessing the quality of negotiated proposals using the REMBRANDT system. European Journal of Operations Research **120**, 162–173 (2000)

Von Winterfeldt, D., Edwards, W.: Decision Analysis and Behavioral Research. Cambridge University Press (1986)

Chapter 15
An Entropy-Weighted Clustering Method for Environmental Pollution Assessment in China

Gang Kou, Qiaoli Sun, and Yi Peng

Abstract Environmental pollution becomes a major problem in China recently. There have been many studies about the interrelationships among environmental pollution, economic development and foreign direct investment (FDI). However, most of the studies only focus on the relationship between environmental pollution and economic development. In this paper, we proposed an entropy-weighted clustering method to assess the impacts on environment using the data of different waste-disposals, GDP and foreign total investment from all provinces in China excluding Tibet between 2002 and 2007. A dynamic synthetic evaluation process which integrates various algorithms such as Dynamic synthetic evaluation, K-means clustering analysis and simple weighted average methods is proposed for the entropy-weighted clustering method. The results indicate that the proposed method can precisely measure the level of environmental pollution and also identify the impacts of economic development and FDI on environment.

Keywords Dynamic synthetic evaluation · Environmental pollution in China · Foreign total investment · GDP · K-means clustering analysis

15.1 Introduction

Environmental pollution is a major problem in China. Along with economic and social development, environmental deterioration threatens national living space. Industrial wastes disrupt agricultural ecological balance seriously, and also impact healthy of human directly or indirectly. As the result of rapid development in foreign investment, some industries with high pollution were transferred to China from developed countries, making environment even worse.

Y. Peng (✉), G. Kou, and Q. Sun
School of Management and Economics, University of Electronic Science and Technology of China, Chengdu, 610054, China
e-mail: pengyicd@gmail.com, kougang@yahoo.com

Y. Shi et al. (eds.), *New State of MCDM in the 21st Century*, Lecture Notes   177
in Economics and Mathematical Systems 648, DOI 10.1007/978-3-642-19695-9_15,
© Springer-Verlag Berlin Heidelberg 2011

There have been many studies about environmental pollution, economic development and FDI. Most of the studies only investigate the relation between two of them. In this research, we aim to assess the difference on waste-disposals, economic development and foreign total investment in different provinces in China. Gross Domestic Product (GDP) and Foreign Direct Investment (FDI) are selected as the indicators for economic development and foreign total investment, respectively.

There are many related studies by Chinese scholars recently. Pan and Yu (2005) tested the relationship between the FDI and the pollution in Jiangsu, Zhejiang and Shanghai and found that the causality really exists in the sample of the aggregated data of the three provinces. Peng and Bao (2006) investigated the dynamic interactions between economic growth and environmental pollution by using a Chinese time series data set of six pollution indicators. Zhang (2007) studied the effect of Chemical Industry FDI on environment in China. Xiong (2008) tested correlatiion of FDI and environmental pollution in China. Guo and Han (2008) constructed a simultaneous model to assess the effect of foreign direct investment (FDI) on environment. Su and Wang (2008) found that the relation of economic development and environmental pollution in Shandong province does not conform to the typical shape of EKC (Environmental Kuznets Curve). Zhou and Ying (2009) structures a framework for analyzing the relationship between foreign direct investment and industrial pollution based on transmission mechanism. He and Ran (2009) analyzed the relationship between environment and per capital income in the east, center and west areas of China. Peng (2010) investigated the difference between eastern and western areas about environmental pollution and economic development.

There are also many researches about environmental pollution, GDP and FDI outside China. Galeotti (2007) analyzed relationship between economic development and environmental quality, and reconsidered the explanations of "Environmental Kuznets Curve". Merican et al. (2007) examined the relationship between pollution and foreign direct investment for five ASEAN nations and found that pollution is linked to FDI activities for Malaysia, Thailand, and the Philippines. Wu and Hsu (2008) examined effect of foreign direct investment (FDI) on economic growth, and found that FDI alone plays an ambiguous role in contributing to economic growth based on a sample of 62 countries covering the period from 1975 through 2000. Ma (2009) tends to study the benefit of China using foreign capitals in perspective of FDI's impacts on GDP according to data from 1985 to 2008. Acharyya (2009) found a statistically significant long run positive, but marginal, impact of FDI inflow on GDP growth in India during 1980–2003. Tamazian et al. (2009) found that both economic and financial developments are determinants of the environmental quality in BRIC economies. Wang (2010) analyzed influence factors, mechanism, environmental regulations and so on of FDI environmental effect, using Spearman rank correlation coefficients.

The contributions and findings of this paper are as follows:

1. In this research, Provinces in China are evaluated based not only on disposal and emissions of industry, GDP, but also on foreign total investment and regional characteristic. Researcher studied relationship between environmental pollution and economic development, or relationship between environmental pollution and

foreign direct investment. But study considering relation among them simultaneously is rather few.

2. Various MCDM and data mining algorithms are integrated In this research, such as dynamic synthetic evaluation, simple weighted average and K-means cluster analysis.

3. Some environment assessment and improvement suggestions are provided according to the research results.

The rest of this paper is organized as: Sect. 15.2 introduces the proposed method, Sect. 15.3 presents details of the experimental study and analyses the results; Sect. 15.4 summarizes the paper.

15.2   Entropy-Weighted Clustering Method

The proposed method is as the following diagram. The details and introductions to the method are listed in Sects. 15.2.1 to 15.2.2 (Fig. 15.1).

15.2.1   Entropy-Weighted Method

"Entropy" was proposed by Rudolf Clausius in 1865 (Goldstein and Joel 2004), and is used to measure the homogeneous degree of energy in space. Then C. E. Shannon, the father of informationism, demonstrated how to calculate the information entropy (Hoffman et al. 1998). In this research, we introduced the concept of entropy to measure the information, which is a term in information theory, also known as the average amount of information.

Entropy is a quantitative measurement of uncertainty. If there was a system with n kinds of results, and each result have a probability $P_i (i = 1, 2 \ldots n)$. Then the entropy of this system is:

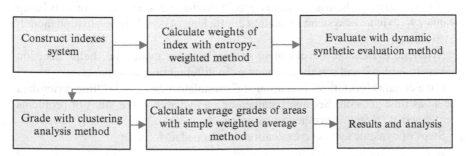

Fig. 15.1 Entropy-weighted clustering method

$$E = -\sum_{I=1}^{n} P_i \ln P_i.$$

Note that $0 \le P_i \le 1$; $\sum_{i=1}^{n} P_i = 1$.

Entropy can be used to calculate objective weights of indexes. For a certain index, if there's much difference among those alternatives, the index will give decision makers much information, and it can be regarded as important factor. While if there's little difference, the index can be treated as useless.

Definition 1. (Entropy of index)(Liang and Wu 2009): Assume that m represents number of alternatives, and n represents number of indexes. In matrix (m, n), entropy of the index j is:

$$H_j = -k \sum_{i=1}^{m} \theta_{ij}^* \ln\theta_{ij} \quad (j = 1, 2, 3, \ldots n.) \tag{15.1}$$

Where $\theta_{ij} = y_{ij} / \sum_{i=1}^{m} y_{ij}, k = \dfrac{1}{\ln m}$. ($y_{ij}$ denotes value of evaluation).

Definition 2. (Entropy-weighted of index)(Liang and Wu 2009): Entropy-weighted of the index j is:

$$w_j = (1 - H_j) / \left(n - \sum_{j=1}^{n} H_j \right) \quad (j = 1, 2, 3, \ldots n) \tag{15.2}$$

Obviously, $0 \le w_j \le 1$, and $\sum_{j=1}^{n} w_j = 1$.

15.2.2 Dynamic Synthetic Evaluation

Generally speaking, there are five concerns in synthetic evaluation: (1) objects being evaluated; (2) indexes system; (3) weight coefficient; (4) synthetic evaluation model; (5) evaluator.

Synthetic evaluation, development of single index evaluation, helps decision makers to evaluate and sort the alternatives in different time and spaces.

For a certain object, there is continued accumulative data called "time series data sheet" as time goes on. Because parameters are dynamic, these kinds of problems are defined as "dynamic synthetic evaluation".

Steps of dynamic synthetic evaluation are defined as follows:

1. Calculate entropy-weighted of indexes

The entropy-weighted of indexes is calculated using entropy-weighted method. Note that weight of a certain index is not the same in different years.

Table 15.1 Reference table assignment of Z

Assignment (Z)	Explanation
0.1	Recent data is extremely important than dated data
0.3	Recent data is slightly important than dated data
0.5	Recent data is as same important as dated data
0.7	Dated data is slightly important than recent data
0.9	Dated data is extremely important than recent data
0.2, 0.4, 0.6, 0.8	Between the neighbor conditions above

2. Calculate time-weight vectors

Time-weight vectors represent the relative importance among samples over time. To compute time-weight vectors, "time dimension" Z is defined as follows:

$$Z = \sum_{t=1}^{q} \frac{q-t}{q-1} \lambda_t^*$$ (15.3)

Table 15.1 shows assignment and explanation of Z which is given by experts, and it's between 0 and 1. Closing to 1 represents decision makers would pay more attention to recent data, but care less for dated data. Simply, when $\lambda = 0.9$, it means the earlier a year is, the more important the data in the year is. When $\lambda = 0.5$, it means all data of different years have the same importance. And when $\lambda = 0.1$, it means only the data of the most recent year will be considered.

When Z was given, time-weight vectors are calculated using nonlinear programming. Time-weight vectors are fixed as long as Z is given. Hence, this method combines subject and object perspective.

Time-weight vectors can be formulated as (q denotes number of years):

$$\max \left(-\sum_{t=1}^{q} \lambda_t * \ln\lambda_t \right)$$
$$s.t \begin{cases} Z = \sum_{t=1}^{q} \frac{q-t}{q-1}\lambda_t \\ \sum_{t=1}^{q} \lambda_t = 1, \lambda_t \in [0, 1] \end{cases}$$ (15.4)
$$t = 1, 2, \ldots, q.$$

In the above function, λ means the importance of time series (Huang 2009).

3. Calculate standard matrix B

Because indexes are different in dimension, original matrixes need to be standardized. There are three kinds of indexes (benefit type, cost type and moderate type) which are standardized as follows:

$$y_{ij} = \begin{cases} \frac{x_{ij}-x_{min}}{x_{max}-x_{min}} & \text{where } x_{max} \neq x_{min} \\ 1 & \text{where } x_{max} = x_{min} \end{cases}$$

$$y_{ij} = \begin{cases} \frac{x_{max}-x_{ij}}{x_{max}-x_{min}} & \text{where } x_{max} \neq x_{min} \\ 1 & \text{where } x_{max} = x_{min} \end{cases} \quad (15.5)$$

$$y_{ij} = \begin{cases} 1 - \frac{|x-x^*|}{x_{max}-|x-x^*|} & \text{where } x_{max} \neq x_{min} \\ 1 & \text{where } x_{max} = x_{min} \end{cases}$$

4. Calculate increase matrix C

In this research, we take into account not only current value but also relative increase value of indexes.

In increasing matrix, elements are denoted as follows:

$$c_{ij}^t = b_{ij}^t - b_{ij}^{t-1} (t = 2, 3, \ldots, q) \quad (15.6)$$

As it is described above, c_{ij}^t represents the increasing of indexes from T_{t-1} to T_t. So increasing matrix can be expressed as follows:

$$C_t = \begin{bmatrix} c_{11}^t & & c_{1n}^t \\ & \ddots & \\ c_{m1}^t & & c_{mn}^t \end{bmatrix} = (c_{ij}^t)_{m*n}, \ t = 2, 3, \ldots, q.$$

5. Combine current and increasing value of indexes

$$e_{ij}^t = \alpha b_{ij}^t + \beta c_{ij}^t \quad (15.7)$$

A novel synthetic evaluating matrix is as follows (S represents objects to be evaluated and h represents indexes):

$$E_t = \begin{array}{c} \\ S_1 \\ \vdots \\ S_m \end{array} \begin{array}{c} h_1 \cdots h_n \\ \begin{bmatrix} e_{11}^t & & e_{1n}^t \\ & \ddots & \\ e_{m1}^t & & e_{mn}^t \end{bmatrix} \end{array} = (e_{ij}^t)_{m*n}, \ t = 1, 2, \ldots, q.$$

Coefficients (α and β) denote the relative importance of current and increasing value of indexes. $0 \leq \alpha, \beta \leq 1$ and $\alpha + \beta = 1$. The higher α is, the more important current value is. On the contrary, the lower α is, the more important increasing value is. If $\alpha = 1$ and $\beta = 0$, it means only current value of index considered; If $\alpha = 0$ and $\beta = 1$, only increasing value of indexes concerned.

To analyze and compute conveniently, we transform E_t into E_i^0 ,which is based on objects being evaluated. (T represents time, and h represents index.)

$$
E_i^0 = \begin{array}{c} \\ T_1 \\ \vdots \\ T_q \end{array} \overset{h_1 \cdots h_n}{\begin{bmatrix} e_{i1}^1 & e_{in}^1 \\ & \ddots & \\ e_{i1}^q & e_{in}^q \end{bmatrix}} = (e_{ij}^t)_{q*n} \ i = 1, 2, \ldots, m.
$$

Positive ideal matrix is composed of the highest value of benefit-indexes and the lowest value of cost-indexes. Negative ideal matrix is composed of the lowest value of benefit-indexes and the highest value of cost-indexes.

6. Calculate distances

$$
d_i^+ = d(E_i^0, E^+) = \sqrt{\sum_{t=1}^q \lambda_t \left[\sum_{j=1}^n w_{tj}(e_{ij}^t - e_{ij}^+)^2 \right]}, \ i = 1, 2, \ldots, m
$$

$$
d_i^- = d(E_i^0, E^-) = \sqrt{\sum_{t=1}^q \lambda_t \left[\sum_{j=1}^n w_{tj}(e_{ij}^t - e_{ij}^-)^2 \right]}, \ i = 1, 2, \ldots, m \quad (15.8)
$$

The relative similarity to ideal solution is:

$$
T_i = d_i^- / (d_i^+ + d_i^-) \tag{15.9}
$$

Alternative is evaluated by its relative similarity T_i. T_i is high when E_i^0 is close to E^+ and far away from E^-. So objects being evaluated get more priority, and they will be sorted in front of others.

15.3   Empirical Study and Results

15.3.1   Construct Indexes System

Data of different waste-disposals, GDP and foreign total investment from all provinces in China excluding Tibet between 2002 and 2007 was collected.

About indexes system, there's no formalism about industrial wastes emissions and disposals until now. So we proposed a new indexes system through the following methods: (1) literatures review; (2) information from the Internet; (3) discussion with experts.

In Table 15.2, B represents benefit-indexes, and C represents cost-indexes. So there are seven benefit-indexes and seven cost-indexes in this system.

Table 15.2 Indexes system

Waste-water	B1 Number of facilities to dispose waste-water
	B2 Standard amount of waste-water's emission
	C1 Overall quantity of waste-water's emission
Waste-gas	B3 Number of facilities to manage waste-gas
	B4 Removal quantity of sulfur dioxide
	B5 Removal quantity of soot
	B6 Removal quantity of dust
	C2 Emissive quantity of sulfur dioxide
	C3 Emissive quantity of soot
	C4 Emissive quantity of dust
Waste-solid	B7 Disposal quantity of waste-solid
	C5 Emissive quantity of waste-solid
Environmental pollution and destroy events	C6 Number of environmental pollution and destroy events
	C7 Direct economic losses of pollution

Table 15.3 Entropy-weighted of indexes

	W02	W03	W04	W05	W06	W07
B1	0.07265	0.07541	0.07188	0.07148	0.07089	0.05615
B2	0.07237	0.07089	0.06624	0.06833	0.06231	0.07722
B3	0.09731	0.07851	0.09189	0.08261	0.08778	0.08385
B4	0.15603	0.17421	0.14997	0.17034	0.15135	0.16277
B5	0.13472	0.14752	0.17004	0.12184	0.09823	0.14177
B6	0.07369	0.06626	0.06864	0.06968	0.07113	0.07985
B7	0.26190	0.26997	0.24281	0.25564	0.28978	0.23550
C1	0.02771	0.01962	0.01832	0.02798	0.03353	0.01949
C2	0.02391	0.02108	0.01897	0.02046	0.02391	0.02449
C3	0.01699	0.01844	0.01702	0.02324	0.02127	0.03122
C4	0.01831	0.01422	0.03095	0.04226	0.04014	0.03623
C5	0.01332	0.01829	0.01317	0.01332	0.01635	0.01530
C6	0.01512	0.01263	0.02124	0.02002	0.02230	0.02422
C7	0.01599	0.01295	0.01886	0.01281	0.01102	0.01196
sum	1.00002	1	1	1.00001	0.99999	1.00002

15.3.2 Calculate Weights of Index with Entropy-Weighted Method

As is shown in Table 15.3, W02 represents weights of 14 indexes in 2002. Obviously, sum of those indexes' weights are approximate to 1.

From Table 15.3, we can see that entropy-weighted of B4, B5 and B7 are higher than others. That is to say, these indexes have significant effects to decision makers' evaluation.

15.3.3   Evaluate with Dynamic Synthetic Evaluation Method

In this research, recent data is extremely important comparing to dated data, so we set $Z = 0.1$. Then time-weight vectors can be calculated through the nonlinear programming as follows:

$$\lambda\,(6, 1) = (0.00302; 0.00852; 0.02543; 0.07537; 0.22372; 0.66391)$$

Obviously time-weight of 2007 year (0.66391) is extremely important than others.

When Combine current and increasing value of indexes, we select three representative groups of parameters: $\alpha = 0, \beta = 1; \alpha = \beta = 0.5; \alpha = 1, \beta = 0$. The first group means considering increasing value only, the second one means increasing value as important as current value, and the last group means considering current value only.

In this research, GDP and foreign total investment are also processed by dynamic synthetic evaluation method. Entropy-weighted and time-weight vectors are assigned for every year.

In Table 15.4, "Disposal01" denotes evaluation of industrial waste-disposals from 2002 to 2007. "FI" indicates evaluation of foreign total investment.

15.3.4   Clustering Analysis (Peng et al. 2008)

To analyze and compare "disposal", "GDP" and "FI" in different provinces in China, results are clustered by K-means algorithm in SPSS. ($k = 3$, maximum iteration $= 20$.)

In Table 15.5, there are three clusters in "Disposal01". Six provinces are ranked as level 1, sixteen as level 2, and eight as level 3. More provinces belong to level 2 than level 1 and 3.

As shown in Table 15.6, disposal of Tianjin is in level 1 when only considering increasing value of indexes, but in level 3 in other conditions. It also means that Tianjin has strong strength in disposing industry wastes at present, but its development trend is not optimistic.

Table 15.4 Results of dynamic synthetic evaluation

	T ($\alpha = 0, \beta = 1$)		
	Disposal01	GDP01	FI01
Beijing	0.4631	0.2942	0.2248
Tianjin	0.4886	0.1212	0.1963
Hebei	0.4524	0.3771	0.0755
......	......	......	......
Ningxia	0.5231	0.0076	0.0128
Xinjiang	0.5000	0.0723	0.0320

Table 15.5 Results of clustering analysis

T α = 0 β = 1	Disposal01	Final cluster centers	0.4402	0.5095	0.4615
		Number of cases in each cluster	8	6	16
	GDP01	Final cluster centers	0.8283	0.1151	0.3528
		Number of cases in each cluster	3	17	10
	FI01	Final cluster centers	0.3454	0.7161	0.0824
		Number of cases in each cluster	4	2	24

Table 15.6 Results of clustering analysis

	Disposal01	GDP01	FI01
Beijing	2	2	2
Tianjin	1	3	3
Hebei	2	2	3
......	......	......	......
Ningxia	1	3	3
Xinjiang	1	3	3

Table 15.7 Average results of provinces in China

	Disposal-ave	GDP-ave	FI-ave
Beijing	2.6667	2.0000	2.0000
Tianjin	2.3333	3.0000	2.3333
Hebei	2.0000	2.0000	3.0000
......	......	......	......
Ningxia	1.6667	3.0000	3.0000
Xinjiang	2.3333	3.0000	3.0000

15.3.5 Calculate Average Levels of Areas with Simple Weighted Average Method

1. Calculate average level of each province with simple weighted average method

To analyze more comprehensively, average level of provinces is computed by simple weighted method. For example, "disposal-ave" of Beijing is average of Disposalo1, Disposal55, and Disposal10. That is $(2 + 3 + 3)/3 = 2.6667$ (Table 15.7).

2. Calculate average level of each area

As we know, there is much difference between east and west area of China, such as economics and population. In this paper provinces are gathered according to Chinese regional characteristic. So "disposal-ave" of Huabei area is average of Beijing, Tianjin, Hebei, Neimenggu and Shanxi province. That is $(2.6667 + 2.3333 + 2 + 1.3333 + 2)/5 = 2.0667$.

15.3.6 Results and Analysis

Average levels are gathered by K-means clustered analysis (k = 3) once more.

1. High GDP area (Huadong area)

East China, the most developed area of this country, owns the highest utilization of funds and resources. Among this area, Jiangsu and Shanghai absorb most of foreign total investment, and both of them are above the average level of Huadong area. However foreign total investment of Anhui province is lower than average level. Disposal of Jiangsu and Shandong province are the worst in Huadong area.

   To sum up, we suggest that waste-disposals should be strengthened in Jiangsu and Shandong province, and foreign total investment should be absorbed more in Anhui province.

2. Medium GDP areas (Huabei area, Huazhong area and Huanan area)

Guangdong and Hainan absorb most of the foreign total investment, followed by Beijing and Tianjin. Obviously, GDP of Guangdong is ahead of others. Waste-disposals of Hubei and Hunan province are the worst.

   So we suggest waste-disposals should be strengthened and more foreign total investment should be absorbed in Hubei and Hunan province simultaneously.

3. Low GDP areas (Dongbei area, Xinan area and Xibei area)

Foreign total investment of these areas is rather few except Liaoning province. And GDP of Liaoning and Sichuan province is better than others.

   In a word, these areas are developing. The most important thing we should do is to promote economical development and attract more foreign investors. Some provinces such as Heilongjiang should reduce the waste-disposals.

15.4 Conclusion

In this paper, an entropy-weighted clustering method is proposed to evaluate the interrelationships among waste-disposals, GDP and foreign total investment in China. There are three groups of results for different parameters, and simple weight average is applied to get synthetic results. According to Chinese regional setting and economic development situation, thirty provinces in China are divided to three regions. The pollution assessment results of different provinces in China in the same region are compared and analyzed.

   The results show that economic development of Dongbei, Huanan and Xibei areas is lower than the average level, and total foreign investment amount in these areas is low. Furthermore, waste-disposals should be reinforced in some provinces such as Heilongjiang, Shanxi, Jilin, Hunan, Hubei province. Besides, some provinces such as Anhui, Hunan and Hubei province should try to attract more foreign investment.

Acknowledgements This research has been partially supported by a grant from the National Natural Science Foundation of China (#70901011), the Fundamental Research Funds for the Central Universities and the Research Project on Humanities and Social Sciences under the Grant No. 10YJC630163, Ministry of Education of China.

References

Acharyya, J.: FDI, Growth and the environment: Evidence from India on CO2 emission during the last two decades [J]. Journal of Economic Development. 2009, 34 (1): 43–58.

Galeotti, M.: Economic growth and the quality of the environment: Taking stock [J]. Environment, Development and Sustainability. 2007:427–454.

Goldstein, S., Joel, L.L.: On the (Boltzmann) entropy of non-equilibrium systems. Physica D: Nonlinear Phenomena. 2004: 53–66.

Guo, H., Han, L.: Foreign Direct Investment, Environmental Regulation and Environmental Pollution [J]. Journal of International Trade. 2008.

He, C., Ran, M.: Environmental Pollution and Economic Growth: Research Based on China's Provincial Data for Difference Areas [J]. China Population Resources and Environment. 2009.

Hoffman, D.K., Wei, G.W., Zhang, D.S., Kouri, D.J.: Shannon-Gabor wavelet distributed approximating functional [J]. Chemical Physics Letters. 1998: 119–124.

Huang Z.: Research on Dynamic Comprehensive Evaluation Performance Evaluation in Enterprise Application: [Master degree theses], Anhui: University of science and technology of China. 2009.

Liang, G., Wu, J.: Job assessment method based on hierarchical entropy-TOPSIS [J]. Information Technology. 2009:158–160.

Ma, X.: An Empirical Analysis on the Impact of FDI on China's Economic Growth [J]. International Journal of Business and Management June. 2009: 76–80.

Merican, Y., Yusop, Z., Zaleha, M. N., Hook, L.: Foreign Direct Investment and the Pollution in Five ASEAN Nations [J]. Journal of Economics and Management. 2007, 1(2): 245–261.

Pan, S., Yu, M.: Causality Test on the FDI and Environment Pollution in Jiangsu, Zhejiang and Shanghai [J]. Journal of International Trade. 2005.

Peng, L.: Comparative study of Eastern and western economy and environment's relation in China: [Master degree theses], Shanxi: Northwest A&F university. 2010: 1–49.

Peng, S., Bao, Q.: China's Economic Growth and Environmental Pollution: An Empirical Test Based on Generalized Impulse Response Function [J]. China Industrial Economy. 2006.

Peng, Y., Kou, G., Shi, Y., and Chen, Z.: A Descriptive Framework for the Field of Data Mining and Knowledge Discovery. International Journal of Information Technology & Decision Making. 2008, 7(4): 639–682.

Su, Q., Wang, L.: Study on the Environmental Kuznets Curve Characteristics of Industrial 'Three Wastes' in Shandong Province. Research of Soil and Water Conservation. 2008.

Tamazian, A., Chousa, J.P., Vadlamannati, K.C.: Does higher economic and financial development lead to environmental degradation: Evidence from BRIC countries. 2009, 37(1): 246–253.

Wang, Y.: The Analysis on Environmental Effect of Logistics Industry FDI. iBusiness. 2010: 300–304.

Wu, J., Hsu, C.: Does Foreign Direct Investment Promote Economic Growth? Evidence from a Threshold Regression Analysis. Economics Bulletin. 2008, 15(12): 1–10.

Xiong, M.: FDI and environmental pollution: [Master degree theses], Hunan: Hunan University, 2008, 1–53.

Zhang, Y.: Study on Environmental Effects of Chemical Industry's FDI in China: [Master degree theses], Zhejiang: Zhejiang University, 2007: 1–65.

Zhou, L., Ying, R.: Foreign Direct Investment and Industrial Pollution. China Population Resources and Environment. 2009.

Chapter 16
Unconstrained Two-Objective Land-Use Planning Based-on NSGA-II for Chemical Industry Park

Ming Xu and Zongzhi Wu

Abstract A model of unconstrained two-objective land-use planning for chemical industry park was constructed applying the theory of multi-objective optimization in this paper and the two objectives were the minimum potential loss of life (PLL) and the maximum total benefit. The optimization process of the model was designed and realized based on non-dominated sorting genetic algorithm-II (NSGA-II) and vector evaluated genetic algorithm (VEGA). Some conclusions were made from this study: (1) The model of unconstrained two-objective land-use planning for chemical industry park proposed in this paper was feasible and NSGA-II that adopted optimization method was effective and all Pareto-optimal solutions could be found. (2) These corresponding land-use patterns had good reference values for land-use planning of chemical industry park.

Keywords Chemical industry park · Land-use planning · NSGA-II · Unconstrained two-objective optimization

16.1 Introduction

Chinese chemical industry parks were developed since 1995 and more than 60 chemical industry parks authorized by the Central Government and provincial people's governments had been built until 2006 (Fang 2007). Once the accidents of fire, explosion or diffusing from leaked hazardous chemicals in chemical industry parks were happened, they would lead to disasters that would made many peoples been dead or seriously injured. Therefore, how to carry out rational land-use planning for

Z. Wu (✉)
China Academy of Safety Science and Technology, Beijing 100012, China
e-mail: wuzongzhi@sina.vip.com

M. Xu
School of Engineering & Technology, China University of Geosciences, Xueyuan Street 29, Haidian District, Beijing 100083, China
e-mail: xuming@cugb.edu.cn

Y. Shi et al. (eds.), *New State of MCDM in the 21st Century*, Lecture Notes in Economics and Mathematical Systems 648, DOI 10.1007/978-3-642-19695-9_16, © Springer-Verlag Berlin Heidelberg 2011

chemical industry parks has become one of core problems needed to be addressed by all levels of governments and managers of parks (Lijun et al. 2007). Industrial locations and determination of optimal land-use patterns are complex multi-criteria decision analysis (MCDA) problems (Ming et al. 2008). The land use planning decisions were made mainly based on safety distances in China and some samples of land use planning were carried out based on quantitative area risk assessment (QARA) in a few areas (Zongzhi et al. 2006). However, those were risk-target single-objective programming. At present, the corresponding research work about multi-objective land use planning for chemical industry park was limited in China. This paper attempted to explore this area. A model of unconstrained two-objective land-use planning for chemical industry park was established applying the theory of multi-objective optimization in this paper. The optimization process of the model was designed and realized based on NSGA-II. Multi-objective optimization problems were described in detail in literature (Augusto et al. 2006; Shi 2009; Shi 2010; Li 2009; Chen et al. 2010). Deb introduced NSGA-II primitively in literature (Kalyanmoy et al. 2002). The robustness of NSGA-II was very good, so it had been applied widely in many fields (Bin and Shifeng 2007).

16.2   Decision Processes of Land-Use Planning for Chemical Industry Park and the Mathematics Model of Two-Objective Optimization

Birgitte Rasmussen (Rasmussen et al. 1999) proposed a decision processes of land-use planning for chemical industry park which included three phases and seven steps. The author considered this decision making procedure included the following four steps (Ming et al. 2008):

- Development of alternatives
- Determination of objectives and consequences
- Generation of Pareto-optimal frontiers
- Determination of the optimum alternative

A general objective in land-use planning for chemical industry park was to manage industrial risks in such a way that net land development benefit was maximized and the various categories of costs and unwanted consequences were minimized. Now only risk objective and economic objective were considered and a two-objective optimization model was established. The risk objective was the minimum total potential loss of life (PLL) and the economic objective was maximum total benefit of land development. The formulation was following as:

$$\min PLL = \iint\limits_{A} IR(x, y) \cdot D_P(x, y) dx dy \qquad (16.1)$$

$$\max Benefit = \iint\limits_{A} b(x, y) dxdy \qquad (16.2)$$

$$s.t. \quad x, y \in A \qquad (16.3)$$

$$PLL \leq LSPLL \qquad (16.4)$$

$$Benefit \geq EBenefit \qquad (16.5)$$

Where *PLL* and *Benefit* were total potential loss of life and economic benefit corresponding an alternative respectively. $IR(x, y)$, $D_P(x, y)$ and $b(x, y)$ were individual risk (IR) function, population density function and economic benefit function of dot (x, y) in the area of concern respectively. *LSPLL* was the limitation standards of *PLL* and *EBenefit* was expected benefit.

16.3 Example 1

16.3.1 Description of Example and Mathematical Model

An example was illustrated in Fig. 16.1. The area of concern region was $100 \, \text{hm}^2$ and it had been divided into 16 equalarea square cells ($250 \times 250 \, \text{m}$) (Number of the cells was illustrated in Fig. 16.1. The origin of the coordinates was the center of No. 4 cell.). The land development types (LDTs) for each cell were undeveloped, industrial, residential and agricultural. Only industrial cells had risk and its risk could impact other cells. Assuming for simplicity that Individual Risk (*IR*) was inversely proportional to the distance squared to the industrial cells, *IR* of 10^{-4} would be attenuated to 10^{-5} along $250 \, \text{m}$. We supposed each cell in this case was a mesh and only calculated the *IR* of each mesh center. It was considered as average risk of this cell. Assuming the population density functions and economic benefit functions of every LDT of each cell were uniform distribution. The basic data was

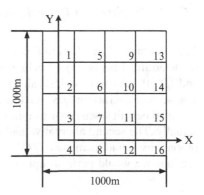

Fig. 16.1 Sketch map of the cells in the area studied

Table 16.1 Data of LDTs

LDTs	Encoding	$IR_{self\,ij}$ (fatalities $\cdot a^{-1}$)	d_{ij} (persons $\cdot$ hm^{-2})	b_{ij} (10^6CNY $\cdot$ hm^{-2})
Undeveloped	0	0	0	0
Industrial	1	10^{-4}	1.2585	744.34
Residential	2	0	600.0000	150.70
Agricultural	3	0	0	1.14

fed from literatures (Shenzhen Municipal Bureau of Statistics 2008) mainly. We had calculated the required data and they were shown in Table 16.1.

The unconstrained two-objective minimizing model was following as:

$$\min PLL = \sum_{i=1}^{4}\sum_{j=1}^{4}(IR_{\text{selfij}}$$

$$+ \sum_{k=1}^{m} IR_{\text{indk}} \cdot 0.1 \cdot (\frac{\sqrt{(X_k - X_{ij})^2 + (Y_k - Y_{ij})^2}}{250})^{-2})D_{P}ij \cdot S_{ij} \quad (16.6)$$

$$\min -Benefit = -(\sum_{i=1}^{4}\sum_{j=1}^{4}b_{ij} \cdot S_{ij}) \quad (16.7)$$

Where *PLL* was total potential loss of life and *Benefit* was economic benefit corresponding to an alternative. IR_{selfij}, D_{Pij}, b_{ij}, S_{ij} were the *IR* of itself produced, population density and economic benefit per cell and the area of the cell that was on the *i*th row and the *j*th column in concern area respectively. IR_{indk} was the *IR* of the *k*th industrial cell had itself. (X_k, Y_k) was the coordinate of the *k*th industrial cell and (X_{ij}, Y_{ij}) was the coordinate of the *i*th row and the *j*th column cell. *m* was the number of industrial cells in one chromosome and its value was a integer from 1 to 16.

16.3.2 Evaluation Criterions of Optimizing Method Effectiveness

The total number of LUPs in this case was $4^{16} = 4294967296$. Three LUPs could be determined easily: ① all cells were undeveloped, ② all cells were residential, and ③ all cells were industrial. The first alternative was no risk and no benefit. The second alternative was maximal benefit when risk was 0. The third one was maximal benefit when risk was minimal (>0). The first one didn't meet the demand actually. The second alternative and the third one were the extremenesses and the probability found them was $1/4^{16}$ using random searching methods. In following sections we would perform optimization using NSGA-II and VEGA and discuss their effectiveness. Therefore we proposed three evaluation criterions of optimizing method effectiveness in term of the laws controlling risk:

1. Two alternatives of all residential cells and all industrial cells could be found.
2. Residential cells and industrial cells could be distinguished effectively and they would be rejection each other.
3. Could find all alternatives including different amount of industrial cells.

16.3.3   Encoding

This paper adapted integer encoding method. The LTDs of each cell were expressed with one integer in range from 0 to 3 and 0, 1, 2 and 3 represented undeveloped type, industrial type, residential type and agricultural type respectively. All 16 cells were arranged by order and a chromosome had 16 bits, it represented an alternative. It was illustrated in Fig. 16.2.

16.3.4   Selection, Crossover and Mutation Operators

Simulated binary crossover operator (SBX) was used to perform cross-operation and parameter-based mutation operator was used to perform mutation-operation (Deb 2000). A binary tournament selection was used to perform selection.

16.3.5   Calculation Results

C++ programming language and Matlab7.5 software were used to program calculation procedure. The parameter settings of NSGA-II were: population size set 100, maximum generations set 200, η_c-the distribution index for SBX set 3, η_m-the distribution index for mutation set 20, p_c-crossover probability set 0.9 and p_m-mutation probability set 0.1, a probability 0.5 of each variable was chosen. The Pareto efficient frontier composed by 14 Pareto optimal solutions (marked with diamond blocks) was illustrated in Fig. 16.3. The abscissa was risk objective (*PLL*,

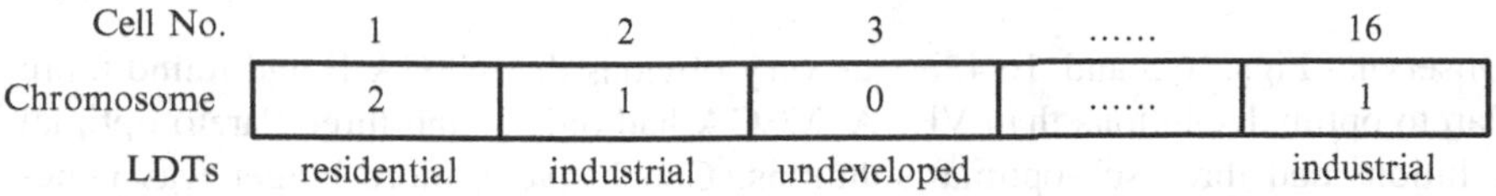

Cell No.	1	2	3	......	16
Chromosome	2	1	0	......	1
LDTs	residential	industrial	undeveloped		industrial

Fig. 16.2 Sketch map of the mode of coding and encoding in one chromosome

Fig. 16.3 Efficient frontier
of *PLL-Benefit*

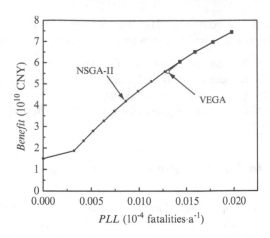

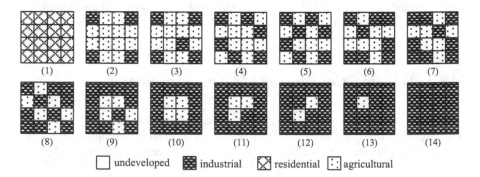

☐ undeveloped　▨ industrial　◈ residential　⠿ agricultural

Fig. 16.4 LUPs corresponding to 14 Pareto-optimal solutions

10^{-4} fatalities·a^{-1}) and the ordinate was economic objective (*Benefit*, 10^{10}CNY). The land use patterns (LUPs) corresponding to 14 Pareto optimal solutions were illustrated in Fig. 16.4. Six optimal solutions (marked with open squares) based on VEGA were illustrated in Fig. 16.3. The parameter settings of VEGA were: population size set 100, maximum generations set 1,000, generation gap set 1.0, p_c-crossover probability set 0.7 and p_m-mutation probability set 0.0219.

16.3.6 Discussion

Observing Figs. 16.3 and 16.4, it was very obvious that NSGA-II had found more Pareto optimal solutions than VEGA. VEGA had only found three Pareto optimal solutions and three sub-optimal solutions. Conclusively, more bigger was benefit, more higher was risk. Control observation to the three evaluation criterions of optimizing method effectiveness proposed in Sect. 16.3.2, we could see NSGA-II satisfied these evaluation criterions completely however VEGA only satisfied these evaluation criterions partly. It indicated that NSGA-II was an effective algorithm to deal with this two-objective optimal model.

The LUPs in Fig. 16.4 were all the optimal solutions. Which alternative should be chosen depends on risk tolerance or expected benefit of decision-makers. For example, if decision-makers could not bear any risk, they would choose No.1 LUP and it was the maximal benefit when risk was 0. If expected benefit of decision-makers was 60 billion CNY, then the No. 11 would be chosen and decision-makers should take a risk of about 143 potential loss of life per 10,000 years. No. 2 LUP showed that if the number of industrial cells in one alternative was less than four, decision-makers would choose No. 1 LUP-development of residential area instead of industrial park.

16.4   Example 2

The area of a chemical industry park in Shenzhen was $2.4\,km^2$, it was illustrated in Fig. 16.5. Each block had seven LTDs: ① storage of inflammable liquid of class A, ② storage of inflammable liquid of class B, ③ storage of inflammable gas, ④ production and usage of inflammable gas, ⑤ production and usage of toxic gas, ⑥ other industrial, ⑦ residential.

Unconstrained two-objective optimization was made using the optimal method proposed in this paper, 256 optimal solutions were get finally. They could be divided into 21 types and these types were illustrated in Fig. 16.6. Two LUPs corresponding to the least $PLL(*.1)$ and the maximum $PLL(*.2)$ of each type were drawn in Fig. 16.6. Optimization results showed that for unconstrained case, only storages of inflammable liquid of class A and B were laid and storages of inflammable liquid of class B were preferred, other industries were rejected. Which alternative should be chosen depends on risk tolerance or expected benefit of decision-makers similarly.

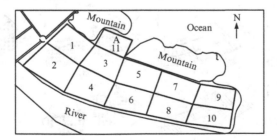

Fig. 16.5 Planar graph of the chemical industry park

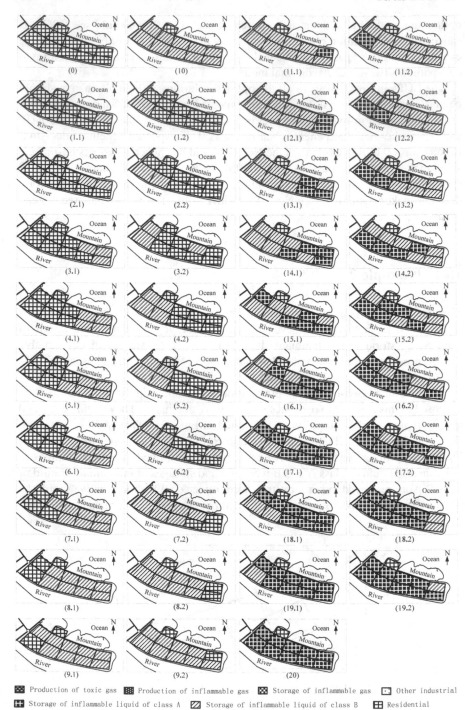

Fig. 16.6 A part of land use patterns

16.5   Conclusions

- The model of unconstrained two-objective land-use planning for chemical industry park proposed in this paper was feasible and NSGA- II that adopted optimization method was effective.
- These corresponding land-use patterns had good reference values to land-use planning for chemical industry park. They could achieve expectant benefits of the park and risk could rest on the acceptable level at the same time.

Acknowledgements This research was financially supported by National Technology R&D Program of China (No. 2006BAK01B02), China Academy of Safety Science and Technology Basic Project (2008JBKY13).

References

Liu Fang "Simply Discuss the Production Safety of Chemical Parks," Fine Chemical Industrial Raw Materials & Intermediates, 37(6), 18–20, 2007

Wei Lijun, Duo Yingquan, Yu Lijian, Liu Ji, Wu Zongzhi, "Research on the Method and Procedure of Safety Planning for Chemical Industry Parks," China Safety Science Journal, 17(9), 45–51, 2007

Xu Ming, Duo Yingquan, Wu Zongzhi, "Review of Multi-Criteria Decision Analysis on Land-Use Planning Vicinity of Chemical Sites," Journal of Safety Science and Technology, 4(6), 37–41, 2008

Wu Zongzhi, Duo Yingquan, Wei Lijun, Guan Lei, "Quantitative Area Risk Assessment Method and its Application in Land Use Safety Planning for Major Hazard Installations," Engineering Science, 8(04), 46–49, 2006

O.B. Augusto, S. Rabeau, Ph Dépincé, F. Bennis, "Multi-objective Genetic Algorithms: A Way to Improve the Convergence Rate," Engineering Applications of Artificial Intelligence, 19, 501–510, 2006

Yong Shi Current Research Trend: Information Technology and Decision Making in 2008. International Journal of Information Technology & Decision Making, 8(1), 1–5, 2009

Yong Shi The Research Trend of Information Technology and Decision Making in 2009. International Journal of Information Technology & Decision Making, 9(1), 1–8, 2010

Deng-Feng Li. Relative Ratio Method for Multiple Attribute Decision Making Problems. International Journal of Information Technology & Decision Making, 8(2), 289–311, 2009

JianYong Chen, QiuZhen Lin and QingBin Hu, Application of Novel Clonal Algorithm in Multiobjective Optimization. International Journal of Information Technology & Decision Making, 9(2), 239–266, 2010

Deb Kalyanmoy, Amrit Pratap, Sameer Agrawal and T Meyarivan "A Fast and Elitist Multiobjective Genetic Algorithm: NSGA-II," IEEE Transactions on Evolutionary Compution, 6(2), 182–201, 2002

Jiang Bin, Liang Shifeng, "Application of Multi-objective Genetic Algorithm in Chemical Engineering," Modern Chemical Industry, 27(7), 66–71, 2007

Birgitte Rasmussen, Ib Bertelsen Vibeke Burchard, et al. "Multi-objective Decisions in Land-use Planning Involving Chemical Sites," Risø National Laboratory, Roskilde, pp. 5–9, 1999

Shenzhen Municipal Bureau of Statistics, "Shenzhen Statistical Yearbook 2008," Beijing: China Statistics Press, pp. 27, 183, 2008

Kalyanmoy Deb, "An Efficient Constraint Handling Method for Genetic Algorithms" Comput. Methods Appl. Mech. Engrg, 186, 311–338, 2000

Chapter 17
Robustness in Economic Development Studies: The Case of Tanzania

Willem Karel M. Brauers and Edmundas Kazimieras Zavadskas

Abstract The definition of robustness in econometrics, the error term in a linear equation, was not only broadened, but in addition moved from a cardinal to an ordinal-qualitative one: the most robust one, more robust than..., as robust as......, robust, weak robust, less robust than..., not robust. This interpretation is tested by an application on the Robustness in Economic Development, namely of Tanzania, while considering multiple objectives for development. For robustness the choice of the objectives has to be non-subjective, which is the case if all stakeholders are involved, and if all possible objectives are represented. Normalization has to be non-subjective too, which is possible by the use of a Multiplicative Form or of MOORA (Multi-Objective Optimization by Ratio Analysis). The last one is composed of ratio analysis "senso stricto" and of the Reference Point Method with the previously obtained ratios as a starting point. In this way, three different methods, controlling each other, form an additional guaranty for robustness.

Keywords Full Multiplicative Form · MOORA · MULTIMOORA · Robustness · Stakeholders
JEL Classification: C44, L52, O41, O55.

W.K.M. Brauers (✉)
Faculty of Applied Economics, University of Antwerp, Birontlaan, 97, 2600 Antwerpen, Belgium
e-mail: willem.brauers@ua.ac.be

E.K. Zavadskas
Vilnius Gediminas Technical University, Sauletekio av. 11, Vilnius, 10223, Lithuania
e-mail: edmundas.zavadskas@vgtu.lt

Y. Shi et al. (eds.), *New State of MCDM in the 21st Century*, Lecture Notes in Economics and Mathematical Systems 648, DOI 10.1007/978-3-642-19695-9_17, © Springer-Verlag Berlin Heidelberg 2011

17.1 Definition of Robustness

In 1969 the statistician Huber (1969) considered robustness as purely cardinal, namely as a compromise between a normal distribution and its light deviations.[1] From the beginning Bayesian analysis has to be characterized as cardinal, nevertheless with a high grade of arbitrariness. This arbitrariness could be softened by considerations on robustness.[2]

However, we observe a move to a more vague and qualitative definition of robustness, namely the most robust one, more robust than..., as robust as......, robust, weak robust, less robust than..., not robust etc.[3] In this way if robustness is indicated as vague or arbitrary is it also not the case with inference statistics (Hoel 1971, 2 versus Hays 1974, 47; Casella and Berger 2002, VII), probability theory (Hays, 47) and statistical specification (Intriligator 1978, 2; Matyas and Sevestre 1992, Chap. 9 versus Thomas 1985, 71; Wonnacott 1970, 312)?

17.2 Conditions of Robustness in Multi-Objective Methods

For the researcher in multi-objective decision support systems the choice between many methods is not very easy. Indeed numerous theories were developed since the forerunners: Condorcet (the Condorcet Paradox, against binary comparisons 1785, LVIII), Gossen (law of decreasing marginal utility, 1853), Minkowsky (Reference Point, 1896, 1911) and Pareto (Pareto Optimum and Indifference Curves analysis 1906, 1927) and pioneers like Kendall (ordinal scales, since 1948), Roy et al. (ELECTRE, since 1966), Miller and Starr (Multiplicative Form for multiple objectives, 1969), Hwang and Yoon (TOPSIS 1981), Saaty (AHP, since 1988), Opricovic and Tzeng (VIKOR since 2004, a new VIKOR method by Yang et al. 2009).

We intend to assist the researcher with some guidelines for an effective choice. In order to distinguish the different multi-objective methods from each other we use the ordinal, qualitative definition of robustness as mentioned above.[4]

The most robust multi-objective method has to satisfy the following conditions:

1. The method of multiple objectives in which all stakeholders are involved is more robust than this one with only one decision maker or different decision

---

[1] At a later time, namely in 1981, Huber (1981) wrote a more complete book on Robust Statistics. In 1994 at the occasion of Huber's birthday his colleagues edited a book on Robust Statistics [editor: Rieder, 1996].

[2] A good overview of this problem of robustness and Bayesian Analysis is brought by Ruggeri (2008).

[3] Cf. Webster's new Universal Unabridged Dictionary: robust: strong; stronger, strongest.

[4] For further information on Robustness and Multiple Objectives, see: Brauers and Zavadskas (2010).

makers defending their own limited number of objectives. All stakeholders mean everybody interested in a certain issue (Brauers 2007, 454–455).

The method of multiple objectives in which all stakeholders are involved, namely also the consumers, has to take into consideration consumer sovereignty too. The method considering consumer sovereignty is more robust than this one which does not respect consumer sovereignty. Community indifference loci measure consumer sovereignty. Solutions with multiple objectives have to deliver points inside the convex zone of the highest possible community indifference locus (these solutions are defined in: Brauers 2008b, 98–103).

No Interactive Methods are examined in which the researcher acts in dialogue with the decision maker and eventually changes his first point of view (the Dialogue Stage after the Calculation Stage). This way of acting is not possible with stakeholders. The stakeholders show a consensus on: the method, the objectives, the importance of the objectives and the alternatives. If afterwards a stakeholder will contest the outcome the whole exercise has to be repeated again. If there is nevertheless a final decision maker which opposes his own stakeholder group then in the case of failure the responsibility will fall entirely on him:

2. The method of multiple objectives in which all non correlated objectives are examined is more robust than this one considering only a limited number of objectives (Brauers and Ginevičious 2009, 125–126).

The objectives have to be non-correlated. Correlation of the objectives is absent or their correlation can not be quantified. Correlation is rather studied in econometric models, either in their autoregressive, reduced or structural form (eventually an econometric model may be a sub-model for multi-objective optimization. For more details, see: Brauers 2004, 17–18):

3. The method of multiple objectives in which all interrelations between objectives and alternatives are taken into consideration at the same time is more robust than this one with interrelations only examined two by two (for the proof of this statement, see: Brauers 2004, 118–122).
4. The method of multiple objectives which is non-subjective is more robust than this one which uses subjective estimations for the choice and importance of the objectives and for normalization.

4.1 For the choice of the objectives and the alternatives

A complete set of representative and robust objectives is found after Ameliorated Nominal Group Technique Sessions with all the stakeholders concerned or with their representative experts (for an example see Brauers and Lepkova 2003).

Subjectivity can still be present in the choice of the objectives and of the alternatives. Political dominance can lead to this choice, either from above in centralization or federalism or from bottom up after the substitution principle or by confederation. In absence of any form of dominance convergence of ideas could lead to non-subjectivity. However, what is meant by non-subjectivity? In physical sciences, a natural law dictates non-subjectivity without deviations. In human sciences, for instance in economics, an economic law will state the attitude of men in general but with exceptional individual deviations. Outside these human laws in the human sciences unanimity or at least a certain form of convergence in opinion between all stakeholders concerned will lead to non-subjectivity. This convergence of opinion, concerning the choice of the objectives, has to be brought not by face to face methods but rather by methods such as the Ameliorated Nominal Group Technique. Convergence on the importance of the objectives is supported by the Delphi Method (for an example see Brauers 2008a, 172).

Alternatives have to be well defined too. If alternatives concern Projects the whole theory on Project Analysis enters into the picture.

We only consider Discrete Optimization and not continuous one. In Continuous Optimization the solution (alternative) originates from the approach itself.[5] For instance linear programming could be used for Continuous Optimization (for an example, see: Brauers 2004, 115–117).

4.2 For normalization

The method of multiple objectives which does not need external normalization is more robust than this one which needs a subjective external normalization (Brauers 2007). Accordingly, the method of multiple objectives which uses non-subjective dimensionless measures without normalization is more robust than this one which uses for normalization subjective weights [weights were already introduced by Churchman and Ackoff (1954) and Churchman et al. (1957)] or subjective non-additive scores like in the traditional reference point theory (Brauers 2004, 158–159).

The Additive Weighting Procedure (MacCrimmon 1968, 29–33, which was called SAW, Simple Additive Weighting Method by Hwang and Yoon 1981, 99) starts from the following formula:

$$Max.U_j = w_1 x_{1j} + w_2 x_{2j} + \ldots + w_i x_{ij} + \ldots + w_n x_{nj} \qquad (17.1)$$

U_j = overall utility of alternative j with j $= 1, 2, \ldots, m$, m the number of alternatives
w_i = weight of attribute i indicates as well as normalization as the level of importance of an objective

$$\sum_{i=1}^{i=n} w_i = 1$$

$i = 1, 2, \ldots, n$; n the number of attributes and objectives
x_{ij} = response of alternative j on attribute i.

---

[5] Hwang and Masud (1979, 6–7) call *Continuous Optimization* rather Multiple Objective Decision Making (MODM) as associated with Design Problems in contrast to MADM (Multiple Attribute Decision Making) being involved with Selection Problems.

Reference Point Theory is non linear, whereas non-additive scores replace the weights. The non-additive scores take care of normalization.

4.3 *For giving importance to an objective*

With weights and scores importance of objectives is mixed with normalization. Indeed weights and scores are mixtures of normalization of different units and of importance coefficients. On the contrary Delphi can determine the importance of objectives separately from normalization. In addition, as all stakeholders concerned are involved, the Delphi method is non-subjective.

5. The method of multiple objectives based on cardinal numbers is more robust than this one based on ordinal numbers: "an ordinal number is one that indicates order or position in a series, like first, second, etc." (Kendall and Gibbons 1990, 1). Robustness of cardinal numbers is based first on the saying of Arrow 1974, 256): "Obviously, a cardinal utility implies an ordinal preference but not vice versa" and second on the fact that the four essential operations of arithmetic: adding, subtracting, multiplication and division are only reserved for cardinal numbers (see also: Brauers and Ginevičious 2009, 137–138).
6. The method of multiple objectives which uses the last recent available data as a base is more robust than this one based on earlier data (Brauers and Ginevičious 2009, 133, 2nd).
7. Once the previous six conditions fulfilled the use of two different methods of multi-objective optimization is more robust than the use of a single method; the use of three methods is more robust than the use of two, etc.

Two methods fulfill the fourth condition of dimensionless numbers: the Full Multiplicative Form and the Multi-Objective Optimization by Ratio Analysis Method (MOORA) on condition that Ameliorated Nominal Group Technique and Delphi are also involved. Starting with the full multiplicative form we shall see if also the other conditions are satisfied and namely on basis of the economic development of Tanzania.

17.3 The Full-Multiplicative Form

The following n-power form is called from now on a *Full-Multiplicative Form* in order to distinguish it from other rather mixed forms (Brauers 2004, 228–229):

$$U_j = \prod_{i=1}^{n} x_{ij}. \tag{17.2}$$

with: $j = 1, 2, \ldots, m$; m the number of alternatives
$i = 1, 2, \ldots, n$; n being the number of objectives
x_{ij} = response of alternative j on objective i
U_j = overall utility of alternative j. U_j is a dimensionless indicator.

With the full-multiplicative form the overall utilities (U_j), obtained by multiplication of different units of measurement, become dimensionless measures.

Accentuating the importance of an objective-attribute can be done by adding a α-term or by allocating an exponent on condition that this is done with unanimity or at least with a strong convergence in opinion of all the stakeholders concerned. Therefore, a Delphi exercise may help (for an example see: Brauers 2008a).

How is it possible to combine a minimization problem with the maximization of the other objectives? Therefore, the objectives to be minimized are denominators in the formula:

$$U'_j = \frac{A_j}{B_j}. \tag{17.3}$$

with: $A_j = \prod_{g=1}^{i} x_{gi}$.

$j = 1, 2, \ldots, m$; m the number of alternatives
i = the number of objectives to be maximized

with: $B_j = \prod_{k=i+1}^{n} x_{kj}$.

$n - i$ = the number of objectives to be minimized
with: U'_j: the utility of alternative j with objectives to be maximized and objectives to be minimized.

17.4   The Full-Multiplicative Form and the Input–Output Structure of Tanzania

Tanzania is a model of stability in East Africa. Bordered by eight nations and with a prime access to the ocean Tanzania is blessed with a strategic geographical setting. Its policy consisted in the protection of its natural resources as the country continued its modernization. Nevertheless poverty, underdeveloped infrastructure with bad roads and an aging rail network, shortage of energy and drinkable water and lackluster resource mobilization asks for new strategies. An effort was made to translate these deficiencies into an input–output table.

The input–output structure consists of a matrix for the totality of the economy in which the deliveries are shown in the rows and the resources in the columns. Both deliveries and resources are interrelated by ratios that are called "technical coefficients". A limited stability of these technical coefficients is assumed and in this way the matrix is applied for prognosis and planning. The input–output table of 1992 for Tanzania was updated to 2002.[6]

---

[6] This technique is explained in Brauers (2004, 281–283). For Tanzania the stability of the technical coefficients of the input-output table can be considered to be valuable for 10 years (Brauers 1995, 33).

Starting from the updated input–output table economic policy may choose between several scenarios. Suppose that the following objectives are advanced for Tanzania, with the scenarios as alternatives:

- Maximization of employment in man-years.
- Maximization of Value Added in the national currency. Why is the maximization of productivity not taken in to consideration? Productivity, defined as value added over employment, would by definition exclude the previous objectives of value added and employment. In a developed country productivity may play a more dominant role, but in a developing country employment comes first. However, also in a developing country one has to be aware of structural development, such as economic growth possibilities. Therefore, the *Internal Activity Multipliers* of Input–Output are taken into consideration.
- Maximization of the internal activity multipliers of the scenarios.
- Maximization of the balance of payments surplus of each scenario.
- Due to shortages.
  - Minimization of the technical coefficient per scenario of electricity and water.
  - Minimization of the technical coefficient per scenario of domestic transportation, linked to bad roads.

The following scenarios are foreseen:
Scenario I, Heavy Industry: installation of a hydro-electrical power station and a steel factory
Scenario II, Agriculture: a new policy for agriculture and fisheries:
- The end of incentives to reduce agricultural production through price controls, export taxes, quotas, import subsidies;
- Removing protection for non-agricultural products, which increases the balance of payments deficit;
- Liberalization of products such as coffee, cacao, cotton and sugar.

Scenario III, Light Industry: installation of a new sugar factory and a cotton mill.
Scenario IV, Tourism: intensified promotion of tourism together with a program for new roads.
The data on these scenarios are assembled in the following numerical illustration on which the full-multiplicative form is applied (Table 17.1).

Does the exercise satisfy the aforesaid robust conditions?

Concerning the first condition, if not so much all stakeholders are involved anyway consumer sovereignty is fully respected by the objectives. The method taking into consideration consumer sovereignty is *more robust than* this one which does not respect consumer sovereignty.

The second condition is fulfilled as all non-correlated objectives are considered, unless mixtures of objectives would be proposed. In this way, the choice of the objectives gives an impression of completeness. The elimination of productivity was defended for a developing country, whereas the objectives only consider economic development. More objectives are perhaps necessary for a broader *Well-being Economy*. Nevertheless, as a pre-determined obligatory filter for all alternatives, the

Table 17.1 Scenarios for an optimal input–output structure in Tanzania

	1. Man-years MAX,	2. Value Added MAX. (in m.Tsh)	3. Techn. coeff. electricity and water MIN.in 0/0000	4. Techn. coeff. transport (domestic) MIN. in 0/0000	5. Internal Multiplier MAX, per 1,000	6. Sectoral Surplus Bal. of Payments MAX. (in m.Tsh)
I/O I	13584	26054	1405	2367	1449	−10247
I/O II	1918702	595480	294	1431	1278	−3559
I/O III	47347	28345	4289	925	1940	28277
I/O IV	165410	75424	1066	1936	1671	143
operations	$(7) = (1)*(2)$	$(8) = (7)/(3)$	$(9) = (8)/(4)$	$(10) = (9)*(5)$	$(11) = (10)*(6)$	RANK
I/O I	353917536	251898.6021	106.4210402	154204.0872	15.04870569	4
I/O II	1.14255E + 12	3886219956	2715737.216	3470712162	975193.0772	3
I/O III	1342050715	312905.2728	338.2759706	656255.3829	18556933463	1
I/O IV	12475883840	11703455.76	6045.17343	10101484.8	1444512327	2

reservation grounds of the Masai Tribe remain closed for all tourists in order to protect its culture and habits. This policy is in sharp contrast with the Kenia policy where tourists are welcomed by Masai dancers and are invited at the Masai Mara Reservation.

No special importance is given to one or another objective by exponents, by adding a α-term or by the introduction of different sub-objectives.

Third, all interrelations between objectives and alternatives are taken into consideration at the same time.

Four, non-subjectivity is satisfied by using non-subjective dimensionless measures.

Five, the multiplicative form of the exercise is based on cardinal numbers.

Six, this method uses the last recent Input–Output tables available in Tanzania.

However, the multiplicative form uses only a single method of multi-objective optimization. On the contrary the multi-objective optimization by ratio analysis, MOORA, is more robust. Indeed, MOORA not only satisfies the first six conditions, but in addition, satisfies the seventh condition by using two different methods of multi-objective optimization. MOORA is the most robust method as no other method up till now exists satisfying the seven conditions better.

17.5 The MOORA Method

The method starts with a matrix of responses of all alternative solutions on all objectives:

$$x_{ij}. \tag{17.4}$$

with: x_{ij} as the response of alternative j on objective i

$i = 1, 2, \ldots,$ n as the objective
$j = 1, 2, \ldots,$ m as the alternatives.

The MOORA method consists of two parts: the ratio system and the reference point approach.

We go for a ratio system in which each response of an alternative on an objective is compared to a denominator, which is representative for all alternatives concerning that objective[7]:

$$x_{ij}^* = \frac{x_{ij}}{\sqrt{\sum_{j=1}^{m} x_{ij}^2}}. \tag{17.5}$$

with: x_{ij} = response of alternative j on objective i

---

[7] Brauers and Zavadskas (2006), prove that the most robust choice for this denominator is the square root of the sum of squares of each alternative per objective.

$j = 1, 2, \ldots, m; m$ the number of alternatives
$i = 1, 2, \ldots, n; n$ the number of objectives
x_{ij}^* = a dimensionless number representing the response of alternative j on objective i.

For optimization, these responses are added in case of maximization and subtracted in case of minimization:

$$y_j^* = \sum_{i=1}^{i=g} x_{ij}^* - \sum_{i=g+1}^{i=n} x_{ij}^*. \tag{17.6}$$

with: $i = 1, 2, \ldots, g$ as the objectives to be maximized

$i = g + 1, g + 2, \ldots, n$ as the objectives to be minimized
y_j^* = the normalized assessment of alternative j with respect to all objectives, can be positive or negative depending of the totals of its maxima and minima. An ordinal ranking of the y_j^* shows the final preference.

Reference Point Theory will go out from the ratios x_{ij}^* found in formula (17.5). In addition, one needs a Maximal Objective Reference Point. The Maximal Objective Reference Point is called realistic and non-subjective as the co-ordinates (r_i), which are selected for the reference point, are realized as an optimum in one of the candidate alternatives. In this way arriving to:

$$\left(r_i - x_{ij}^* \right). \tag{17.7}$$

with: $i = 1, 2, \ldots., n$ as the objectives

$j = 1, 2, \ldots., m$ as the alternatives
r_i = the ith co-ordinate of the reference point
x_{ij}^* = a dimensionless number representing the response of alternative j on objective i as found in formula (17.5) then this matrix is subject to the *Min–Max Metric of Tchebycheff* (Karlin and Studden (1966) [8]:

$$\underset{(j)}{Min} \left(\underset{(i)}{max} |r_i - x_{ij}^*| \right). \tag{17.8}$$

$|r_i - x_{ij}^*|$ means the absolute value if x_{ij}^* is larger than r_i for instance by minimization.[9]

In order to give more importance to an objective its responses on the alternatives could be multiplied with a Significance Coefficient. The Attribution of

---

[8] Brauers (2008b) proves that the Min-Max metric of Tchebycheff is the most robust choice between all the possible metrics of reference point theory.

[9] Many methods link multi-objective approaches to Tchebycheff. For instance Soylu links Tchebycheff to Promethee II (Soylu 2010).

Table 17.2 Ranking with MULTIMOORA

Scenarios	Multiplicative form	MOORA ratio system	MOORA reference point	MULTIMOORA
(III) Light industry	1	2	1	1
(IV) Tourism	2	3	2	2
(II) Agriculture	3	1	3	3
(I) Heavy industry	4	4	4	4

Sub-Objectives represents still another solution. For instance, for employment two sub-objectives replace a significance coefficient of two and in this way characterize the direct and indirect side of employment.

Appendix A shows the results of the MOORA application on Tanzania.

17.6 MULTIMOORA as a Combination of the Full Multiplicative Form and of MOORA

Table 17.2 shows the combination of the Full Multiplicative Form with MOORA under the name of MULTIMOORA.

Despite a small deviation between the two methods of MOORA one may say that the development of new industry under the form of a sugar factory or/and a cotton mill ranks first, whereas reform of agriculture, the setting up of a hydro-electrical power station and a steel factory, seem less significant. Promotion of tourism is handicapped by the fact that a network of new roads is a preceding condition. This new roads program needs more imports, counterbalancing the balance of payments surplus of tourism revenues. The full multiplicative form is more explicit than MOORA in saying that the development of light industry dominates the other scenarios.

Aggregation of the two approaches under the name of MULTIMOORA forms a possibility to increase the robustness of the results. In addition MULTIMOORA would bring the fulfillment of the seventh robustness condition on the basis of three different methods.

17.7 Conclusion

In a country the national economic development can depend on the reactions per sector on the objectives. Does the economic development of Tanzania satisfy the seven conditions of robustness which were discussed above?

Concerning the first condition, if not so much all stakeholders are involved anyway consumer sovereignty is considered by the objectives. The method taking into consideration consumer sovereignty is *more robust than* this one which does not respect consumer sovereignty.

The second condition is fulfilled as all non-correlated objectives seem to be present, unless mixtures of objectives are proposed. Anyway if the choice of the objectives gives impression of completeness only economic development is covered. Indeed more objectives are probably necessary for a broader Well-Being Economy, for more sustainable development. Nevertheless, as a predetermined filter in all scenarios, the reservation grounds of the Masai Tribe have to remain out of bounds for all tourists, protecting in that way the well-being of the Masai people.

No objective received more importance than the others by exponents, by adding a α-term or by the introduction of different sub-objectives.

Thirdly, all interrelations between objectives and alternatives are taken into consideration at the same time.

Fourthly, non-subjectivity is satisfied by using non-subjective dimensionless measures, which does not need further normalization.

Fifthly, the Full Multiplicative Form and MOORA are based on cardinal numbers.

Sixthly this method uses the last recent available data as a base as no more recent Input–Output tables are available in Tanzania.

Despite a small deviation between the two approaches of MOORA one may say that the development of new industry by way of setting up a sugar factory or/and a cotton mill ranks first. The full multiplicative form is more pronounced to say that the development of light industry dominates the other scenarios. For that reason one could think of aggregating the Full Multiplicative Form and MOORA in one multi-objective system, for instance called MULTIMOORA. In this way MULTIMOORA would become the fulfillment of the seven robustness conditions on the basis of three different methods.

Does the recent development correspond to the policy proposed by MULTI-MOORA based on the input–output table? The light industry will indeed be promoted on basis of sugar-cane. Much riceland is even replaced by sugar-cane plantations. However, due to the shortage of mineral oil ethanol refineries on basis of sugar-cane will replace the new sugar factories.

Nevertheless a change in the traditional policy is possible, a sustainable development which input–output can not foresee. The protection of Tanzania's natural landscape comes in danger. Here the traditional policy would change. Plans for a highway through the area of 24,000 square km of Serengeti Park will bring a better link between Victoria lake and the Ocean and will boost the economy and promote tourism but will be a disaster for the wild life in the park and will disturb the Masai population. It would be better to have a road south of the park much longer but safeguarding much more the well being of the population, protecting the wildlife and perhaps also better economically.

Appendix: MOORA and the Input–Output Structure of Tanzania

On basis of the data given in Table 17.1 of the main text the following table shows the MOORA results (Table 17.3).

Table 17.3 MOORA applied on input–output structure of Tanzania

	1 MAX.	2 MAX.	3 MIN.	4 MIN.	5 MAX.	6 MAX.	Sum	Rank
17.3a – Matrix of responses of alternatives on objectives: (x_{ij})								
I/O I	13584	26054	1405	2367	1449	−10247		
I/O II	1918702	595480	294	1431	1278	−3559		
I/O III	47347	28345	4289	925	1940	28277		
I/O IV	165410	75424	1066	1936	1671	143		
17.3b – Sum of squares and their square roots								
I/O I	184525056	678810916	1974025	5602689	2099601	105001009		
I/O II	3.68142E + 12	3.54596E + 11	86436	2047761	1633284	12666481		
I/O III	2241738409	803439025	18395521	855625	3763600	799588729		
I/O IV	27360468100	5688779776	1136356	3748096	2792241	20449		
Σ	3711204096369	361767460117.0000	21592338.000000	12254171.000000	10288726.0000	9172766668.000000		
root	1926448.571	601471.08	4646.755642	3500.595806	3207.604402	30286.57571		
17.3c – Objectives divided by their square roots and MOORA								
I/O I	0.007051317	0.043	0.302361499	0.676170609	0.452	−0.338	0.1637727	4
I/O II	0.995978833	0.990039288	0.063269951	0.408787555	0.398428185	−0.117510809	2.2669355	1
I/O III	0.02457735	0.047126123	0.923009586	0.264240732	0.604812738	0.933647972	1.6101642	2
I/O IV	0.085862661	0.125399213	0.229407372	0.553048711	0.520949528	0.004721564	0.7369330	3

17.3d – Reference Point Theory with Ratios: co-ordinates of the reference point equal to the maximal objective values

	1 MAX.	2 MAX.	3 MIN.	4 MIN.	5 MAX.	6 MAX.
r_i	0.995978833	0.990039288	0.0633	0.2642	0.604812738	0.933647972

17.3e – Reference Point Theory: Deviations from the reference point

	1 MAX.	2 MAX.	3 MIN.	4 MIN.	5 MAX.	6 MAX.	Max.	Min.
I/O I	0.988927516	0.94672216	0.2391	0.4119	0.153073739	1.2720	1.2720	4
I/O II	0	0	0.0000	0.1445	0.206384553	1.0512	1.0512	3
I/O III	0.971401484	0.942913165	0.8597	0.0000	0	0.0000	0.8597396	1
I/O IV	0.910116173	0.864640075	0.166	0.289	0.08386321	0.928926409	0.9289264	2

References

Arrow K.J. (1974). General Economic Equilibrium: Purpose, Analytic Techniques, Collective Choice, *American Economic Review*, 256.

Brauers, W.K. (2008a). Group Decision Making With Multi-Objective Optimization, *Foundations of Computing and Decision Sciences*, Vol. 33, N° 2, Poznan Technical University, 167–179.

Brauers, W.K. (2008b). Multi-Objective Decision Making by Reference Point Theory for a Wellbeing Economy, *Operations Research International Journal*, 8, 89–104.

Brauers W.K. (2007). What is meant by normalization in decision making? *International Journal of Management and Decision Making*, ISSN 1462–4621. 8, 5/6, 445–460.

Brauers W.K. (2004). *Optimization Methods for a Stakeholder Society. A Revolution in Economic Thinking by Multi-Objective Optimization*, ISBN 1–4020–7681–9, Kluwer Academic Publishers and Springer, Boston.

Brauers W.K. (1995). *Prévisions économiques à l'aide de la méthode entrées-sorties* (Economic Forecasting assisted by the Input-Output Method) Economica, Paris.

Brauers, W.K., E. K. Zavadskas, (2010). Is Robustness really Robust? Robustness from the Point of View of Statistics and Econometrics, *Multiple Criteria Decision Aiding*, Editors C. Zopounidis, M. Doumpos et al. ISNB 978–1–61668–231–6, NOVA Science Publishers, Chapter 2, 17–42.

Brauers W. K., Ginevičious R. (2009). Robustness in Regional Development Studies. The Case of Lithuania, *Journal of Business Economics and Management*, ISSN 1611–1699, 10(2), 121–140.

Brauers W.K., Zavadskas E. K. (2006). The MOORA Method and its Application to Privatization in a Transition Economy, *Control and Cybernetics*, Systems Research Institute of the Polish Academy of Sciences, ISSN 0324–8569, 35, 2, 445–469.

Brauers W.K., Lepkova N. (2003). The Application of the Nominal Group Technique to the Business Outlook of the Facilities Sector of Lithuania over the Period 2003–2012, *International Journal of Strategic Property Management*, Vol. 7, N° 1, Vilnius, Gediminas Technical University, Lithuania and Napier University, Scotland, 1–9.

Casella G., Berger R.L. (2002). *Statistical Inference*, Second Edition, Duxbury, Thomson Learning Pacific Grove, Ca, US.

Churchman C.W., Ackoff R.L., Arnoff E.L. (1957). *Introduction To Operations Research*, Wiley, New York.

Churchman C.W., Ackoff R.L. (1954). An Approximate Measure of Value, *Operations Research*, 2, 172–180.

Condorcet, M. (1785). *Essai sur l'application de l'analyse à la probabilité des décisions rendues à la pluralité des voix*, Paris, l'Imprimerie royale.

Gossen, H H. (1853). *Entwicklung der Gesetze des Menschlichen Verkehrs und der daraus Flieszenden Regeln für Menschliches Handeln*, 3 Auflage, Prager, Berlin, 1927.

Hays W.L. (1974). *Statistics for the Social Sciences*, Holt, Rinehart and Winston, London.

Hoel P.G. (1971). *Elementary Statistics*, Wiley, New York.

Huber P.J. (1981). *Robust Statistics*, Wiley, New York.

Huber P.J. (1969). *Theorie de l'Inférence Statistique Robuste*, les Presses de l'Université de Montreal, Montreal.

Hwang, C.-L., Yoon, K. (1981). *Multiple Attribute Decision Making, Methods and Applications*. Lecture Notes in Economics and Mathematical Systems, 186, Berlin, Springer.

Hwang, C.-L., Masud A. S. Md. (1979). *Multiple Objective Decision Making, Methods and Applications*, Lecture Notes in Mathematical Systems, N° 164, Berlin, Springer.

Intriligator M.D. (1978). *Econometric Models, Techniques and Applications*, North Holland, Amsterdam.

Karlin, S., Studden, W. J. (1966) *Tchebycheff Systems: with Applications in Analysis and Statistics*, Interscience Publishers 278–280, New York.

Kendall, M. G. (1948). *Rank Correlation Methods*, Griffin, London.

Kendall, M. G.; Gibbons, J. D (1990) *Rank Correlation Methods* Edward Arnold, London.

MacCrimmon, K.R. (1968). Decisionmaking among Multiple Attribute Alternatives. A Survey and Consolidated Approach, RM-4823-ARPA, the Rand Corporation, Santa Monica (CAL).

Matyas L., Sevestre P. (1992). *The Econometrics of Panel Data. Handbook of Theory and Applications*, Advanced Studies in Theoretical and Applied Econometrics, Vol. 28, Kluwer Academic Publishers, Dordrecht.

Miller, D.W., Starr, M.K. (1969). *Executive Decisions and Operations Research*, 2nd Edition, Prentice-Hall Inc. Englewood Cliffs (N.J.).

Minkowsky, H. (1896). Geometrie Der Zahlen, Teubner, Leipzig.

Minkowsky, H. (1911). Gesammelte Abhandlungen, Teubner, Leipzig

Opricovic, S., Tzeng, G.-H. (2004). Compromise solution by MCDM methods: a comparative analysis of VIKOR and TOPSIS, *EJOR*, 445–455.

Pareto, V. (1906). *Manuale di Economia Politica*, Translation revised by Pareto Himself: *Manuel d'économie politique*, Second Ed., Paris (1927).

Rieder H. Editor (1996). *Robust Statistics, Data Analysis and Computer Intensive Methods*, Springer, New York.

Roy, B., Benayoun, R., Sussman, B. (1966). *ELECTRE*, Société d'Economie et de Mathématique appliquées, Paris.

Ruggeri F. (2008). Bayesian Robustness, *European Working Group, Multiple Criteria Decision Aiding*, Series 3, 17, 6–10.

Saaty, T. L. (1988). *The Analytic Hierarchy Process*. Mcgraw-Hill, New York.

Soylu B. (2010). Integrating Promethee II with the Tchebycheff function for Multi Criteria Decision Making, *International Journal of Information Technology and Decision Making*, 9, 4, 525–545.

Thomas R.L. (1985). *Introductory Econometrics*, Longman, London.

Wonnacott R.J., and T.H. (1970). *Econometrics*, Wiley, New York.

Yang Y.-P. O., Shieh H.-M., Leu J.-D., Tzeng G.-H. (2009) A VIKOR-based Multiple Criteria Decision Method for improving information security risk, *International Journal of Information Technology and Decision Making*, 8, 2, 1–21.